M000119720

ALONG THE STREETS OF BRONZEVILLE

THE NEW BLACK STUDIES SERIES

Edited by Darlene Clark Hine and Dwight A. McBride

A list of books in the series appears at the end of this book.

ALONG THE STREETS OF BRONZEVILLE

Black Chicago's Literary Landscape

Elizabeth Schroeder Schlabach

University of Illinois Press
Urbana, Chicago, and Springfield

Library of Congress Cataloging-in-Publication Data
Schlabach, Elizabeth Schroeder.
Along the streets of Bronzeville : black Chicago's literary landscape /
Elizabeth Schroeder Schlabach.
pages   cm. — (The New Black Studies Series)
Includes bibliographical references and index.
ISBN 978-0-252-03782-5 (cloth : acid-free paper)
ISBN 978-0-252-09510-8 (ebook)
1. American literature—Illinois—Chicago—History and criticism.
2. American literature—African American authors—History and criticism.
3. African Americans—Illinois—Chicago—Intellectual life. 4. Chicago (Ill.)—
Intellectual life—20th century.
I. Title.
PS285.C47S35   2013
810.9'977311—dc23   2013012803

For my family—past, present, and future.

CONTENTS

PREFACE

Gwendolyn Brooks, a lifelong resident and Bronzeville native, once wrote, "If you wanted a poem, you had only to look out of a window. There was material always, walking or running, fighting or screaming or singing."[1] Brooks did an interview much later in life where she was asked if she were disturbed by this environment to which she replied, "In my twenties when I wrote a good deal of my better-known poetry I lived on 63rd Street—at 623 East 63rd Street—and there was a good deal of life in the raw all about. You might feel that this would be disturbing, but it was not. It contributed to my writing progress. I wrote about what I saw and heard in the street. I lived in a small second-floor apartment at the corner, and I could look first on one side and then on the other. There was my material."[2] She recalled receiving the letter at this address from publisher Harper and Brothers accepting *A Street in Bronzeville* for publication, after which she ran into her kitchenette apartment building's "community bathrooms, locked the door, and gasped through the gold of a firm acceptance."[3]

Poverty-stricken, segregated, and bursting at the seams with migrants— Brooks's Bronzeville is the community that provided inspiration, training, and work for an entire generation of diversely talented African American authors and artists who came of age during the years between the two world wars. Willard Motley, poet, novelist, and nephew of famed painter Archibald Motley Jr., the first African American trained at the Chicago Art Institute, wrote, "There is a small group of young Negro artists in Chicago that will be heard from one of these days. At present they are struggling in garage and top-floor tenement studios. . . . They paint for the love of it. There is much talent in the group."[4] Many of these artists and authors went on to become the leading names in their fields and in so doing earned for the United States a reputation as the creative wellspring of twentieth-century African American art and literature. Yet, until late, the majority of Chicago's

African American writers and artists and their Renaissance movement had remained in relative scholarly obscurity.

Along the Streets of Bronzeville fills this void in African American cultural arts' scholarship while it delineates new modes of artistic thought and aesthetics. The project contributes both to current efforts to expand upon the history of African American cultural production during the twentieth century and to theories of race, identity, and geography. Reading across a wide range of visual, literary, and popular texts, from some of the world's most popular African American authors and artists, *Along the Streets* reads the artistic legacy of the Chicago Black Renaissance as a configuration of subjectivity and identity that retheorizes the relationship between artistry and place. This project demonstrates what Chicago's artists, authors, and musicians were doing that pushed Harlem to the background and Chicago to the foreground of black cultural production. It shows that Bronzeville, specifically, became a distinctive place with a distinctive aesthetic for African American Cultural production in the mid–twentieth century.

The Chicago Black Renaissance had a unique Midwestern conceptualization of space, which enables a new understanding of African American cultural and literary history. Part of recovering the Chicago Black Renaissance means adding important dimensions of study to this space—describing a Midwest artistic movement where artists and authors such as Gwendolyn Brooks are fully at home and artistically potent in the segregated urban metropolis. This study finds that Chicago's African American artists and authors shared a common question, a common theme, and a common politics—that their art should always present black reality from the vantage point of African Americans in Bronzeville. Thus the movement is richly textured by its sociohistorical setting; the South Side of Chicago's streets, alleyways, and institutions are the threads that bind the Chicago Black Renaissance. Together these arguments map Chicago as the logical hotbed of African American Renaissance creativity—unrivaled by any city throughout the mid–twentieth century.

As a conceptual category, the "Chicago Black Renaissance" first gained prominence in 1986, when it was articulated by Robert Bone, a scholar of African American literature.[5] Since then, the Renaissance has been the subject of much scholarly discussion, but it remains largely unknown to the public, even in Chicago itself. Samuel Floyd summarized the situation in his book *The Power of Black Music*: "Like the Harlem movement, the Chicago Black Renaissance was a flowering of Afro-American arts and letters. Unlike the Harlem manifestation, however, in which recognition and theorizing took place simultaneously with its activity, recognition of and theorizing about the Chicago Black Renaissance is only now beginning."[6] This lack of acknowledgment is part of a problematic black mythical geography heavily reliant on the divisions of north/south, east/west, and urban/ rural. Chicago, more broadly conceived as the Midwest, finds itself caught between these spaces and has been vastly undertheorized, making it an invisible black space. Part of recovering the Chicago Black Renaissance means adding important dimensions of study to this invisible space—describing a Midwest artistic movement where blacks are fully at home in Bronzeville. Retheorizing the Chicago Black Renaissance enables a different conceptualization of space, and subsequently a new understanding of African American cultural and literary history. An expansive narrative serves scholars well in leading the challenge against the simplistic rigid geographical axes and strict periodizations along which we have typically studied black cultural output.

Several scholars have worked to fill this vacuum and help to outline this movement in interesting and productive ways. Here the work of Robert Bone and Richard Courage's book *Music in Bronzeville* looms as the most recent publication on a distinct Bronzeville Renaissance. This book is Bone's own answer to his call that there was something in fact going on in Bronzeville that merited larger and focused study.[7] Bone and Courage's book outlines the Chicago Black Renaissance by mentioning its patrons, artists, authors—it is a brilliantly comprehensive tour of the movement and its origins. Annie Meis Knupher's book *The Chicago Black Renaissance and Women's Activism* highlights African American Women's groups' participation in the movement— she engages the topic through the lens of civics, respectability, and gender. Carla Cappetti situates the literature of the Renaissance amid the rubric of the Great Migration specifically and more generally among literature by immigrants. Bill Mullen's *Popular Fronts* provides a Chicagocentric moment as he demonstrates that Chicago was the preeminent site of African American social realism in both the 1930s and the 1940s. Drawing his central trope of a political front from a *Chicago Defender* editorial, Mullen provides readers with an ideological, political, cultural synthesis that defined Chicago's black cultural and political production after World War I and during World War II.

Any attempt to define or delineate a new black literary movement or shed light on an overlooked decade of African American cultural production must carefully and thoughtfully explore artisans' own understanding and navigation of their relationships within a racially volatile city such as Chicago. The work of Adam Green, Davarian Baldwin, Madhu Dubey, and Carlo Rotella serve this narrative well in their precedents for thinking about the relationship between the urban world and the literary fictive world. Their works tackle Chicago's dilemma of representation, inclusion in American's literary canon, and the delineation of new modes of artistic thought in their call that Bronzeville's literature and art must be evaluated in terms of the geographic and sociohistorical settings, and "texts" of the major authors, artists, musicians, and journalists. Ultimately, it is my hope that by tracing African American cultural production throughout this exciting period of history, with the aid of these scholars, *Along the Streets* sheds light on the dynamism and multiplicity of artistic and literary expression permeating these decades of Chicago's history.

To explore these modes of expression, *Along the Streets* situates black cultural production in relation to two categories conditioned always by race—aesthetics and geography. I take a methodological and theoretical lead first and foremost from Bronzeville's South Side Writers Group, organized by Richard Wright in 1936. Under the helmsmanship of Wright, noted authors such as Frank Marshall Davis, Margaret Walker, Chester Himes, and Arna Bontemps politicized the African American writer's project in a seminal document of literary theory: "Blueprint for Negro Writing." Radically, "Blueprint" demands that Chicago Black Renaissance writers reject what had been for them their only "black" literary and aesthetic history—the Harlem Renaissance—for a more authentic one. Wright, the most noted author to hail from the movement, called upon them to learn to view and to present black reality exclusively from the vantage point of African Americans in Bronzeville, something that had not been done by previous literary generations. The group showed to the world that Bronzeville's artists were rising; as a backdrop to their ascension, Bronzeville's social ferment and the Chicago Black Renaissance cultural explosion, an aesthetic ideology of this "different kind of youth," seems to have been born.

Second, *Along the Streets* leans heavily on the spatial theses from scholars investigating the relationship between space and cultural production. Chicago was very much both a home for its authors and artists as a fact of their upbringing as well as a vibrant aesthetically generative space. With this as *Along the Streets'* foundational principle, the book demonstrates the existence of a Black Cultural Renaissance with a collation of literary and visual art figures, residents of Bronzeville, their lives and their crafts embedded in a series of institutional networks, producing a clear and distinct cultural aesthetic.

Who, then, were these youth? What are their stories? The creative output of Chicago-based writers during the Renaissance included some of the greatest names in African American literature: Richard Wright, Gwendolyn Brooks, Margaret Walker, Arna Bontemps, William Attaway, Willard Motley, Frank Marshall Davis, Fenton Johnson, Theodore Ward, and, according to lead archivist Michael Flug at the Chicago Public Library's Vivian G. Harsh Research Collection of Afro-American History and Literature, a host of lesser-known writers. Langston Hughes and Owen Dodson, though not Chicagoans, each made important contributions to the movement during their years in Chicago. Richard Wright is at the center of the Chicago Black Renaissance, the towering figure whose achievement first forced the world to pay attention to what was taking place in black Chicago. Wright used Chicago as a starting point in his epochal novel *Native Son*, and in his *12 Million Black Voices*, the great essay and photographic work on the Great Migration. Both drew from his experience on Chicago's South Side. It was out of this experience also that he wrote the Introduction to St. Clair Drake and Horace Cayton's *Black Metropolis*, the 1945 sociological classic. Wright's career is one of the prime examples of the remarkable interplay between creativity, place, scholarship and radical politics that formed the core of the Chicago Black Renaissance.[8]

Talented poets, artists, journalists, sociologists, and jazz musicians emerged during the Renaissance as well. Margaret Walker's first collection of poetry, *For My People*, won the Yale Younger Poets award in 1942. Frank Marshall Davis, who worked for the Associated Negro Press, published four volumes of poetry. Gwendolyn Brooks's first book of verse, *A Street in Bronzeville*, appeared in 1945. In 1949, Gwendolyn Brooks appeared at the "Book Review and Lecture Forum" at the George Cleveland Hall Branch Library to read from *Annie Allen*, her second book of poetry. The next year she was to win the Pulitzer Prize for poetry. Brooks became the first black writer to win the most prestigious creative award in the United States, an achievement that marked the culmination of the extraordinary literary output of black Chicago during the Chicago Black Renaissance. In 1944, Alice Browning and Fern Gayden, both members of the prestigious South Side Writers Group, launched the Chicago-based journal *Negro Story*, an important but little-known creation that published both poems and short stories.[9]

Today the names of Chicago Black Renaissance visual artists—Richmond Barthe, Margaret Taylor Goss [Burroughs], William Carter, Eldzier Cortor, Charles Davis, Ramon Gabriel, Joseph Kersey, William McBride, Archibald Motley, George Neal, Gordon Parks, Charles Sebree, Charles White, and a host of others—loom large in the history of American art. Their works span the full range of artistic endeavor. These new Bronzeville artists made names for themselves in oil paintings and watercolors, sculptures and murals, lithographs and photographs. They also created a close and supportive community of artists and institutions, such as the South Side Community Arts Center, and a shared sense that they were developing something new. For many of them, however, the creative environment that stimulated their work extended beyond the ranks of visual artists to the political awareness then deepening in black Chicago. Charles White put it bluntly: "I feel that the job of everyone in a creative field is to picture the whole social scene. . . . Paint is the only weapon I have with which to fight what I resent. If I could talk I would talk about it. Since I paint, I must paint about it."[10]

According to Chicago Public Library archivist Michael Flug, music was the precocious discipline of the Chicago Black Renaissance; the explosion of Chicago's black musical creativity did not wait for the 1930s and 1940s.[11] Chicago was a blues recording center in the 1920s. Classical music, already rooted in the community, gained impetus with the formation of the National Association of Negro Musicians in 1919. Maude Roberts George, one of its early presidents and music critic for the *Chicago Defender*, ceaselessly promoted classical music schools and concerts. Early in the century, Chicago's churches were renowned for their choirs.

But it is for jazz that Chicago's South Side musicians first gained national, and even international, recognition. During the Great Migration, the sounds of New Orleans jazz and Mississippi blues began to take over clubs and dance halls, and in the process merged with influences from Northern cities. Most early Chicago jazz performers came to the city from 1917 to 1921, from New Orleans or Memphis, drawn by jobs in the rapidly expanding network of clubs, theaters, and dance halls in Chicago's "Stroll" district at 35th and State Streets. Three New Orleans musicians—King Oliver, Louis Armstrong, and Johnnie Dodds—and one Memphis performer, Lil Hardin, led a movement that dramatically reshaped jazz. "It was in Chicago," wrote Samuel Floyd Jr. in *The Power of Black Music*, "that Armstrong became the world's most influential jazzman, developing his art and technique to a level that was then unapproachable by other trumpet players."[12] More importantly, music operated a central position in the political consciousness of many African Americans; as Ralph Ellison attests, jazzmen were the arbiters of this consciousness:

> Looking back, one might say that the jazzmen, some of whom we idolized, were in their own way better examples for youth to follow than were most judges and ministers, legislators and governors. . . . For as we viewed these pillars of society from the confines of our segregated community we almost always saw crooks, clowns or hypocrites. Even the best were revealed by their attitudes toward us as lacking the respectable qualities to which they pretended . . . while despite the outlaw nature of their art, the jazzmen were less torn and damaged by the moral compromises and insincerities which have so sickened the life of our country.[13]

Historian Rebecca Sklaroff notes that although this portrayal is rather romantic, Ellison nevertheless taps into the political power of cultural figures whose music spoke more directly and uncompromisingly about the most serious issues concerning African Americans.[14]

When "swing era" jazz was revolutionized by bebop, Chicago was at the center of the new developments.[15] Earl Hines's band with Dizzy Gillespie and Charlie Parker, at the height of its popularity during World War II, led the experimentation. One observer of the scene, when asked about the origins of bebop, provided a reply that it was simplicity in itself: "Bird [Parker] was responsible for the actual playing of it, and Dizzy [Gillespie] put (i.e., wrote) it down."[16] After World War II, Miles Davis's innovations were added to Chicago's bebop development. Depicted in paintings by Archibald Motley, and lauded in poems by Langston Hughes, the music that came to be known as "Chicago Jazz" was at the heart of the Chicago Black Renaissance.[17]

Chicago, in the period of the Renaissance, was the center of black journalism in the United States. Bronzeville's residents could choose their newspapers from among the *Chicago Defender*, the Chicago edition of the *Pittsburgh Courier*, the *Chicago Bee*, the *Chicago Whip*, and several smaller community papers. All of these papers printed articles from the national Black wire service, Claude Barnett's widely respected Associated Negro Press, also a Chicago-based institution.[18]

News of African Americans in the South and across the nation was carried regularly in the newspapers, often with emphasis on the home states of many Chicagoans. It was through these papers that Bronzeville's residents learned about the Scottsboro boys, the war in Ethiopia, the unionization of the sleeping-car porters, and a host of other national and international stories. Leading social scientists of the Chicago Black Renaissance presented their views to the community in regular newspaper columns. Each of the papers also carried news and information about Bronzeville. A great deal of space was given to news of meetings held by organizations and lodges; music, literature, and art events; women's and social clubs; and churches. The black press served as both the "town crier" for events and as the recorder of the community's social, cultural, and intellectual life.[19]

Columnists played a major role in the African American newspapers of the time. Political analysis often merged with literary efforts in the columns. In 1943, Langston Hughes introduced his famous character, Jess Semple, in his *Defender* column. Gwendolyn Brooks's first published poetry appeared in the *Defender* from 1934 to 1936. The *Chicago Whip*'s columnists campaigned for jobs for Bronzeville's residents, while the *Chicago Bee* sought to raise the consciousness of its readers by selling black history and literature books through the paper.[20]

At the beginning of World War II, a young man from Arkansas, John H. Johnson, launched a small black magazine-publishing venture with the appearance of *Negro Digest*. Operating at first out of Johnson's office in the Supreme Life Insurance building, and funded on a shoestring budget, this risky experiment proved to be the birth of a publishing giant. By 1945, Johnson added what was to become the most widely read black magazine anywhere, *Ebony*, followed six years later by the pocket newsmagazine, *Jet*.

In time, Johnson Publishing Company would have the most far-reaching impact of any of the ventures in black journalism that emerged from the Chicago Black Renaissance.[21]

Film and theater developments during this era hailed new opportunities for black actors and the black community as a whole. Work by Rebecca Lauren Sklaroff, Clovis Semmes, and Jacqueline Najuma Stewart attest to the role and unique position offered to the black community through the patronage of cinemas and theaters first along the Stroll and then in the heart of Bronzeville by 1945. *Along the Streets* looks toward Bronzeville's theaters as locations through which to examine the crossroads of aesthetics and political consciousness—whether by acting on stage or taking action by attending the theater and demanding representation through leisure and consumer culture. Hollywood and the politics of audience illustrate African Americans' interrogation of the larger history of representation and discriminatory practice, as well as the search for "truth" in cultural representation. The general excitement films brought about in the black press and the community indicates, as Sklaroff concludes, that they had significant meaning for the larger freedom struggle.[22]

Nearly all of the artists were supported, financially and spiritually, by the institutions with which they worked and/or the federal government; those who did not see funds from these federal initiatives received support from philanthropist and friend to Booker T. Washington, Julius Rosenwald. One federal initiative was a national New Deal creation, the Federal Art Project of the Works Progress Administration, an extension of the government's impulse to rely on cultural programs as a political tactic.[23] Several key institutions nurtured the literary atmosphere in Chicago. At Hall Branch Library's "Book Review and Lecture Forum," created by librarian Vivian G. Harsh to highlight the "Special Negro Collection" she was building, writers could meet and share their literary creations with everyday citizens. Informal gatherings among writers were further galvanized by the WPA-sponsored Illinois Writers Project and its celebrated "Negro in Illinois" study, which employed many of these writers.[24]

Additional support came from the Federal Art Project but served as a uniquely homegrown development—the South Side Community Art Center. Together with the South Side Writers Group, variously helmed by Richard Wright and Margaret Walker, the two provided literary and artistic crucibles for the emergence of African American literature, arts, and activism in Chicago. The Writers Group included Frank Marshall Davis, Ted Ward, Fern Gayden, and other young black writers. In May 1941, the formal dedication of the South Side Community Art Center by Eleanor Roosevelt was accompanied by an exhibition of paintings, sculpture, and drawing by Chicago's new black artists. The exhibition, entitled "We Too Look at America," offered a full range of works by all the artists of the Chicago Black Renaissance for the first time in a single show. The institutions of the Chicago Black Renaissance offered sites where writers, artists, musicians, and social scientists could present their latest work to Bronzeville's citizens for discussion, appreciation, and criticism. At the same time, they brought artists together with writers, musicians with journalists, sociologists with political activists. The interchange of ideas helped power the creative surge of the period. The character of the institutions helped make the Chicago Black Renaissance a truly multidisciplinary movement—unified, however, by an artistic consciousness that did a different sort of "race work."[25] Further studies must be done to speak to the contested nature and racialized power dynamics of these sources of philanthropy.

Along the Streets proceeds through the following scope: it begins much as a traveler would to any neighborhood by exploring Bronzeville's physical spaces and artistic spaces. It then moves to explore the lived experiences of Bronzeville's vibrancy. It draws to a narrower focus in its examination of two of Bronzeville's lives, Richard Wright and Gwendolyn Brooks, and then closes with a discussion of the distinct aestheticsm of the movement, that which set it apart from all other surges of African American production. Finally, an epilogue serves to conclude the project with a reexamination of the artistic legacy of Chicago's confluence of artists, writers, and streets—the physical spaces conditioned by the unforgiving twentieth-century urban racism of the North—where craft and life coexisted for a time and then dropped off toward the advent of the 1960s.

Chapter One charts the complex interplay and intersection of race, geography, and cultural criticism that permeated the Renaissance as a whole. Starting with the categorization of the neighborhood as the Black Belt and ending with heralding itself as "Bronzeville," this chapter explores the interfacing of newly arrived migrants with previously settled African Americans that bloomed into an exciting community. Specifically, this chapter examines two popular intersections in the South Side of Chicago—the "Stroll" district (the intersection of 35th and State Streets) during the early 1920s and the intersection at 47th and South Parkway. During the 1930s, the Savoy Ballroom, the Regal Theater, and South Center Department Store were located there. This intersection along with the Stroll served as foundations and sources of work for famed African American musicians, artists, and writers, such as Richard Wright, Langston Hughes, and Gwendolyn Brooks, themselves migrants or the daughters and sons of migrants. This chapter articulates an awareness of Chicago's African American urban landscape, with its hallmark intersections and institutions such as the Savoy Ballroom and South Center Department Store; it evidences Chicago Black Renaissance artists' and writers' critical interrogation of a black self and racial identity for the South Side and, with the gaining popularity of the Chicago Black Renaissance, the world.

Chapter Two covers the South Side Community Art Center and the South Side Writers' Group that predate the fame of Richard Wright and Gwendolyn Brooks. Pillars of the Bronzeville's community, these institutions of art and literature engendered a unique aesthetic consciousness/political ideology for which Chicago Black Renaissance would garner much fame. This chapter of *Along the Streets* emphasizes how the artists of the South Side Community Art Center and authors of the South Side Writers' Group evidenced a strong commitment to and conditioning by the streets and people of Bronzeville. It finds that the aesthetic formula characterized by these visual arts and literary groups collided and intersected in interesting ways that always articulated a vital political and modern consciousness sustaining the Renaissance movement into the 1940s.

Chapter Three introduces the many spheres of policy gambling, a game that rose to prominence between 1908 and 1955. This chapter reads policy as performance art, as informing black cultural production throughout Bronzeville, and as a patron and fiscal support of the Chicago Black Renaissance. Most importantly it seeks to demonstrate the relationship between lived actual realities of Bronzeville's mass culture of games and luck, and the grist mill that it was in that the game and its derivative culture provided for both the people in Bronzeville who hoped to imagine themselves beyond their existence and writers and artists who recognized the rich cultural material that was the policy game, its kings and queens, and the vernacular of luck in a world of harsh racism.

Chapter Four explores the rise and fame of Richard Wright and Gwendolyn Brooks through the particular genre of autobiography. Wright's *Black Boy (American Hunger)* and Gwendolyn Brooks's *Report From Part One* evidence these authors' awareness of spatial realities and how they transformed the city of fact into the city of feeling, to borrow from Rotella, into their writing. This chapter charts the dialogue between Wright's and Brooks's fiction and their urban surroundings as residents and then prize-winning authors. Through various literary and sociological projects, Wright and Brooks commenced an investigation of place, coherency, and consciousness in Chicago's flats, alleyways, blocks, and one-room kitchenette apartments.

Chapter Five continues this investigation of the moment's primary spearheaders with a comparison of Wright's 1941 photographic essay *12 Million Black Voices* and his final literary publication, *The Outsider*, set in Chicago and Harlem, to Brooks's 1945 collection of poetry, *A Street in Bronzeville*, and her only novel, published in 1953, *Maud Martha*. Brooks's and Wright's narratives rest on an axis of place and on assertions of racial identity and consciousness. Wright and Brooks offer a virtual tour of African American urban life at street level. Often one can imagine their characters brushing past one another on these harsh streets. This chapter argues that migration to the city and its unkept promise of freedom left African Americans on Chicago's South Side suspended between two planes of existence. The harshest loci of this suspension were the one-bedroom kitchenette apartments that began to burst at the seams as more and more migrants poured into Bronzeville. Brooks and Wright illustrated an acute consciousness of the symbiotic relationship between the streets of Bronzeville—the lived Bronzeville—and opportunities for cultural production. Their work serves as prime examples of the dynamics of this process that would be operationalized, in many different ways, by African Americans of the Chicago Black Renaissance.

Finally, the project closes with the epilogue assessing Bronzeville's and the Chicago Black Renaissance's narrative of decline. It is tempting to view this Renaissance's story as encompassing the rise and fall of Black community—tempting, but misguided.[26] The experience of Bronzeville's residents during this period was not one of unmitigated triumph followed by unfortunate demise; instead it was a contradictory blend of expansion, progress, and stagnation.[27] From 1910 to 1950 neighborhood residents produced and witnessed a remarkable growth in cultural, economic, and political institutions designed to serve their growing needs. Thus, the history of the neighborhood is an uncomfortable and conflicting mixture of opportunity and subjugation. As an ending note, this section focuses on the changes, urban and ideological, happening in Bronzeville as the neighborhood's heyday and the arts movement's momentum wound down. As its closing note, *Along the Streets* concludes by coming to terms with the *actual* existing economic, political, and cultural relations of the period as well as any ambiguities that follow. It tells the story of decline through the same spatial lens that governs the previous chapters to show how the once vibrant neighborhood succumbed to the pressures of segregation and economic disparity—that moment when the unforgiving streets that once provided fonts of material for writers and artists lent to the Renaissance movement's end but left an enduring legacy in a few surviving institutions.

Along the Streets reads the texts—literary, visual, and musical—of the Chicago Black Renaissance through such a lens, tying the remarkable cultural production of African Americans in Chicago to the materials or environment informing the literature and arts. *Along the Streets* surpasses the fragmented perspective offered by current scholarship in the field[28] by replacing it with a perspective stressing geographic continuities running through Chicago's black aesthetic production. This complex combination, anchored by Bronzeville as a thematic referent, drove the Chicago Black Renaissance movement's remarkable cultural creativity to such a degree that Bronzeville easily assumed the title of America's most thriving center of African American culture and arts in the mid–twentieth century.

ACKNOWLEDGMENTS

I have been so fortunate to have had the guidance and encouragement of many while writing this book. As a graduate student at Saint Louis University, I enrolled in a seminar on W. E. B. DuBois, and from then on I was hooked. I found an intellectual home in American Studies methodology, Women's Studies, African American history, urbanism, thought, and expressive culture. Little did I know that those many Monday evenings, surrounded by a gifted cohort, would have such a profound effect on the next ten years of my life. I was lucky enough to take this class from Jonathan Smith and Shawn Michelle Smith. Joseph Heathcott and Matt Mancini also deserve accolades for their valuable guidance during my time at SLU and beyond. I value their sustained friendship and guidance as I progress to further levels in my career. Thank you for being role models, superlative scholars, and caring friends.

I am grateful to Lehigh University's American Studies Program where I received my first taste of interdisciplinary thought and methodology. I especially thank John Pettigrew and Dawn Keetley. Thank you both for encouraging me to stay the course; thank you for providing me with intellectual confidence and maturity.

Most of my research took place in Chicago. I thank the curators at the Chicago History Museum and the Chicago Public Library. I especially thank Michael Flug, Cynthia Fife-Townsel, and the staff at the Vivian G. Harsh Research Collection of Afro-American History and Literature, Carter G. Woodson Regional Library. The South Side Community Art Center, University of Chicago's Special Collections, Newberry Library, and the Abraham Lincoln Presidential Library, Springfield, Illinois, and Hampton University Museum, Hampton, Virginia, deserve special thanks as well.

Since 2008, my academic home has been the History Department and American Studies Program at the College of William and Mary. I thank my colleagues for their advice, guidance, humor, and devotion while I charted into unknown territory with my book—especially Jody Allen, Cindy Haha-movitch, and Scott Nelson. I also extend thanks to those colleagues who read the manuscript and encouraged me to submit it as far and wide as possible. Thank you for being so welcoming and supportive. I thank the librarians at the Earl Gregg Swem Library—especially Martha Higgins—for their help. If I ever need to find anything I will come to you; you can be certain of that.

I would like to thank Joanne Catapano for giving *Along the Streets* its home and Larin McLaughlin and Dawn Durante, at the University of Illinois Press, for seeing it through to publication. Thank you.

Finally, none of this would be possible without the love, unwavering en-couragement, and generosity of my family, to whom this book is dedicated. Mom and Dad: thank you for everything you have done to get me to this place; I hope to make you proud. Joel: thank you for joining me on this crazy journey. I love you.

CHAPTER I

FROM BLACK BELT TO BRONZEVILLE

The South Side of Chicago was dubbed the Black Belt during the late teens. Crowds of people milled about day and night. Popular in the late teens and 1920s, the Stroll—South Parkway Avenue (presently Martin Luther King Jr. Boulevard)—was the center of Chicago's Black Belt. The Stroll served as inspiration for famed African American musicians, artists, and writers, such as Richard Wright, Langston Hughes, and Gwendolyn Brooks, themselves migrants or the daughters and sons of migrants. This chapter considers these specific sites, even addresses, as geographies of culture production—places where migrants to and residents of Black Chicago experienced the intersection of race, geography, and culture production in early-twentieth-century Chicago. The cultural formations powerfully link the various mappings of the Black Metropolis.[1]

As a prime destination for black migrants from the South, Chicago's "Black Belt" quickly grew into a segregated Black Metropolis where African American entrepreneurship, entertainment culture, and political activity thrived in the face of hostile "native" and ethnic white resistance to Black insurgence and racial integration.[2] Moving to Chicago signified a move into urban industrial modernity, a move and consciousness explored thoroughly in the scholarship of Adam Green, Davarian Baldwin, and Jacqueline Najuma Stewart; as a result, black migrants discovered and contributed to a dynamic, confident Black urban community that traced a third transition from "Black Metropolis" to "Bronzeville." Heralding the community as the locus of shining bronze faces, beautiful bronze faces, the neighborhood's transition through a variety of appellations evidences a complex interplay between hope, reality, and the triumph over the segregation and racial decimation that comprised Black migration—all captured in the dynamic cultural production of the Chicago Black Renaissance. These traditions, beginnings, and movements of black bodies from the Stroll southward to

47th Street and South Parkway map Chicago as the logical hotbed of African American Renaissance activity. Moreover, a careful rendering, geographically and fictionally, of these topographies finds "a city within a city" following the Depression as Bronzeville became the capital of Black America.[3]

Between 1910 and 1950 Chicago was the crossroads of northern urbanity.[4] The first mass movement of black southerners to northern cities occurred during and immediately after World War I. Participants in this "Great Migration" left their southern homes but brought with them, as Richard Wright noted in his 1945 autobiography *Black Boy (American Hunger)*, the "scars, visible and invisible," of southern boyhood.[5] Wright was both fascinated and intimidated. "I was seized by doubt," he recalled of the moment he walked out of the railroad station in Chicago. "Should I have come here? But going back was impossible. I had fled a known terror, and perhaps I could cope with this unknown terror that lay ahead."[6] Along with the unknown terror[7] of the big city came the liberating realization that a white man sitting beside him on the streetcar seemed unconscious of his blackness. "Black people and white people moved about," he noticed, "each seemingly intent upon his private mission. There was no racial fear. Indeed, each person acted as though no one existed but himself."[8] The new rules would require adjustment, but they also promised hope. Despite the fact that he grew disillusioned rather quickly, Richard Wright did not regret coming to Chicago in 1927. For in the South, an ambitious black American could find even less nourishment for hopes and dreams than in the North.

Black southerners "recognized that their future lay in the North."[9] The migrants brought with them experiences, memories, and expectations similar to Richard Wright's. Many had more modest goals—but they likewise had decided that the North was a land of opportunity. During World War I, northern cities were just that, especially compared with the South and within the context of the migrants' short-term expectations and early experiences.

With Northern employers unwilling to hire blacks as long as white immigrants from Europe remained available, northward migration had played little role in southern black life until World War I shut off immigration. Catalyzed in early 1916 by recruiters from northern railroads suffering from the wartime labor shortage, the Great Migration soon generated its own momentum. "Northern fever" permeated the black South, as letters, rumors, gossip, and black newspapers carried word of higher wages and better treatment in the North. Approximately one-half million southerners—both black and white—chose to say farewell to the South and start life anew in northern cities during 1916–1919, and nearly one million more followed in the 1920s, making it, according to Henry Louis Gates Jr., "the largest movement of Black bodies since slavery."[10]

For many migrants, the promise of the "North" and "the city" contained the dream of being liberated from the abuses and restrictions that characterized life in the South, lives once structured so strictly by the rhythms of a slave past.[11] Therefore, from cities, towns, and farms, they poured into northern cities. The lure of higher-paying work and freedom from social and political restrictions drew many southern blacks away from sharecropping and tenant farming toward the northern "land of promise."[12] According to Robin Bachin's study *Building the South Side*, an addition to these factors fueling the expansion of the Black Belt specifically was the availability of less expensive housing before World War I. This concomitance with job opportunities that would arrive with the war led the black population of Chicago to increase by 148.5 percent between 1910 and 1920 alone.[13] In these early periods, as historical and literary accounts of the Harlem Renaissance attest, Harlem became the mecca of black culture, home to such luminaries as W. E. B. DuBois, James Weldon Johnson, and Marcus Garvey. But in much of the Deep South, the Midwest—and as the 1930s neared—it was Chicago that captured the attention and imagination of restless and fed-up black Americans. The title of cultural mecca shifted to the Midwest.[14]

Among the many cities offering new employment and opportunities, Chicago represented a logical destination for black men and women preparing to leave homes in southern communities. Meatpacking firms were known even in the rural South, where their storage facilities dotted the countryside. Many black southerners had heard of the "fairyland wonders" of Chicago's spectacular 1893 Columbian Exposition.[15] Others knew of Chicago as the home of the Overton Hygienic Manufacturing Company, maker of High Brown Face Powder. Baseball fans might have seen or heard of Chicago's American Giants, the black team that barnstormed through the South every summer in a private railroad car.

Finally, the city was easily accessible via the Illinois Central Railroad, whose tracks stretched southward from Chicago into rural Tennessee, Mississippi, and Louisiana, with easy access from adjoining states as well. Regardless of where someone "stopped on the way," recalled one migrant from Mississippi, "the mecca was Chicago."[16] From 1916 to 1919, thousands more passed through the city before moving on to other locations in the North.[17]

Chicago became the symbol of the promise of the North for those who stopped there and passed through, and even for those who migrated elsewhere. As trains approached Chicago, the migrants' hope and excitement began to mix with awe, trepidation, and sometimes disappointment. Most railroad routes passed through the steel towns lying south and east of Chicago, offering initial views dominated by the gray pall that usually hung over the mills and the rickety houses of Gary, Indiana, and South Chicago.

To those arriving at night, the sight could have been particularly impressive and disorienting; the fiery smokestacks never rested, denying the natural rhythms of night and day that ruled migrants' agricultural pasts. Finally the train rolled into one of Chicago's railroad depots. Migrants fortunate enough to have someone to meet them might have been unsettled by the crowds but were soon reassured by the sight of a familiar face. Those migrants who were not met at the train by a friend were immediately faced with the problem of finding their own way to the South Side. They had to look for assistance; several black institutions met them during their first hours in the city, in effect providing the first connective tissues for a coherent political and artistic renaissance. Black porters and doormen assisted migrants and both white and black Travelers Aid assistants referred people with problems either to the Urban League or the black branch of either the Young Men's Christian Association or Young Women's Christian Association.

Newcomers experienced a series of shocks as they emerged from the railroad station. Many gazed at the immense structures, the concrete and iron materials that seemed to be everywhere, and the swift motion of people, automobiles, and trolleys. Richard Wright was taken aback by the "towering buildings of steel and stone"[18] and by elevated trains that occasionally shook the ground. The screeching of streetcars and honking of horns augmented the awesome sights. Scurrying residents seemed oblivious not only to their environment but to other people as well, and their "clipped speech"[19] was incomprehensible to Wright.[20]

Despite the dissonant urban environment, migrants could expect clarity in Chicago's color line. Shaped by both the circumscribing influences of the white city that surrounded it and the demands of the migrants and "Old Settlers" who inhabited it, by 1920 the emerging Black Metropolis on the South Side divided along lines of class, religion, and even age. But it remained a community nevertheless, unified by the implications of racial taxonomies. Beginning at the edge of an industrial and warehouse district just south of the Loop (Chicago's central business district), black Chicago stretched only a few blocks wide except at its northern end. In 1910, 78 percent of black Chicagoans lived on the South Side in a narrow strip of land known to whites as the Black Belt. From 1916 until 1948, racially restrictive covenants were used to keep Chicago's neighborhoods white. In language suggested by the Chicago Real Estate Board, legally binding covenants attached to parcels of land varying in size from city block to large subdivision prohibited African Americans from using, occupying, buying, leasing, or receiving property in those areas.[21]

Up to 1947, restrictive racial covenants covered large parts of the city and, in combination with zones of nonresidential use, almost wholly surrounded the African American residential districts of the period, cutting off corridors of extension. Davarian Baldwin, in his study *Chicago's New Negroes: Modernity, the Great Migration, and Black Urban Life*, defines restrictive covenants as legally binding documents, usually between white real estate agents and owners, to prevent the renting or sale of housing to nonwhites, with threat of civil action.[22] The rationale was to protect property values by keeping areas all white. For example, the University of Chicago grew concerned over the growing fear of declining property values around their South Side campus just east of the Black Belt neighborhood that was rapidly expanding during and after World War I. It has already been mentioned that Chicago's black population skyrocketed 148.5 percentage points between 1910 and 1920; its white population increased only 21 percent. Bachin charts the settlement patterns of migrants decade by decade alongside whites' response: "Before 1900, African Americans lived primarily on the South Side but were scattered in various neighborhoods. After 1900, and clearly by 1915, the narrow Black Belt south of the central business district, bounded by 12th and 39th Streets, State Street and Lake Michigan, solidified. White residents from these areas, fearing the 'Negro Invasion,' moved southward into neighborhoods around the University of Chicago."[23] The University supported neighborhood organizations pushing for racial restrictions in their homeowners' associations such as the Hyde Park Protective Association (HPPA). These associations worked with the Chicago Real Estate Board to ensure that African Americans could not "invade" white areas of the city. Bachin cites a 1920 formal scheme of racial segregation where the Board voted to expel "any member who sells a Negro property in a block where there are only white members."[24] These covenants with redlining tactics and virulent protests[25] in white neighborhoods would exacerbate conditions brought on later during the Great Depression, as competition increased for jobs, decent housing, and social and health services.[26] The housing left to black residents was in some of the city's most dilapidated neighborhoods. With the restrictive covenants, landlords could extract the highest rents for the worst housing from the most economically disenfranchised population.[27]

Many of the neighborhoods encumbered with racially restrictive covenants were subsequently settled by a second wave of the Great Migration during and after World War II,[28] only by this time the covenants had been declared unconstitutional. As part of the budding civil rights movement in the North, the National Association for the Advancement of Colored People (NAACP) put their focus on the covenants. On a local level, Chicago's branch of the NAACP assisted Carl Hansberry in a challenge to restrictive covenants on the South Side in a court battle his daughter Lorraine would fictionalize in her play *A Raisin in the Sun*.[29] The young and intrepid Hansberry serves as a model of the aestheticism of the Chicago Black Renaissance: the lived experiences of authors, artists, and musicians translated well into fictional renditions of the South Side's ugliness and chaos that would have powerful nonfictive consequences. In fact, on a nationwide scale, NAACP lawyers crafted what historian Thomas J. Sugrue called a "social scientific case—drawing from cutting-edge work in urban sociology and economics—about the negative consequences of restrictive covenants."[30] Emphasizing chaotic overcrowding, poor health conditions, and crime as results of the covenants, lawyers were successfully able to convince the Supreme Court to reconsider racial restrictions in the 1948 *Shelley v. Kraemer* case involving covenants in Detroit, St. Louis, and Washington.[31]

As troubling and disorienting as navigating the urban landscape was, it was thrilling as well. Upon initial arrival, migrants generally headed straight for Chicago's famous South Side ghetto where the bright lights and commotion introduced them to the rhythms of their new home. Langston Hughes recalled the thrill of his arrival in Chicago in 1918, before he became influential in the Harlem Renaissance of the 1920s: "South State Street was in its glory then, a teeming Negro street with crowded theaters, restaurants, and cabarets. And excitement from noon to noon. Midnight was like day. The street was full of workers and gamblers, prostitutes, and pimps, church folks and sinners."[32] The *Chicago Whip*, a black newspaper, agreed with Hughes's assessment, describing the Stroll as a cosmopolitan "Bohemia of the Colored folks," where "lights sparkled, glasses tinkled," and one could find bootblacks and bankers dressed in finery.[33] Looking east from the busy corner, a newcomer with an eye for the symbolic might have compared past and future, because five blocks away the Plantation Café's bright neon sign suggested dissonant images of the rural South and urban North.[34] At the turn of the century, Black Chicagoans enjoyed a whole range of leisure activities—a world of things to see and do[35]—that were available or highly restricted in other parts of the country, particularly the South. Migrants to Chicago frequently cited increases in leisure time and disposable income and the wider choice of recreational activities as major improvements in their daily lives, alongside better educational opportunities and greater political participation that this northern city afforded.[36]

Public space such as the Stroll showed African Americans as laborers as well as leisure seekers in the urban landscape. In the 1910s and 1920s, thanks to the publicity efforts of the *Chicago Defender*, it was the best-known street in African America, rivaled only by Seventh and Lenox Avenues in Harlem. The Stroll was where the action was. In the evening the lights blazed and the sidewalks were crowded with patrons attending the jazz clubs and those just gazing at all the activity. During daylight hours it was a place to loiter, gossip, and watch the street life. Black Chicagoans were on show, and they dressed up and acted accordingly.[37]

The Stroll marks a *starting point* in the evolution of Chicago's Black Renaissance patterns in which African Americans begin to use the black public space in their lives to construct themselves—physically and metaphysically—in a new and often hostile urban environment.[38] Stewart's book, *Migrating to the Movies*, focuses on the cinemas that lined the Stroll and argues simply that the sidewalk "served as a contested discursive and physical space in which black public spheres were constructed and interpreted, empowered and suppressed. What resulted were new things to continually reinterpret—the Black subject's highly contested public roles, rights and responsibilities—the public dimension of black entertainment in light of heated debates about black migration and leisure to Chicago."[39] This chapter takes such analysis by Stewart, and similar analysis of leisure sites by Adam Green and Davarian Baldwin, a step further; Chicago enables us to see, in dramatic and documented form, the high stakes of defining the racial boundaries of urban leisure for migrants seeking new "modern" freedoms and opportunities, for whites seeking to maintain racial hierarchies, and for Black Old Settlers seeking to police and distinguish themselves from recent arrivals from the South. This chapter shows the impulses both to control and to flaunt African American physical presence on urban scenes such as the Stroll and then at Bronzeville's 47th and South Parkway intersection. Chicago Black Renaissance artists, musicians, and authors demonstrate a relationship between their creative worlds and this highly contested social scene; this is evidenced through the development of jazz on the South Side, the visual art of Archibald Motley, and the fiction of Richard Wright and Gwendolyn Brooks.[40]

African Americans of all classes attended attractions on the Stroll much to the credit of the pages of the *Chicago Defender*, which was widely regarded as the country's leading "race" newspaper.[41] According to historian James Grossman, the *Chicago Defender* "grew into the largest-selling black newspaper in the United States by World War I, with two-thirds of its circulation outside of Chicago."[42] The *Chicago Defender*, the most widely read newspaper in the black South, afforded thousands of prospective migrants glimpses of an exciting city with a vibrant and assertive black community.

The newspaper, whose offices were along the Stroll,[43] ran occasional features that extolled the virtues of the Stroll, the commercial strip of cafes, dance halls, poolrooms, and theaters[44] that attracted seemingly ever-increasing numbers of African Americans seeking to see and be seen during their leisure hours. *Chicago Defender* contributor Columbus Bragg's column "On and Off the Stroll" along with Tony Langston's weekly "Review of the Theatres," inaugurated May 1914, provide a picture of Black patronage and commercial amusements near the Stroll.[45] The *Chicago Defender* credits the Stroll as a major cultural force in African American life in general and a major advocate of Black Belt amusements. For example, an article about the intersection of 31st and State Streets that appeared in the *Chicago Defender* in 1910 describes the vibrant social interaction that took place outside the Stroll's places of amusement: "Every young man of color in Chicago, young or old, if he has any leisure time generally wends his way to this interesting corner. Why? Because here he can meet all of his friends and here he can talk 'shop' to his 'heart's content' and learn in an hour everything of interest that has occurred during the last day, week, or year. Here congenial souls in all walks of life meet in a happy half hour's chat."[46] Stewart observes that in some ways this description of the typical character strolling through the Black Belt, reminiscent of Wright's Bigger Thomas, brings to mind Walther Benjamin's flaneur.[47] However, unlike the white male with his individualized, distracted, and dreamlike gaze, Wright gave Bigger a heightened awareness, a capitulation to conscious and restless viewing. Scholars Shane White and Graham White observe, "What was valued highly on the Stroll was not only the stylish way young black men-about-town presented their bodies but also their verbal agility and quickness of wit."[48] The Stroll provided a unique space for the elaboration of modern, African American experience in a stretch of urban sidewalks replete with amusements, commodities, and other sights. But the new, mobilized ways of looking and modern subjectivities that were developed along the Stroll were never completely divorced from a sense of engagement and participation in a new Black public, a heightened personal and political awareness of how one performs and interacts with others in that public. Jazz's evolution on the South Side provides a remarkable opportunity to examine this heightened awareness and how that developed into a uniquely Bronzeville aesthetic.

William Howland Kenney, in his study *Chicago Jazz*, references what anthropologist Clifford Geertz called the "flow of social action" and the "conceptual structures" in his close analysis of the Stroll as a particular place during a time widely recognized to have been important to the evolution of jazz.[49] As mentioned earlier, during and after World War I, the Stroll came alive with a fast-moving, free-spending night life. In the early years of this century, South Side night life first focused on the intersections of South State with cross streets numbered in the twenties, the area of the old vice district called the Levee.[50] This sin and entertainment district south of the Loop had grown up to service a transient population that circulated around the South Side terminals of the city's railroad, elevated, and trolley lines. Stretching from Van Buren or Harrison on the north to 22nd Street to the south, and from Michigan or Dearborn on the east to Clark or the meandering Chicago

River on the west, it encompassed almost a full square mile of the city's South Side heartland.[51] The Levee red-light district made up twenty square blocks; this vice district comprised 500 saloons, 6 variety theaters, 1,000 "concert halls," 15 gambling houses, 56 pool rooms, and 500 bordellos housing 3,000 female workers.[52] The showplace of the Levee had been the internationally famous Everleigh Club at 2131–2133 Dearborn Street. Run by two Kentucky sisters, Ada and Minna Everleigh, the club had even used hidden wall devices to shoot perfume into the rooms. Three African American brothels featuring "Colored Gay Ladies of the Night" made themselves available to free-spending Caucasian customers. Several madams of color maintained lucrative establishments and expected healthy profits from the 1893 World's Fair.[53] Thanks in part to the Everleigh's flaunting disdain for reformers, the Levee had been officially closed by Mayor Carter Harrison in 1912; but the move had succeeded only in moving such activities to other areas of the city and even into the suburbs.[54]

In his study of the World's Columbian Exposition of 1893, hosted by Chicago, Christopher Robert Reed stresses that African Americans who lived in the Levee red-light district, essentially a slum area, came to represent white Chicago's number-one social problem. The small enclave dominated by African Americans took on the nickname of "Cheyenne" because of this section's resemblance to the wild west. One guide to pleasure spots for the wicked recommended that "if this locality is visited at all, it should be in broad daylight and in good company."[55] But as the black population grew on the South Side and the mayor's vice commissions escalated, the center of the black bright-light district moved southward away from the area of the Pekin Inn on 27th Street to 31st Street (Elite Café No. 1, Grand Theater, Royal Gardens Café) and then to 35th Street, where much of the influential jazz activity and the heart of the Stroll would take place—in the Elite Café No. 2, DeLuxe Café, Dreamland Café, Sunset Café, Plantation Café, and Apex Club.

White jazz personality Eddie Condon later claimed that in 1924–1926, in the height of the Jazz Age, a trumpet held up in the night air of the Stroll would play itself.[56] Stores remained opened twenty-four hours a day to serve those enjoying urban life after years of rural tranquility. During the day, women leaned from tenement windows while small groups of men asserted a more public presence on the sidewalks. This evidences Stewart's assertion that there were women on the Stroll but it was a place that displayed an aggressively masculine ethos.[57] At night the crowded sidewalks rang with music and laughter, the cabarets, vaudeville, and movie theaters interspersed with "gaudy chile, chop suey, and ice cream parlors" around the clock.[58]

The Stroll and the southward-moving South State Street bright-light district, which would be centered at 47th and State Streets by the end of the decade, created an enterprise in racial entertainment serving the tourist market on two fronts—first, many black customers were tourists from different points throughout the Midwest; second, the arrival of so many migrant blacks in Chicago stimulated the curiosity of whites, who came to the Stroll to experience something of "race" life in the north. Racial tourism on the Stroll was governed by white American attitudes toward African Americans. The mixture of fascination and fear that often gripped whites when they turned their attention on blacks had a long historical tradition about which the Stroll's entrepreneurs—most of whom were white—could scarcely have been ignorant.

Chicago historian Allan H. Spear points out that African Americans were completely excluded from most commercial amusements—skating rinks, dance halls (nightclubs), and amusement parks elsewhere in the city.[59] The one amusement park for blacks—Joyland Park at 33rd and Wabash—never became a major force in South Side enterprise.[60] Given the lack of city-financed recreational facilities, a larger role was played in young people's leisure-time plans and employment opportunities by sports venues, cabarets, dance halls, movie theaters, and pool halls. Black youth tended to concentrate on what was available to them: vaudeville theaters and cabarets. Chicago's most widely discussed Jazz Age cabarets were the "black-and-tans," South Side clubs where black performers played and blacks and whites interacted in certain stylized ways, talking, flirting, drinking, dancing, and listening to music. Alain Locke asserted that "jazz took up more or less permanent residence in Harlem and Chicago"; he wrote of the latter, "Chicago became the reservoir of the rowdy, hectic, swaggering style of jazz that has since become known as 'hot jazz.'"[61] This blend of heat, beat, and interracial proximity led to much more intimate social contacts and helped inform a uniquely Bronzeville musical, literary, and visual aesthetic captured by the Chicago Black Renaissance.

During the late twenties, white gangsters, who had always been a force in the Black Belt, tightened their grip on the Stroll. The Al Capone syndicate reputedly bought the Plantation Café. Joe Glaser had also bought into the Plantation. Ed Fox owned the Grand Terrace. As the noose of federal prohibition tightened, business fell off and competition became violent. Bombs ripped through the Plantation and the recently renovated Café de Paris. The most famous South Side cabarets became increasingly notorious as gangland properties, cutting themselves off from legitimate businessmen in both the black and white communities. Gangsters' prohibition brought an end to the South Side's cabaret culture. Clubs successfully defied prohibition as long as prosecutors remained unable to prove that illegal alcohol, discovered and then confiscated on the premises, had been sold by, or even in, the club. But in December 1926, this legal loophole was closed when federal judge Adam C. Cliffe heard the appeal of Chicago's Moulin Rouge, Friars Inn, and Al Tierney's Town Club—three of the Loop's leading night clubs—and ruled that the Volstead Act outlawed not just public places that actually sold illegal beverages but also "places where people carrying liquor congregate."[62] This national campaign, dubbed the "hip flask ruling," successfully closed nearly all of the cabarets. *Variety* began to talk about Chicago's jazz cabarets in past tense: "Chicago was once the hottest café town in the United States, famous for sizzling music, torrid night life, a great little spot for the great little guys. But that's history now. Night by night it gets tougher for the cabarets."[63] The groundswell of sensibility about urban leisure time was far too powerful, however, to be completely arrested by the Depression and federal prohibition. The cabaret business survived on a smaller and far less remunerative scale. This did not satisfy the wallets of Chicago's jazz musicians. Many, like Benny Goodman, Louis Armstrong, and Eddie Condon, found themselves at a stage in their careers where working for a few dollars and drinks in an obscure neighborhood apartment was unacceptable. What jazz needed was a change of venue. Some of the more technologically advanced Chicago jazzmen of both races might have turned from small cabaret bands to the movie theater pit orchestras. But the arrival in Chicago during the summer of 1927 of new technologies, marketed by Vitaphone and Movietone, brought mechanically produced sound to the movies that eliminated these paychecks as well.[64]

Even though prohibition politics, radio, movie soundtracks, jukeboxes, and a reeling economy destroyed much of Chicago's cabaret business after 1920, peculiarly, most of the dance halls survived. The larger, more prestigious dance halls had already established a privileged position among Chicago's urban reformers, and therefore they largely escaped the local political heat that the reformers had turned on the cabarets in 1927. As reform pressure increased on cabarets and speakeasies in the late 1920s, the relative innocence of dance halls recommended itself to reformers and politicians. They also appealed to out-of-work jazz men who were technically prepared and ready to take hold of the opportunities dance halls provided.[65]

Kenney stresses that "the core cultural and musical synthesis that produces Chicago jazz of the twenties emerged in the cabarets from 1904 to 1929."[66] Historically, mostly white Chicagoans danced to Jazz Age music in the large Loop hotels and in the large dance halls built in the major north side and west side bright-light districts. Only one of these more sizable institutions—the Savoy Ballroom—was built in the Black Belt. Before the cracking of its foundation, the large commercialized dance hall was overwhelmingly a white phenomenon that catered to a craze among the white population for social dancing. But as the Stroll's cabaret era ended, Bronzeville's dance hall era began.[67] The opening of the hugely successful Savoy Ballroom at 47th Street and South Parkway in 1927 created a new center of black nightlife that effectively killed off the Stroll.

In 1927, as part of a chain of dance halls opening in black neighborhoods across the country, dance hall entrepreneur I. Jay Faggen and a group of white investors undertook to build a state-of-the-art dance hall deeper into Chicago's South Side. Faggen owned New York City's Roseland (after 1924, the Arcadia), the Dance Hall at 53rd and Broadway, the Rosemont Ballroom in Brooklyn, Harlem's Savoy Ballroom, three Roseland ballrooms in Philadelphia, and the Cinderella Ballroom at Madison and Central Streets in Chicago. He associated with white Chicago dance-band leader Ray Miller to form the Cosmopolitan Orchestras Booking and Promotion Offices, which controlled and promoted the bands serving his own and others' dance halls. The Savoy was opened on Thanksgiving night in 1927 at 47th Street and South Parkway, and the Regal Theater opened on February 4, 1928. Throughout its existence, the ballroom and theater served the predominantly African American neighborhoods between 23rd and 63rd Streets and helped anchor the 47th and South Parkway bright-light district. The Savoy secured its reputation as one of the city's top night spots by showcasing the nation's hottest jazz bands in a refined setting that appealed to upwardly mobile black Chicagoans.

Plans for the construction of a large, $1 million deluxe theater, ballroom, and department store near the southeast corner of 47th Street and South Parkway were announced in 1926 by a syndicate headed up by real estate developers Harry M. and Louis Englestein. The *Chicago Tribune* reported: "What easily stands out as the most ambitious building project so far contemplated for Chicago's ever growing colored district is announced by a white syndicate for the southeast corner of South Parkway (formerly Grand Boulevard) and 47th Street. Harry M. and Louis Englestein head the syndicate. Louis Khan, former of Becker Ryan and Co. [a department store chain], is part of it."[68] The work was to begin December 7. Having already acquired several properties on the site, they planned to replace the existing structures with an expansive three-story structure that would include space for a theater, ballroom, department store, drugstore, bowling alleys, billiard rooms, offices, and as many as fifty smaller stores. Construction on the project began toward the end of 1926, with the ballroom slated to be the first part of the project completed. The most elegant, elaborate, and expensive entertainment complex ever built in black Chicago, the Regal/ Savoy pulled bright-light entrepreneurs away from the Stroll and created a new center of black Chicago nightlife for the thirties.[69]

The Savoy outshone all of the smaller South Side dance halls along the Stroll, and its success killed the 35th and South State Streets entertainment district. With more than a half-acre of dancing space, the Savoy had a capacity of over four thousand persons. The ballroom's name recalled the enormously popular and highly regarded dance palace of the same name in New York's Harlem, which had opened a little more than a year earlier. Opening night featured a gala ball that attracted hundreds of community leaders, theater celebrities, star musicians, and their most ardent followers. On stage for the festivities were Sammy Stewart, Charles Elgar, and Clarence Black and their orchestras. Comedians Moss and Frye also performed.[70] This lively atmosphere became the grist mill for many of Archibald Motley's Depression-era paintings. Formally trained at the Art Institute of Chicago, Motley powerfully depicted African American nightlife in his paintings *Black Belt* and *Barbecue* (both in 1934); nightclub and vaudeville scenes in *Blues* (1929), *Saturday Night* (1935), and *Between Acts* (1935); and Sanctified church life in *Tongues (Holy Rollers)* (1929).[71] The evolution of jazz work shows a link between the contextual world of jazz—the South Side cabarets, black-and-tans, and ballrooms—and Bronzeville's unique ("hot" even) aesthetic. Motley's themes illustrate the ways in which jazz entertainers, Bronzeville residents, and racial tourists traversed, navigated, and brought together overlapping locales; indeed his work captured the beauty of Condon's standing self playing the trumpet.

In its review of the Savoy, the *Chicago Defender* extolled the modern features of the new ballroom:

> Never before have Chicagoans seen anything quite as lavish as the Savoy ballroom. Famous artists have transformed the building into a veritable paradise, each section more beautiful than the other. The feeling of luxury and comfort one gets upon entering is quite ideal and homelike, and the desire to stay and dance and look on is generated with each moment of your visit. Every modern convenience is provided. In addition to a house physician and a professional nurse for illness or accident, there is an ideal lounging room for ladies and gentlemen, luxuriously furnished, a boudoir room for milady's makeup convenience, an ultra modern checking room which accommodates 6,000 hats and coats individually hung so that if one comes in with his or her coat crushed or wrinkled it is in better condition when leaving.[72]

Such modern amenities not only lent an "atmosphere of refinement" to the ballroom that reflected the class pretensions of upwardly mobile black Chicagoans, but also decreased the likelihood that the Savoy would draw fire from those advocating the closure of disorderly dance establishments. An adjacent one-thousand-space parking lot also likely appealed to more prosperous black Chicagoans.

Black newspapers also praised the Savoy management for its fair hiring policies. "In operating this smart ballroom," the *Chicago Defender* reported, "more than 150 will be employed. Not only will all of the help be Race people, but wherever it is possible for the management to distribute money by means of purchases it will be among our people."[73]At a time when most of the city's ballrooms, theaters, and department stores excluded African Americans from positions involving contact or interaction with customers, the ballroom's managers drew no such color line, albeit with the expectation that most of the Savoy's customers would themselves be black.

Under Faggen's management, the Savoy hosted a wide variety of jazz bands and other entertainers: some black, some white, some from Chicago, some making their Chicago debut. In 1928, the popular all-white orchestra of Paul Ash, famous for its performances at the predominantly white McVickers and Oriental Theaters in Chicago's Loop, played a stint at the ballroom. But the majority of bands to appear at the Savoy were black, beginning with Charles Elgar and Clarence Black's orchestras in 1927. Faggen revolutionized the urban scene for African American leisure-seekers further when he pursued a two-band policy at the Savoy from 1927–1929. He began this new format with the well-established dance orchestras of Charles Elgar and Clarence Black. The former was soon replaced with the Carroll Dickerson Orchestra featuring Louis Armstrong and drummer Zatty Singleton. The Dickerson orchestra became the hottest dance band on the South Side and in 1929 broadcast nightly over WMAQ, the Chicago Daily News affiliate. Armstrong showed particular musical acumen with the new dance hall orchestra formats. The trumpeter and vocalist became the star attraction in the newest, largest, and best-connected dance hall in black America, playing to packed houses and rave notices with the Dickerson band at the Savoy. South Siders could count on Armstrong's reassuring ability to outshine the top white solo instrumentalists; according to the *Chicago Defender*, "Louie poured plenty of oil and it soaked in too. The crowd gathered around him and wildly cheered for more and more."[74] Two bands were engaged every night to permit continuous dancing. When one band took a break, another was on hand to play on. This excitement would sustain the black community into the thirties with appearances by Duke Ellington, The Walter Barnes Orchestra, and Cab Calloway and Benny Moten's orchestras making appearances there in 1931. The music never stopped at the Savoy. From 1927 until 1940, the Savoy was open seven days a week, with matinees on Saturdays and Sundays.

The Savoy, however, was more than just a ballroom. It doubled as a community center and spectator sports venue for black Chicago, serving as further evidence that Chicago provided the connective tissue to put together a fertile cultural renaissance. The South Side Chamber of Commerce and the board of directors of the black-owned Binga State Bank held banquets there during the late 1920s. The ballroom hosted the *Chicago Defender* benefit ball in 1928 and a celebration of black achievement in 1931. Other events during the ballroom's early years included community mass meetings to discuss pressing political issues, boxing matches, and roller-skating parties.

Basketball became a part of the Savoy's offerings in 1927, when the management, looking to increase ballroom attendance, began hosting semiprofessional basketball matches two nights a week. To put together a team to play as the home side, they turned to local sports promoter Abe Saperstein. Saperstein selected five of the best black basketball players from the South Side to play on the ballroom's team, which became known as the "Savoy Big Five." After a short stint at the Savoy, Saperstein took his team on the road, where they played local basketball teams in highly publicized matches. To drum up local enthusiasm for the matches, he dropped the "Savoy Big Five" and renamed his team the "Harlem Globetrotters."

Next door to the Savoy Ballroom was the Savoy Outdoor Boxing Arena, seating about five thousand. The admission ran nearly forty cents for amateur boxing bouts. Admission consisted of ten boxing bouts and two wrestling matches. Adjoining the arena was a training headquarters where Joe Louis worked out for his fight with King Levinsky.[75]

By day, the Savoy Complex or the "South Center Building"—a large commercial real estate development project including the South Center Department Store, the famous Regal Theater, and 47th Street and South Parkway—was a vibrant commercial district. The *Federal Writers' Project: Negro Studies Project* described the intersection as

> A point easily accessible from the Loop by bus, elevated train, and street car. . . . Tourists will find the South Center Building on the southeast corner of 47th Street and South Parkway a very entertaining spot. They will see the South Center Department Store, a real commercial community center with colored and white salespeople, managers, etcetera, working together throughout the store. Also in this building is the Regal Theater, one of the largest and finest, on the largest and finest in the South Side. Near the Regal Theater is the Savoy Ballroom, where there are boxing matches, wrestling, basketball, and dancing.[76]

Clovis Semmes, in *The Regal Theater and Black Culture*, called the Regal "the greatest movie-stage-show venue in the United States ever constructed to specifically service a major African American community."[77] White investors built this state-of-the-art entertainment complex; it was without question the largest, the most technologically advanced, and the most architecturally ornate movie house in the Black Belt. In his book, Semmes describes Bronzeville as a political and economic colony, existing (financially) for the benefits of whites, who lived elsewhere. The history of the Regal Theater confirms this.[78]

Regal shows, furnished stunning pageantry, and Regal management extended every consideration and courtesy to ensure the enjoyment and comfort of its patrons. Regal shows were large, lavish productions organized around an artistic theme; titles included: "Midnight Follies," "Bag of Tricks," and "So This is Venice."[79] In the first two years of operation, Regal management produced live shows on a very frequent basis, probably averaging two or more weeks of shows per month. Also, major films came to the Regal after completing their first run at the downtown houses.[80] A famous scene from Wright's *Native Son* takes place inside the Regal Theater where Bigger Thomas took in a double feature: *The Gay Woman* and *Trader Horn*.[81]

The Regal as a commercial venture, Semmes tells his readers, stood in contrast to the fact that it was not uncommon for white-owned entertainment venues and other business establishments in black communities to treat Blacks as second-class citizens by maintaining Jim Crow policies. What was even more remarkable was that Blacks could work for the Regal in nearly every capacity. Semmes stresses that these egalitarian practices were less the result of a new moral fervor by white businessmen, and more a consequence of the emergence of Blacks as an important consumer class; of an increasingly competitive business climate where white businesses had to compete (generally with each other) for Black patrons; and of activism on the part of blacks who began to boycott white businesses in their communities when they were denied employment based on race.[82] This activism met an organizational climax in the *Chicago Whip's* "Spend your Money Where You Can Work Campaign," which targeted boycotts at chain stores that would serve but not hire blacks. The campaign registered some successes, but according to historian Christopher Reed, "the response from the white store owners was neither enthusiastic nor cooperative even in instances where the businesses were predominantly African American."[83] The movement spread rapidly to other cities, drawing support from the major civil rights organizations. In 1931 black ministers, politicians, and businessmen published appeals in Harlem newspapers to follow Chicago's example. Calls for boycotts came from the Harlem Business Men's Club and from supporters of the black nationalist Marcus Garvey. Harlem Reverend John H. Johnson of Saint Martin's Protestant Episcopal Church formed the Citizens League for Fair Play and used Harlem newspapers to promote its picketing efforts. In 1933 in Washington, D.C., the New Negro Alliance, Inc., created the motto "Buy Where You Work—Buy Where You Clerk." Responding to layoffs of black workers at a Washington hamburger grill, the alliance targeted such black district stores as Kaufman department stores, the A&P, and the High Ice Cream Company stores. Overall, the alliance developed a comprehensive agenda advocating increased black employment, opportunities for black advancement and promotion, combined African Americans' purchasing power, and the creation of larger black businesses.[84]

After great anticipation and fanfare, the Regal opened its doors on February 4, 1928. The *Chicago Defender* helped engender the excitement:

> This new and magnificent structure will be open to the public in a few weeks. It has been built to serve citizens of all races and will be dedicated to the showing of the finest motion pictures and high-class stage productions. It is located on the southeastern corner of 47th street and South parkway, and will be complete in every respect, having spacious lobbies, lounging and waiting rooms, modern fresh air plants, a huge stage with a hydraulic curtain, and a grand organ that will rise and lower by electricity. The refinement, charm, and beauty of Moorish architecture will predominate throughout the theater. The huge auditorium will be topped with a grand canopy effect.[85]

This intersection, from its consistent mention in the *Chicago Defender*, was becoming quite famous. Richard Wright called this stretch, in his Federal Writers' Project piece, the "promenade."[86] The area housed the most fashionable shops and stores. On holidays such as Easter and Christmas, "Negroes parade up and down here, dressed in their best finery."[87] *Black Metropolis* explains:

> There is continuous and colorful movement here—shoppers streaming in and out of stores; insurance agents turning in their collections at a funeral parlor; club reporters rushing into a newspaper office with their social notes; irate tenants filing complaints with the Office of Price Administration; job-seekers moving in and out of the United States Employment Office. Today a picket line may be calling attention to the "unfair labor practices" of a merchant. Tomorrow a girl may be selling tags on the corner for a hospital or community house. The next day you will find a group of boys soliciting signatures to place a Negro on the all-star football team.[88]

No longer were educated blacks limited to jobs at the post office—doctors and lawyers could set up their practices on 47th Street. The first twelve black certified public accountants in America had their offices in the Savoy Complex. A small but vibrant black leisure class was emerging, and 47th Street offered black Chicagoans a sense of freedom and purchasing power they couldn't find anywhere else in America at that time. For example, the largest African American–owned department store, South Center, enjoyed much success in a white-dominated business climate. *Black Metropolis* offers an excellent description of South Center Department Store's location:

This is Bronzeville's central shopping district, where rents are highest and Negro merchants compete fiercely with whites for the choices[t] commercial spots. A few steps away from the intersection is the "largest Negro-owned department store in America," attempting to challenge the older and more experienced white retail establishments across the street. . . . Within Black Metropolis, there are neighborhood centers of activity having their own drugstores, grocery stores, theaters, poolrooms, taverns, and churches, but "47th and South Park" over-shadows all other business areas in size and importance.[89]

Clearly, something was happening that had never occurred before on the South Side of Chicago—or in the Midwest, for that matter.

Table 1.1, adapted from the 1938 "Negro in Illinois Papers," delineates the number of businesses operated by Negro and white Proprietors on 47th Street between State and Cottage Grove:[90]

Table 1.1. Number of businesses operated by Negro and white proprietors on 47th Street between State and Cottage Grove[*]

	Negro	White
Food stores	3	45
Business services	4	15
Automotive	1	3
General merchandise	1	16
Clothing stores	8	49
Furniture and household appliances	0	15
Hardware stores	0	4
Prepared food	8	13
Drug stores	0	9
Other retail stores	7	22
Personal service	42	36
Bookies	1	1
Repair services	2	7
Miscellaneous	6	2
Totals	83	237

* Federal Writers' Project: Negro in Illinois Papers, Vivian Harsh Collection, Carter G. Woodson Regional Library, Courtesy of the Chicago Public Library, Chicago.

Thus South Center Department Store was the first store where the people of Bronzeville could shop in a store catering to their needs, owned by a member of the race, where they could be helped by a majority of black salesmen and saleswomen. South Center opened in March 1928 with nine thousand square feet of floor space, an African American store doctor, and an African American law firm handling their business. The Federal Writers' Project reported:

The South Center Department Store Inc. . . . employs more Negroes than any other firm of its kind in the United States. There are approximately four hundred persons employed and 49 percent are women and 51 percent are men. Their ages range from eighteen years to fifty-five years old. After one year's service each employee is eligible for ten days vacation each subsequent year with pay. All work eight hours a day. The minimum salary is $15.00 a week. . . . Sixty-nine percent of the women employed are Negroes and 31 percent are white women. And 51 percent of the men are Negroes and 49 percent are white men.[91]

In addition to the Savoy Complex's sporting and entertainment offerings, African Americans exercised their purchasing power at its department store. South Center Department Store was the first store where people of Bronzeville could shop in a store catering to their needs, operated by a member of the race, Richard Lee Jones,[92] and where they could be helped by a majority of black salesmen and saleswomen.

The South Center Department Store serves as evidence of a powerful African American public self and Bronzeville's functionality. African Americans took great pride in their South Side communities and institutions and this pride would not only spill onto canvases, pages, and music sheets but into community practices as well. In 1930, the black newspaper, the *Chicago Sunday Bee*, held a contest to elect a mayor of Bronzeville. The whole "mayor" idea was the brainchild of one of Bronzeville's most beloved sons—James "Jimmy" Gentry, who since 1916, or thereabouts, bankrolled the annual Miss Bronze America beauty pageants. In fact the name Bronzeville is rooted in those very beauty pageants, which gave rise to common expressions like "Bronze-beauties of Bronze-ville." Gentry, a theater editor for Anthony Overton, the cosmetic king and publisher of the *Chicago Sunday Bee*, suggested that they use his coined word *Bronzeville* to identify the community, since it more accurately described the skin tone of most of its inhabitants. Overton supported the idea and in 1930 his newspaper sponsored an unsuccessful Mayor of Bronzeville contest.

In 1932 Gentry left the *Chicago Bee* and carried his Mayor of Bronzeville idea to *Chicago Defender* publisher Robert S. Abbott. Abbott jumped at Gentry's idea. Charles Browning, the *Chicago Defender*'s promotional genius, developed the Mayor of Bronzeville contest into the newspaper's second most profitable promotion—second to The Bud Billiken Club and parade—the oldest African American parade in the country.[93] With the blessings and backing of Robert Sengstacke Abbott—founding Publisher of the *Chicago Defender* newspaper—the title "Mayor of Bronzeville" was created. As framed in its charter mission statement, the Mayor of Bronzeville was conceived to elevate an outstanding citizen to heights beyond imagination and to make of him a symbol for the city. Gentry set up shop in Suite 47 in the Liberty Life Insurance Company building at 35th Street and South Parkway to run the campaign, which was to coincide with his annual Miss Bronze America beauty pageant. Posters and ballot boxes were set up in every drugstore, restaurant, boutique, barber shop, garage, church, grocery store, and newspaper stand in Bronzeville, and nomination ballots ran in the *Chicago Defender*. Scores of community activists and ward precinct captains took to the streets of Bronzeville to hype the campaign. Before long the mailroom at the *Chicago Defender* was flooded with nomination ballots.[94]

Notable among the finalists were Savoy Ballroom announcer Eddie Plique, controversial union boss J. Levitt Kelly, and Thomas Smith, owner of Smith Transportation Company. But on Saturday night September 22, 1934, behind the walls of the Eighth Regiment Armory on Giles Street, Tiny Parham's Orchestra rocked the house as Pullman-porter-turned-leading-businessman James E. Knight was elected as the first-ever Mayor of Bronzeville. Known affectionately as "Genial Jim," Knight was a ranking member of the Masonic order and one of the architects of the "new downtown Black America" on 47th Street. James Knight was the founder of the world-famous Palm Tavern at 446 East 47th Street, a Bronzeville landmark still open for business today and for decades a key social and civic center. Knight went on to found the Knight-Young Shoe Stores with *Chicago Defender* sportswriter Frank "Beansy" Young and was the first African American representative at the national shoe-store owners' convention, then held annually at the Palmer House. Parades and parties followed the announcement, hallmarking a new era in "race progress," a phrase that was popular in that day to denote the improvement of the condition of African Americans. The annual election of the "Mayor of Bronzeville" grew into a community event with significance far beyond that of the circulation stunt, in which tens of thousands of people used to participate.

As Mayor of Bronzeville, Knight would add his voice to the issue of jobs for the black man in the construction of what was to become the Ida B. Wells Homes; but the post was clearly a paper tiger with no official city status. However, it was highly respected because the Bronzeville Mayor was chosen by popular vote of the people, void of political party influence. As such, when the Mayor of Bronzeville talked issues with outside business and political leaders, his words were taken in a sense that this person truly spoke for the concerns of the community. And over the years many of the community's most respected people would have the privilege of serving, including two noted physicians and a top radio personality.[95]

The renaming of the community as "Bronzeville" held deep political and social significance. It was no longer known as the "Black Belt," a term used by sociologists and vice commissions to highlight increased rates of delinquency, dependency, and crime.[96] Drake and Cayton used the term *Black Belt* to engage and challenge outsiders' observations on the community that it was merely one thing—homogeneously black. They contrasted this "Black Belt," as the outsiders' assertion, with "Bronzeville," the insiders' assertion—championing the race. Bronzeville, then the largest black community in the country, signified a collective spirit, with its own legendary mayoral elections. As such, Bronzeville became one of the centers, if not *the* center, of African American culture, the perfect setting for a renaissance.

Bronzeville's position as the center of black life—its amazing brightness and vibrancy—in the twentieth century was complex and desperately in need of critical elaboration. With popularity came the necessity of critique. It is important to recall Drake and Cayton's assessment that Bronzeville was a community of stark contrasts, the facets of its life as varied as the colors of its people's skins.[97] By 1930, the area had become almost completely segregated, with dilapidated tenements, high rentals, and crowded flats divided into kitchenettes. Those fortunate enough to buy homes found their choices limited by the restrictive covenants. Migrants brought to the North an understanding of racial categories and they found them reinforced. Bronzeville's racial conditions offered an odd blend of comfort, familiarity, and utter newness that soon led to migrants' disappointment.

Writers and artists of the Chicago Black Renaissance offered, for the first time, a critical interrogation of this synthesis through their art and literature. Gwendolyn Brooks best summarized it through a cast of interesting black men and women in her 1945 collection of poetry *A Street in Bronzeville*. She executes a geographic and artistic methodology that interprets the urban landscape of Black Chicago by rendering individuals traversing its streets. For example, in her 1945 poem, "The Sundays of Satin-Legs Smith," Brooks investigates the relationship between Chicago's migration history, its urban landscapes, and the captivating individuals along 35th and State Streets or shoppers in South Center Department Store. Broadly stated, the question occupying this poem and every poem in her collection *A Street in Bronzeville* is, how important is the outside (Black Chicago) to the inside (its people)?

"Sundays" explores the gestures between the streets and the poem's protagonist Satin-Legs Smith. It starts with migration, as the poem reminds us that Smith has a "heritage of cabbage and pigtails;"[98] it then reminds readers of migrants' awkward tendencies and hardships or unfamiliarity in the urban scene by stressing Smith's "old intimacy with alleys, garbage pails."[99] With time, however, Smith wises up; readers see this in his adoption of urban dress. This serves as one of several benchmarks of his evolution from southern "cotton seed" to urban zoot-suiter. Brooks described this character in her autobiography *Report from Part I:* "You probably don't remember the zoot-suiters; they were still around in the early forties. They were not only black men but Puerto Ricans, too, who would wear these suits with the wide shoulders, and their pants did balloon out and then come down to tapering ends, and they wore chains, perhaps you've seen them in the movies. That's the kind of person I was writing about in 'The Sundays of Satin-Legs Smith.'"[100] Aside from dress, another marker of his urban transformation and relinquishment of all things southern is Satin-Legs Smith's Sunday morning stroll. Black magazines like *The Age* documented the Sunday tradition where "the crème de la crème" mingled with the "has-beens" and the "would-bes."[101] It is difficult to know exactly how to categorize Smith, but one may judge from his choice of prostitutes and dining locations that he is closest to a "would-be," what Harlemites would call a "striver."[102] The Sunday stroll became an unquestioned tradition, and one did not have to look far to find its practical benefits. Smith's mission must have been to socialize, to fraternize, to strut his stuff. It was the relaxed, neighborly quality of the stroll that mattered most.[103] James Wendell Johnson located and detailed the custom in Harlem in the following manner:

> One puts on one's best clothes and fares forth to pass the time pleasantly with friends and acquaintances and, most important of all, the strangers he is sure of meeting. One saunters along, he hails this one, exchanges a word or two with that one, stops for a short chat with the other one. . . . He passes on and arrives in front of one of the theatres, studies the bill for a while, undecided about going in. He finally moves on a few steps farther and joins another group and is introduced to two or three pretty girls who have just come to Harlem, perhaps only for a visit; and finds reason to be glad that he postponed going into the theatre. The hours of a summer evening run by rapidly. This is not simply going out for a walk; it is like going out for an adventure.[104]

Johnson's description captures the flavor of the event, but quite possibly mystifies it at the same time. The point of the exercise, as it is on Sundays everywhere in the Christian world, is to look well before the Maker. Sunday emphatically is not, as a reader might first anticipate, a day of worship and prayer for Smith. It is rather the day when he steps out on the town with a woman and eventually takes her to bed. "The Sundays of Satin-Legs Smith" is all about the dignity of its title character. His strutting is not about spiritual hunger or strivings—it is about sexual potency or manhood on parade. Black public space works for him in this way; he uses his element the best way he knows how. As a stroller on the sidewalks of State and 47th Streets, Smith feels good about himself. He is his own man. He is proud of his race, as his showboating demonstrates. Persistent regal imagery in the poem highlight this

Sunday pride: Smith feels "royal"[105] on Sundays: "he designs his reign,"[106] lives out the full significance of his "title"[107] as ladies' man. If on Sundays he feels "royal," this temporary elevation of mood stands in contrast to the other days of the week: six days of the week for Smith are "shabby," filled with "intricate fear . . . / postponed resentments . . . prim precautions."[108] Smith's activities are shadowed against this bitter backdrop—the ongoing powerlessness he experiences as a black man earning a precarious living in a white-dominated socioeconomic system: the Chicago of the 1940s.[109]

Brooks rather than Smith, narrator rather than protagonist, takes readers on an illuminating guided tour of this socioeconomic system. Satin-Leg's stroll provides, simultaneously, a celebratory picture of Black Chicago and a stinging critique of twentieth-century civilization, with its manifest social, ethical, and spiritual problems. Smith's trip to the movies is a case in point. The movie scene further defines the dangers and humiliations to which racial prejudice exposes him, e.g., "the heroine / Whose ivory and yellow it is sin / For his eye to eat of."[110] In this section tone is arguably at its bitterest as Brooks briefly sketches out the backdrop against which Smith's triumphantly fulfilling Sunday activities occur. But Brooks does not surrender Smith's ego to his environment. Instead of signaling surrender to the hardships of urban migration and segregation, Smith exits the streets to his bedroom for a night's success—he does, after all, get the girl in the end.

The narrator implores readers to join her in examining the details of one particular black man's Sunday: from his wardrobe, a source of the very real pride he achieves despite limited opportunities and his heritage of cabbage and pigtails, to his stroll through town to a night of love in his tenement apartment. Brooks does not lump the built environment over her characters; rather she explores the contours of city geography through the faces, closets, and bedrooms of its people. Her interdisciplinary methodology allows us to critically interrogate the built environment—the Stroll district and Bronzeville's 47th and South Parkway—more effectively. Brooks exposes readers to Bronzeville, built and peopled, at the same time. This is why Satin-Legs Smith must be set in Chicago; and why Chicago stood as the epicenter or mecca of African American cultural production for the mid–twentieth century.

Smith's scene is Black Chicago—its eateries, clubs, cabarets, dance halls, what was all the rage, what seemed real; that is what he would have been raised with or found when he stepped off the train in one of Chicago's bustling depots. To answer the lingering questions from the beginning of this chapter, "Why Chicago?" or "Why Bronzeville?" and "What invigorated the South Side?" this chapter turned to these "other" cultural institutions that, as much as women's clubs, black churches, and social settlements, flourished and reinvigorated Chicago's South Side and inspired the creativity of many. Dance halls, theaters, cabarets, black-and-tans, and jazz clubs, feeling pressure from the Great Migration, put black public space to work first with the Stroll section in the early twenties and then 47th and South Parkway into World War II. Every night couples flocked to the Savoy Ballroom to dance to big-band and scat music or even watch a boxing match. When the Regal Theater opened in 1928, South Side residents could sit under a domed ceiling awash with painted stars and listen to Duke Ellington, "Fatha" Hines, Fats Waller, and King Oliver. African Americans found black salesmen and saleswomen catering to their needs and sensibilities at the South Center Department Store. Sundays also offered cultural edification as well, including the gospel music of Mahalia Jackson and her chorus at the Ebenezer Church.

To these entertainments and sensibilities were added a constellation of venues and groups for the appreciation of history, sociology, literature, art, and politics connecting African Americans in Chicago and African Americans throughout the nation through the mediums of literature, art, and music.[111] Bronzeville's spatial concentration as a neighborhood lent itself to the success of artistic centers such as the South Side Community Art Center and the South Side Writers group discussed in the preface. Writers and artists could live, and many did, in the Parkway Community House or attend workshops at the YMCA or Hall Branch Library—one could walk to any of these institutions and not get tired. The walks between these institutions—the urban promenades of Bronzeville, the clubs, danc-ing, and movie theaters—starkly contrasted against, but conscious of, the poverty of Bronzeville, became the artistic legacies of the Chicago Black Renaissance. Subsequent chapters show that institutions such as the South Side Community Art Center, with help from the Federal Writers' Project, and groups such as the South Side Writers Group, the Book Review and Literature Forum of the Hall Branch Library, and the journal Negro Story fostered a criticism much needed for the bustling, vivacious, rich cultural scene that was Bronzeville in the 1930s and 1940s.

Specifically black public space—in this case the intersection of 47th and South Parkway of the twenties and thirties—heavily influenced and crafted an evolving conceptualization of a black public self that would flourish in Bronzeville. An awareness of Chicago's African American urban landscape, with its hallmark institutions such as the Savoy Ballroom, the Regal Theater, and South Center Department Store, buttresses Chicago Black Renaissance artists' and writers' critical interrogation of this black self and racial identity for the South Side.

CHAPTER 2

THE SOUTH SIDE COMMUNITY ART CENTER AND SOUTH SIDE WRITERS GROUP

> We believed that the purpose of art was to record the times.
> As young black artists, we looked around and recorded in our
> various media what we saw. It was not from our imagination
> that we painted slums and ghettos, or sad, hollow-eyed black
> men, women and children. They were the people around us.
>
> We were part of them. They were us. Thus, the coming of this
> Community Art Center has opened up new hope and vista to all
> of us.
>
> —"Defense of Culture," Margaret Burroughs, the dedication of the
> South Side Community Art Center, May 7, 1941

During the Chicago Black Renaissance, there were many community institutions that cultivated the arts, nurtured a budding African American modern consciousness, and carved the way for future generations of migrants, Chicagoans, and African American artists and authors. These institutions included the South Side Community Arts Center (SSCAC),[1] what Anne Meis Knupfer terms "the first black art museum in the United States,"[2] and the South Side Writers Group (SSWG). These were the intellectual and community centers and arteries of knowledge, culture, and artistry for Bronzeville; these sustained the Chicago Black Renaissance as a whole. Thus informed by these literary and historical traditions, the beginnings of the South Side Community Art Center and the South Side Writers Group show a sense of continuity amid the literature and visual art of the Chicago Black Renaissance.

Artists in Chicago found momentum at an enlightened point in American history by the direct intervention of the federal government in the form of the Federal Art Project of the Works Progress (later Projects) Administration (FAP/WPA), created October 14, 1935.[3] Under this program thousands of artists and authors—black and white—were given the opportunity to feed their families, practice their crafts, and hone their talents through interaction with their peers at community art centers established by FAP/WPA throughout the nation.[4] With the stock market crash of 1929 and the onset of the Great Depression, the nation went into a sharp decline that saw the unemployment rate reach the fifteen million mark, over one-fourth of the labor force by 1933. Franklin D. Roosevelt was swept into office on his promise to reverse this downward spiral of the nation's economy and belief in its role as world leader. The new president recognized that until the private sector recovered from the shattering effects of the Crash the federal government would have to shoulder the responsibility for putting the country back to work. Conservative critics of this New Deal approach questioned the constitutionality of using federal funds for local undertakings, but Roosevelt was to prevail. WPA became a reality; the nation's artists and authors, black and white, joined the ranks of employment.

Although there were other government projects that brought relief to artists during the Depression years, WPA/FAP was the largest and most well known. A staggering amount of art was produced nationwide including 108,000 paintings, 18,000 sculptures, 2,500 murals, and thousands of prints, posters, and photographs.[5] At the Federal Writers' Project's height in 1936, payrolls included 6,471 names; by 1938, when congress had dramatically reduced relief allocations, the number employed was approximately 3,500. FWP historian Monty Penkower estimates that in its four-year span, an average of 4,500 to 5,200 people worked for the project consistently.[6]

Officials couched the blueprints for the FAP in the language of relief, and 90 percent of all FAP employees were required to come from welfare rolls. Yet, this emphasis, Sklaroff stresses, should not obscure the aesthetic goals of the administration. Under the leadership of Harry Hopkins (governor of New York), art was understood as a tool of reform: "Mr. Hopkins has opened the door, a crack, but opened to this great field of human interest and thought. The world of the creative impulse, without which people perish."[7] Couched in this creativity, described by sculptor Gutzon Borglum, Hopkins believed that devotion to aesthetics could improve living in lower-income regions. As a democratizing force, a federal arts program would create a community of "cultural consumers," whose lives would be enriched by access to literature, music, theater, and visual art.[8] The success and longevity of the FAP in Bronzeville, however, was unpredicted.

In addition to this federal largess, Chicago Black Renaissance artists and authors found Julius Rosenwald a great source for funding. The Rosenwald foundation, administered by Edwin Embree, provided fellowships for one thousand promising African Americans from 1928–1948, many of whom, as a result, went on to compose the infrastructure of black culture and arts. Among the Chicago-based authors who received Rosenwald fellowships were (for literature) William Attaway, Arna Bontemps, Frank Marshall Davis, Willard Motley, and Margaret Walker.[9] Together the WPA and the Rosenwald Foundation helped underwrite a variety of community groups alongside the sweat equity of local figures.

Chicago's unique contribution to the story of African American aestheticism[10] leans on a blend of historical studies and theoretical discourse and values articulated in decisive essays by two different generations: Alain Locke, Langston Hughes, and W. E. B. DuBois and then a "different kind of youth" emerging during the Great Depression: Richard Wright and the South Side Writers Group. Arnold Rampersad points out in "W. E. B. DuBois as a Man of Literature" that DuBois' imaginative writings anticipate the writings of many who became the most significant figures in twentieth-century black literature—this "different kind of Youth"—writers and artists coming with the advent of literary and artistic Chicago with different political, emotional, and aesthetic aspirations. Both Hughes and DuBois established a literary and aesthetic framework that would inform the movement, but Bronzeville's artists and authors would deliver the content in their own unique ways. Therefore Chicago's "different kind of Youth," to which DuBois refers, crafted a complex aesthetic consciousness unique to the Chicago Black Renaissance. This consciousness is informed by an appreciation of the beauty of their works but conscious of the forces, institutions, and previous aesthetic traditions that drove them to create—informed by what Carlo Rotella deemed Chicago, in his fantastic study *October Cities*, a city of both fact and feeling.[11] These African American intellectuals, intrinsically valuable to and actively influential during the period in question, provide a foundation for various jeremiads developed by the South Side Community Art Center and the South Side Writers Group that craft the theory of black aesthetics articulated by the Chicago Black Renaissance.

This aesthetic mindset reflects a shift in leadership that changed soon after the turn of the century from the accomodationist policy of Booker T. Washington to the radical protests and artistic talents of both W. E. B. DuBois and Langston Hughes. African Americans became racially conscious and self-assertive, affirmed their humanity, and demanded respect. Hughes's "The Negro Artist and the Racial Mountain" is an archetypal statement of this determination:

> We younger Negro artists who create now intend to express our individual dark-skinned selves without fear or shame. If white people are pleased we are glad. If they are not, it doesn't matter. We know we are beautiful. And ugly too. The tom-tom cries and the tom-tom laughs. If colored people are pleased

we are glad. If they are not, their displeasure doesn't matter either. We build
our temples for tomorrow, strong as we know how, and we stand on top of the
mountain, free within ourselves.[12]

Hughes's statement is among the most defiant. He granted African American
artists permission to demand respect, affirm their humanity, and unabashedly
create art. By contrast, W. E. B. DuBois expressed a similar determination,
and, although it lacked the mass and radical appeal of Hughes's declaration,
DuBois in his essay "The Criteria of Negro Art" made clear the necessary relationship between art and propaganda—all art must be propagandistic—but
also the odd relationship between racial identity and aesthetics.[13] Hughes gave
African Americans permission to express themselves while DuBois supplied
the prescription for these expressions.

DuBois' political life championed blacks, but his creative work had trouble
finding beauty across the entire spectrum of blackness—primarily in terms of
physical beauty, but certainly not limited to it. He wove these complexities
into a theory of black aesthetics explored in his fiction, which was widely
popular during the Harlem Renaissance but that carried resonance over to
the Chicago period (*Darkwater: Voices from Within the Veil*, published in
1920, and *Dark Princess: A Romance*, published in 1928). In these works
DuBois pioneered an articulation of a theory of art developed from the
perspective of African Americans that attempted to utilize a wider definition
of aesthetics pushing against dominant white notions of beauty in art and
life. This attempt was plagued by a prescription he made that literature by
blacks must be unflinchingly true to African American life, while simultaneously he demanded that such descriptions be unflinchingly beautiful—even
in the portrayal of the ugly and unheroic. He tried to find or create a faithful
literary process invested in an honest description of African Americans that
possessed qualities serving his devotion to racial uplift to bring out a sort
of beauty of the heart and not of the eye.

Many of the apparent contradictions in DuBois' views on black aesthetics
found expression not only in his fiction but are expressed in the pages under
his editorship of *Crisis* as well, particularly in the period from 1919–1933.
These thoughts stemmed from his ambivalence about the developments in
expression and publication of the Harlem Renaissance and the Chicago
Black Renaissance. He wrote in a 1926 issue of *Crisis*:

> We want especially to stress the fact that while we believe in Negro art we
> do not believe in any art simply for art's sake. . . . We want Negro writers to
> produce beautiful things but we stress the things rather than the beauty. It is
> Life and Truth that are important and Beauty comes to make their importance
> more visible and tolerable.

Write then about things as you know them. . . . In *The Crisis*, at least, you do not have to confine your writings to portrayal of beggars, scoundrels and prostitutes; you can write about ordinary decent colored people if you want. On the other hand do not fear the Truth. . . . If you want to paint Crime and Destitution and Evil paint it. . . . Use propaganda if you want. Discard it and laugh if you will. But be true, be sincere, be thorough, and do a beautiful job.[14]

In a June, 1921, opinion piece, "Negro Art," DuBois wrote against reducing art to propaganda, calling it "wrong and in the end . . . harmful."[15] At that time he was forcefully proclaiming the need for all avenues of artistic expressions to be inclusive of African American artists and all themes of human experience to be employed by those same artists. Then, in 1926, he insisted with equal rigor that "all art is propaganda," and "I do not care a damn for any art that is not propaganda."[16] In any attempt to think about African American cultural production, both of these pieces from *Crisis* are crucial in explaining the significance of DuBois' work toward a black aesthetic. Ambivalent about the role of art and propaganda from the start, his development of a black aesthetic stemmed from an unstable foundation.[17] Nonetheless, he worked to enunciate black experience and expand and explode old definitions of blackness:

> Such is Beauty. Its variety is infinite, its possibility is endless. In normal life all may have it and have it yet again. The world is full of it. . . . Who shall let this world be beautiful? . . . We black folk may help for we have within us as a race a new stirrings; stirrings of the beginning of the new appreciation of joy, of a new desire to create, of a new will to be; . . . and there has come the conviction that the Youth that is here today, the Negro Youth, is a different kind of Youth, because in some new way it bears this mighty prophesy [*sic*] on its breast, with a new realization of itself, with new determination for all mankind.[18]

His mission became apparent, Arnold Rampersad tells readers; it was "the bounded duty of black America" to create, preserve, and realize "Beauty" for America, for the aim of art and political struggle was not black power in isolation but a philosophically reconstructed universe. The tools in the creation of beauty had always been and must be, he said, truth—"the highest hand-maid of imagination . . . the one great vehicle of universal understanding"; and goodness, "in all its aspects of justice, honor and right—not for sake of an ethical sanction but as the one true method of gaining sympathy and human interest." Thus, DuBois went on, "the apostle of Beauty . . . becomes the apostle of Truth and Right not by choice but by inner and outer compulsion."[19] Chicago's authors, artists, and musicians would develop their own understanding of this relationship between beauty, truth, and right, one that would always have Bronzeville as a referent. As Margaret Burroughs commented at the opening of the SSCAC—"We believed that the purpose of art was to record the times."

A synthesis of DuBois' seemingly contradictory *Crisis* editorials might be reached by reading a third publication, a July 1926 piece entitled, "Krigwa Players Little Negro Theater."[20] According to historian Rebecca Sklaroff, during the 1920s Harlem became home to the Krigwa Players, a theater group founded under the auspices of *Crisis*, dedicated to an "organic black theater." The Krigwa Players espoused a mission to produce plays written by, for, and about African Americans. By their second season in 1927, DuBois served as general chair, and a small company had been established. Their success led many, especially DuBois, to engage in a discussion about the benefits of an independent black theater. In *Crisis* and *Opportunity*, DuBois and Alain Locke set forth criteria for black drama. Decrying the fact that black actors, relegated to demeaning roles, could earn a living only by solely catering to an "alien group" (white audiences), DuBois pronounced that "the best of the Negro actor and the most poignant Negro drama have not been called for."[21] He believed that a successful black theater must produce plays by black playwrights, about black life, and in black neighborhoods. Along similar lines, Locke advocated a laboratory where all dramatic and technical skills could be cultivated. "Not that we would confine the dramatic talent to the . . . plant-rooms of race drama," he explained, "but the vehicle of all sound art must be the native group—our actors need their own soil, at least for sprouting."[22] With Bronzeville booming, the soil was rich for budding artists and authors; there was plenty of material for Chicago's artists and writers. Poet Gwendolyn Brooks relayed it quite nicely: "If you wanted a poem, you had only to look out a window. There was material always, walking or running, fighting or screaming or singing."[23] This quote delicately illustrates an acute consciousness of the symbiotic relationship between the streets of Bronzeville—the lived Bronzeville—and an opportunity for cultural production. She hints at how dynamic this process was that African American artists and writers operationalized, in many different ways, in Chicago during the 1940s. This method produced a uniquely Chicago aesthetic consciousness or ideology for which Chicago Black Renaissance institutions, such as the South Side Community Art Center and the South Side Writers Group, would garner much fame.

Officially, the SSCAC was a product of the WPA's Community Arts Center Program, which during its tenure opened more than eighty community art centers around the country. Peter Pollack, a North Side gallery owner, who in 1938 was a staff member on the Illinois Federal Art Project, described the Community Art Center Movement as such:

It has often been said that it is useless to bring culture to people who have not been prepared for it. The Community Art Center movement of the Works Project Administration believes that the converse of this view is a more accurate estimate. . . . The more than eighty centers of the Community Art Center Program established in the American communities of widely divergent geographic and historical backgrounds have developed, from common experience, a new approach to the cultural needs of the people. The purpose of the Art Center movement is not to superimpose preconceived ideas of art but rather to find, develop and broaden the indigenous culture of the community . . . to advance the cultural level of the nation as a whole.[24]

The WPA targeted the Bronzeville community of Chicago as a site for a community art center.[25] Bill Mullen credits the decision of the WPA to establish a Community Arts Center in Bronzeville to Pollack and Illinois Art Project director George Thorpe. Margaret Burroughs remembered Pollack as a progressive Jewish American whose North Michigan Avenue gallery had been the first to exhibit South Side black artists on the North Side, including herself, Bernard Gross, Charles Sebree, and Joseph Kersey.[26] Pollack saw the Center as "the cornerstone of what may shortly become a national center for Negro art" moving "closer to the mainstream of a democratic and ever growing people's art. As we establish a cultural unity and exchange among the peoples of this country, we lay the basis for unity and understanding on other levels of our national life."[27] Pollack saw art as a democratizing medium; he saw the day of "art for the few" as having passed. He began his speech at the SSCAC's dedication, "It is a truism that art in this country, if it is to survive, must have its base as close to the democratic idea as we would have our economic, political, and social life."[28] These sentiments fell synonymously with the Community Art Center Movement whose social thinking represented an attempt "on a broad scale to build a basis for art, created, supported, and understood by the whole American people."[29]

With this in mind Pollack turned to members of Bronzeville's community to head the Center's Officer's Cabinet. Pauline Kligh Reed, president of the SSCAC Officer's Cabinet, invited four friends—Frankie Singleton, Susan Morris, Marie Moore, and Grace Carter Cole—to meet Pollack. Other women assisted in the Center's development: Irene McCoy Gaines attended the organizational meetings and gave her full endorsement. She, along with Margaret Goss Burroughs, Mrs. Gonzelle Motts, Pauline Jackson Lawrence, and K. Marie Moore, became members of the first board of directors. Most of the SSCAC's officers were professional women. President Reed was a social worker; second vice president, Ethel Hilliard, was a school teacher, also known for her fund-raising skills with the Chicago NAACP. Margaret

Goss Burroughs, an art teacher with recent degrees from the Chicago Normal College and the Chicago Art Institute, became the Center's recording secretary and one of the "house" artists.[30]

The founders also realized the import of including prominent men in the Center's organization. As Reed recalled, "We went around the room and named twelve men each—sixty men—who together comprised a spectrum of the South Side society at the time."[31] One of those men was Golden Darby, owner of an insurance company and chair of the board of directors of the South Side Settlement House (SSSH). The settlement, among its other activities, had offered art classes attended by Burroughs and other aspiring young black artists. When Darby spearheaded the idea of a young artists' contest, with monetary awards and certificates, Burroughs was one of many contestants.

Knupher stresses that the SSCAC's sponsorship by the FAP proved to be a mixed blessing. It underwrote the SSCAC's teaching and administrative staff. Twenty-four teachers were furnished by the Illinois Art and Craft Project of the WPA.[32] The government agency's philosophy, at least on paper, was similar to the staff's. The SSCAC staff had already embraced the FAP's central tenet, that art centers "return art to the people—to all the people."[33] The FAP's stipulation that art centers educate community members through free exhibits, lectures, films, classes, workshops, and cultural events was already in place at the SSCAC. Similarly, the SSCAC's facilities were available to other community groups for meetings. Finally, the FAP's intention to financially "jumpstart" community centers in hopes that communities would seek local support had already happened.[34]

Although the government was instrumental in initiating the SSCAC, an already thriving artist group within Bronzeville played an integral part in establishing the Center. Chicago's black artists had already organized themselves into what was known as the Arts Crafts Guild. Organized by painter George E. Neal in 1932, the Guild was the only active group of African American visual artists in the community. Its charter membership included such notable artists as Margaret Taylor (later Goss Burroughs), Eldzier Cortor, Bernard Goss, Charles White, William Carter, Joseph Kersey, and Archibald Motley Jr. A diverse approach and broad aestheticism is reflected in this selection of artists, but one thing remained: their work reflected the lived experiences of Bronzeville.

In 1938 and 1939, according to Burroughs, more than forty planning meetings were held at various South Side locations including the Urban League and a funeral parlor at 55th Street between Michigan and Wabash Avenues. Persons attending included George F. Thorp, state director of the Federal Art Project of Illinois, Pollack, and many Guild members. The first meeting was productive. Committees were established, active roles were assumed, and plans began to unfold. All members of the Arts Craft Guild were in attendance, except George E. Neal, a painter, who had died two months earlier.[35]

Committee members began the task of raising capital from the residents of Bronzeville, who gave generously of their time and money to a variety of fund-raising events: theater performances, card parties, and a "Mile of Dimes" street-corner campaign. Margaret Burroughs recalled, "I well remember that I was twenty-one years old, and I stood on the corner of 39th and South Parkway (now Martin Luther King Jr. Drive) collecting dimes in a can. . . . I collected almost $100 in dimes."[36] Additional fundraising lectures and exhibitions were held in churches, community centers, schools, and clubhouses. The most spectacular and successful event was the first annual Artists and Models Ball held on October 23, 1939, at the Savoy Ballroom beside the Regal Theater at 47th and South Parkway.[37] In style, esprit, and turnout the first annual gala dance called the "Artists and Models Ball" put to work a multitalented collective of young artists for which they designed elaborate costumes and awarded prizes for the best creations. The ball featured a combination of local food and politics, music and art, highbrow social posturing, and grassroots cultural work.[38] The 1938 ball, for example, coordinated by black society woman Frances Moseley Matlock, featured costumes, decorations, and artwork by Burroughs, Kersey, and William Carter. These balls were an immediate success drawing large crowds from Bronzeville's black bourgeoisie. They helped raise the down payment on a once elegant brownstone at 3831 South Michigan Avenue previously owned by the Comiskey family and located on what had been the Gold Coast of old Chicago white society prior to the influx of African Americans into the area. Only a few blocks from the mansion was one of the most exciting streets in Chicago—47th Street—brought vividly to life by SSCAC member Archibald Motley's *Gettin' Religion* (1948).[39]

Stores of every variety, taverns, and restaurants lined both sides of the street for several blocks. On Michigan Avenue, just south of 47th and a few blocks from the Art Center, was the Hall Branch Library, which served as a literary cultural center for many Bronzeville authors; a little further south, at 51st Street, was Washington Park, which offered playing fields and paths to run and bicycle (Fig. 2.1). Florence Hamlish Levinsohn, author of Harold Washington's biography, called the area "raucous, exciting, stimulating, liberating. Politics, religion, sex, music, film, art, photography, books, sports, commerce, the practice of law and medicine were all there in that little metropolis where friends met every weekend to talk, argue, shop, listen, watch, to absorb and participate in the life of the African-American community."[40] It was in this atmosphere that the SSCAC was founded and had its most vital years.[41]

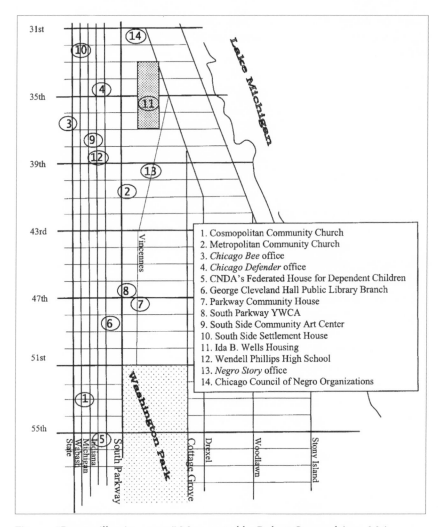

Fig. 2.1. "Bronzeville, circa 1945." Map created by Robert Cary and Anne Meis Knupher. Reprinted from Anne Meis Knupher, *The Chicago Black Renaissance and Women's Activism*. Urbana: University of Illinois Press, 2006.

Between June and December 1940, WPA funds, Julius Rosenwald Fellowships, and the sweat equity of South Side artists transformed the mansion, including the painters and sculptors who scrubbed floors and walls in preparation for the scheduled May 7, 1941, dedication. Prior to the dedication, however, these same artists received the first fruit of their labor at the informal opening of the SSCAC in December 1940. Charles White, Henry

Avery, Charles Davis, Archibald Motley Jr., Eldzier Cortor, William Carter, Joseph Kersey, Raymond Gabriel, and Bernard Goss were featured in a show of seventeen artists and forty-two oils and watercolors. The inaugural exhibition was a survey show of prominent local painters and sculptors.[42]

The show marked not only the successful remodeling of the mansion but another step in the ongoing renovation of the black artists initiated by other showcases of African American art in Chicago, such as Chicago's 1940 American Negro Exposition and Alain Locke's book *The Negro in Art: A Pictorial Record of the Negro Artist and of the Negro Theme in Art*. Central to Locke's book and the Exposition were Chicago artists such as Henry Avery, William Carter, John Collier, Edward T. Cortor, Eldzier Cortor, Charles Davis, Katherine Dorsey, Raymond Gabriel, Bernard Goss, Margaret T. Goss, Charles T. Haig, Fred Hollingsworth, Joseph Kersey, Clarence Lawson, Frank Neal, George Neal, Marion Perkins, Charles Sebree, Earl Walker, and Charles White (Fig. 2.2).[43]

Locke's celebration of northern black urban artists and the move toward the creation of public black space for the arts connected him intimately with what was going on in Chicago. Mullen stresses that Locke's "wistful, and wishful, celebration of northern black urban artists and Art Centers as the new homes of the black 'folk' encapsulated ideological and historical revisions in the black aesthetic Chicago's South Side arts scene embodied."[44] These revisions included articulations of a new communal space meant to mark the end of one historical journey—the Great Migration—and the beginning of another. In the minds of Chicago painters and members of the SSCAC the time had come to historicize, house, protect, and reproduce racial experience, from field to factory, cotton to canvas. The SSCAC's membership and leadership and the artists' work, shows, and exhibitions evidence a strong commitment to the Chicago Black Renaissance aesthetic.

Dozens of poor painters and cultural workers saw the SSCAC as a chance, in Burroughs's words, "to stop shining shoes all week and just paint on Sundays."[45] Unfortunately, this transition would not be easy. Many such artists found themselves pushed to the margins by the numerous black socialites who had come to attach themselves to this sudden institutionalization of black culture. Prior to the SSCAC's 1941 dedication, with First Lady Eleanor Roosevelt slated to speak, the artists were told that they would not be able to speak formally as part of the ceremony. Burroughs hurriedly wrote out a "Statement" on behalf of the artists present and asked David Ross, a fellow painter, to read it to Mrs. Roosevelt and the crowd:

> Now, in this period of wartime, we have our own plans for a defense—a defense of culture.

Fig. 2.2. "American Negro Exposition." Poster 1940. Claude A. Barnett Papers. Courtesy of the Chicago History Museum, Chicago.

* * *

We were not then and are not now complimented by the people who had the romantic idea that we liked to live in garrets, wear off clothes and go around with emaciated faces, painting for fun; living until the day we died and hoping that our paintings would be discovered in some dusty attic fifty years later and then we would be famous.

* * *

We believed that the purpose of art was to record the times. As young black artists, we looked around and recorded in our various media what we saw. It was not from our imagination that we painted slums and ghettos, or sad, hollow-eyed black men, women and children. They were the people around us.

We were part of them. They were us. Thus, the coming of this Community Art Center has opened up new hope and vista to all of us.[46]

Burroughs's call for a "defense of culture" was not simply an injured artist's response to a social slight, but a rallying cry to Chicago's black visual artists. The manifesto made a commitment to the shared struggle with the many migrants and inhabitants of the South Side. Mullen insists that Burroughs's demand that the Chicago's South Side public space serve as the site and source for the "defense of culture" was itself a metonymy for the seizure and transformation of the former Comiskey mansion into a site of black struggle and creative work. This was visually reaffirmed in the art featured at the Center's dedication. The exhibition, *We Too Look at America*, included many of the local artists represented in the inaugural exhibition of the previous December in addition to works by nationally known artists and members of Chicago's white art community: Gertrude Abercrombie, Margaret Brundage, Emil Armen, Si Gordon, Julia Thecla, Sophie G. Wessel, and others.[47] Among the works selected for exhibition were Charles Davis's "Back Streets," and Burroughs's (then Goss) "Street Scene" and "Neighborhood." Like the poems of Gwendolyn Brooks's *A Street in Bronzeville* these paintings visually foretold while they deployed tensions between the potential of Bronzeville with the isolation and encroaching despair of race-based poverty endemic to it.[48] All that was real to Bronzeville, all that made the Chicago Black Renaissance aesthetic so full of tension and dynamism.

The Center was officially dedicated May 7, 1941, by Mrs. Eleanor Roosevelt[49] and Dr. Alain Locke, Professor of Philosophy, Art and Humanities at Howard University (Fig. 2.3). Michigan Avenue was cordoned off from traffic, and crowds thronged the streets to see the First Lady. After the tour and the ribbon cutting, a police-led motorcade escorted her to the Savoy Ballroom for the dedication banquet. Guests numbering in the hundreds

Fig. 2.3. "Commemorative booklet, Eleanor Roosevelt dedication of the South Side Community Art Center," May 7, 1941. William McBride Papers. Courtesy of the Vivian G. Harsh Research Collection, Carter G. Woodson Regional Library, Chicago Public Library, Chicago.

heard Mrs. Roosevelt and Dr. Locke give celebratory speeches. Mrs. Roosevelt expressed her belief in the value of art and creativity:

> I think we now realize . . . in this country that . . . we need to . . . develop an audience for our artists of every kind [and] that the power to appreciate is often just as important as the power to actually create. . . . [By] fostering that in this way all over the country we create a democracy in art. . . . This is one of the thing[s] which this center is going to do . . . and so it is with great pleasure that I dedicate this building to the greater appreciation of art and the greater development of artists in our country.[50]

Dr. Locke, perhaps, gave a more electrifying charge to the artists, notables, and others in attendance at the ceremony. He saw, in the Foreword of the *We Too Look at America* catalogue, the opening as an opportune occasion for cooperation between younger Negro artists of Chicago as contributors toward "racial and national objectives"; for the good of both causes the Center would serve as a place for continuous and harmonious cooperation "toward increasing Chicago's quota of vitally representative contemporary American art."[51] Only then would the Center "assume its true and correct significance."[52] It is worth quoting him at length:

> For the first time, at least on such a scale with prospects of permanency, a practicing group of Negro artists has acquired a well-equipped working base and a chance to grow roots in its own community soil. Not only will it increase and deepen their own creative activity, but it will enable them, through teaching, to recruit their ranks with the hitherto undiscovered and unencouraged talent which must exist in a community that, without such facilities and encouragements, already has turned out a score of promising young artists, nearly half of whom have a fighting chance to gain national place and importance. Furthermore, this Center can and will radiate into the community an appreciation of what is good in art, and what is the social and racial significance and function of the artists.[53]

Locke's speech captures it best in his use of the word *community*—indeed Bronzeville had already turned out, and with the help of such urban arts institutions like SSCAC and the SSCAC, a new and different youth would continue to explore and figure the relationship of urban visual art and literature to the cities it draws upon for inspiration.[54] Institutions such as these provided a home base of sorts for urban intellectuals to craft their artistic and literary texts that investigate and charge the personal and political contexts in which urban intellectuals work.

The SSCAC delivered. The SSCAC divided itself into three major divisions: exhibits, lectures, and education. In general, it called for its exhibitions "to convey the broadest possible picture of art, bringing out the development of art in all media and the relation and uses of art as an influence in our social structure."[55] In an effort to preserve this mandate, the SSCAC strove to exhibit work by artists of the past and present; work by local and national artists; historic art, crafts, and industrial art; and the related arts. Through its lectures, gallery talks, and other educational activities, which included community participation and a free art school offering instruction in fine and applied arts to both adults and children, the Center strove to integrate art as a useful cultural influence on Bronzeville—staking out an important relationship between cultural production and place. There were theater classes and poetry classes from which emerged such luminaries as Gwendolyn Brooks and Margaret Danner; writers Richard Wright and Willard Motley achieved national recognition while associated with the Center's writers' forum.[56] The Center served as a public place where young black artists met respected elder artists such as Archibald Motley Jr.; where students met mentors; where artists, writers, and dancers—black and white—mingled and exchanged ideas. Full, bustling weeks at the Center were capped by the smooth jazz sounds of the Nat "King" Cole trio on some Saturday nights.[57] It also drew internationally famous stars like Josephine Baker to its doors. Margaret Burroughs was not being facetious when she said, "Any artists, black or white, who amounted to anything, passed through the doors of the art center."[58]

In its report "The First Year's Work," the SSCAC dubbed 1941 as "the most enterprising first year in the life of the South Side Community Art Center."[59] In 1941, it catalogued more than 50,000 visitors to its exhibitions (Fig. 2.4). *American Magazine of Art*, the *Art Digest*, and the *Art News* and other art magazines as well as the critics from the daily and weekly press reviewed its exhibitions, devoting "much space to the analysis of the Negro's contribution to American culture."[60] The SSCAC extended its influence into a booming Bronzeville community when it formed an advisory committee composed of schoolteachers affecting cooperation between the Board of Education Art Department and the SSCAC, assuring the Center of student attendance from the school system. A luncheon was held in November 1941 for the principals of the thirty-two schools on the South Side. The Chicago Art Institute School of Fine Arts agreed to send senior students to the Art Center for their practice teaching credits. The Center relied on volunteer instruction such as this due to the waning WPA employment rolls. These volunteer-led classes included fashion illustration, poetry, and a children's theater workshop. During the year 1941, 2,169 students under 16 and 647 adults attended classes.[61] Demand for such specialty classes increased, as the report notes: "There is no room in the main building to accommodate a class in weaving though a number of students have applied. There is also a great demand for classes in wood

Fig. 2.4. "Chicago, Illinois. An art exhibition at the South Side Community Art Center." April 1942. Jack Delano. Farm Security Administration–Office of War Information Photograph Collection. Courtesy of the Library of Congress. LC-USW3-000707-D (black and white film negative).

sculpture, wood carving and repair of furniture, upholstery, etc. In connection with a wood shop design unit experimenting in wood and plastics should be imitated. These two departments could be installed in the rear building of the Art Center."[62] Such a detailed report exhibits the dedication the Art Center felt by "offering to the community a completely well rounded program in the teaching of the arts and crafts."[63]

It had taken a long time for the Chicago artists to realize their goal and provide a place where Gordon Parks, Charles White, Margaret Burroughs, and Archibald Motley would come together to work in an atmosphere of shared creative excitement. World War II and the termination of WPA would soon scatter them, many into artistic obscurity. The enthusiasm and fanfare of the Center's first months of operation soon gave way to wartime priorities. The nation's entry into the war in 1941 curtailed WPA Federal Arts Project expenditures. In 1943 all federal funding ceased. In addition to the cessation of these funds, many of the Center's native sons left the Chicago area to fulfill military obligations or to seek career opportunities in other cities (e.g., Eldzier Cortor, Jones, Sebree, Parks, and White). The downward spiral in the life of the Center and the Chicago Black Renaissance began with the "Red Scare" of the early 1950s. In a move to curtail rumors of "un-American" activities at the Center, the executive board made the decision to banish artists and their associates from the Center. Other black artists involved with the Center left Chicago to pursue other interests. Margaret Burroughs joined her friend and fellow artist Elizabeth Catlett in Mexico City. Despite these events, the SSCAC would stand as the only place in Chicago where minorities could regularly exhibit. The lifelong supporters—Wilhelmina Blanks, Fern Gayden, and Grace Thomspon Leaming—almost single-handedly kept the doors from closing. The Civil Rights movement in the 1960s resulted in a new interest in black art and greater opportunities for African American artists to exhibit their work.[64] Although its activities paled in comparison to its earlier years, art shows, and educational programming would continue and do continue at the SSCAC to this day.[65]

Throughout its thick and thin years, the Center remained true to its mission. It stands today as an institution that continues to cultivate the talents of African American artists and an entire community. The Chicago Black Renaissance's artists would take pride in having launched an institution proving to be a dynamic force in the black cultural life of Chicago. The SSCAC offered African American artists access to professional training and economic security at a crucial point in African American cultural and artistic history. The WPA Centers provided the opportunity for young African American men and women to work together during their formative years in an environment that they charged with the electric energy of their creativities. This contributed to the genesis of the Chicago Black Renaissance and helped establish it as an important era in American art.[66] Bill Mullen wrote in *Popular Fronts* that the "obscurity of the story of the South Side Community Art Center reflects the extent to which Chicago's black 'renaissance' has been narrowly construed in previous cultural histories."[67] The history of the SSCAC exists mostly in internal commemorative records produced by the Center, its surviving members, and the city of Chicago itself. Yet arguably no black cultural institution better documents both the midcentury absorption and revision of 1930s American cultural and political radicalism into black public space. No Chicago institution, Mullen concludes, reflects more overtly the enduring scars of internal black struggle for provenance and sovereignty over the direction of postwar political black culture.[68] The South Side Community Arts Center is located in the heart of Bronzeville—to this day. This Center claimed significant numbers of African American artists who would play pivotal roles in the Chicago Black Renaissance; but the SSCAC itself played a pivotal role in the Renaissance as well. It served as a cultural marker and incubator of the artistic and literary rumblings of the Renaissance at its most embryonic stage. The Center and the South Side Writers Group, also bolstered by WPA funds, figured as wellsprings of artistic and literary talents that would take the Renaissance to its most potent levels.

Margaret Walker, on assignment for the FWP and then a later member of the SSWG, called the FWP "an artistic appendage to the tremendous socioeconomic program of the Works Progress Administration."[69] This program was created by Roosevelt in his third year of his first term in office. He proposed this social legislation to the Congress early in the spring of 1935, and after Congress passed it the program began operation early in the fall of 1935. It was designed to give employment to impoverished or needy, but capable, writers, some of whom had even published books that were no longer selling, and to such professionals and amateurs who were talented but so down on their luck they were near starvation.

With the help of these funds and Richard Wright's leadership, African American writers helped initiate what Arna Bontemps, Wright's colleague on the project, believed was a reawakening of the Harlem Renaissance. Walker realized the great significance of the marriage of WPA funds and African American creativity:

> Looking back to that time I slowly realize the great significance of the WPA. It had more than economic importance—providing subsistence pay for unemployed, impoverished, and promising writers—though that was first. It had political and social significance in a period when communism and fascism were threatening American democracy. Marxism, the intellectual fad, was an idea that spread throughout the Federal Arts Projects. But the greatest significance of the WPA was that it accomplished what nobody believed was possible at that time—a renaissance of the arts and American culture, with the appearance of spectacular artists or artistic figures, phenomenal programs, and immortal creative work.[70]

The first office of the Chicago Writers Project was on the north end of the Loop in the 1000 block of Wells Street. Walker remembered seeing Richard Wright, a fellow WPA employee like herself, in an elevator once or twice in the Chicago offices. Wright's original appointment was with the Federal Theatre Project and not the Writers Project. Here he served as a writer in public relations. While in Chicago, Wright wrote "The Ethics of Living Jim Crow" and the stories that were published in his first book, *Uncle Tom's Children* (1938). Wright also laid the groundwork for the books that most explicitly engage his Chicago experience: *Native Son* (1940), *12 Million Black Voices* (1941), and *American Hunger* (1977), the continuation of his autobiography *Black Boy* (1945). Informed by Marxist politics and sociological theories developed at the University of Chicago, these books strongly express Wright's sense of being an outsider in white America. Though Wright had escaped the overtly racist South and found Chicago exhilarating, he struggled to find his place as an African American writer in an alienating urban culture. Nevertheless, Wright, Bontemps, and other writers associated with the project, such as William Attaway, Willard Motley, Margaret Walker, and Frank Yerby, invigorated the literary scene on the city's South Side.

Riding the 1930s wave of African American literary popularity, Wright was planning a writers' group for the National Negro Congress, in which the Communist party assumed an aggressive role of leadership and sought to unify black and white labor with black intellectuals. An outgrowth of the National Negro Congress was the South Side Writers Group (SSWG). Margaret Walker recalled receiving a penny postcard inviting her to the first meeting of the SSWG at the South Parkway home of Bob Davis, television and movie actor known as Davis Roberts. Davis, at that time, was writing poetry and publishing in the magazine *New Challenge*. Walker related her nervousness but desire to connect with the budding South Side literary notables: "Twice I left the house and turned back, the first time out of great self-consciousness because I felt I looked abominable. I had nothing to wear to make a nice appearance, and I was going to the far South Side, where I felt people would make fun of me. But my great desire to meet writers and end my long isolation conquered this superficial fear. I made myself go."[71]

Subsequent meetings took place at the Abraham Lincoln Center (ALC) on Oakwood Boulevard where the Illinois Writers Project was housed.[72] Walker described the dynamics of these meetings: "I was surprised to see they did not cut me down. Ted Ward and Dick Wright were kind in their praise. I remember Russell Marshall and Edward Bland were also there. Bland was killed in the Battle of the Bulge. I was completely amazed to hear Wright read a piece of prose he was working on. Even after I went home I kept thinking, 'My God, how that man can write!'"[73] Walker and Wright established a mutual admiration for one another and established quite a close relationship based on their love of writing. Suspended in time between the WPA and the SSWG, three forms of writing took place in their consciousness, conversations, and actions. They would sit together and work on the forms of Walker's poetry, the free verse things, and come up with forms and revisions. Likewise they sat together and worked on revisions of "Almos' a Man" and *Lawd Today*. Relationships such as these sprung up across the SSWG much the same way artists got to know one another at the SSCAC. In addition to their work on the WPA, writers influenced one another through their own writers' groups such as the SSWG and John Reed Clubs. Literary and intellectual discussions took place at the South Parkway

Community Center as well as the Hall Branch Library—Bronzeville was a space rich with outlets and spaces for literary discussion, revision, and review. Bronzeville's pens and typewriters were busy.

Twice a month, at least fifteen members of the SSWG met at the ALC. Many of its members were established writers, at least in Chicago. For example, Fenton Johnson had already written four volumes of poetry and two books of prose. Wright was revising his first novel. Frank Marshall Davis had written two books of poems; Perkins had written two plays. Dorothy Sutton, a law student and minister, had published some of her poems in literary magazines.[74] The long isolation of the "Negro artist" ended with the advent of such groups and centers; there was a great deal of mingling and mixing of artistic and literary talent, a great deal of exchange between writers, artists, actors, and dancers.[75]

Wright would write about this in his speech "The Isolation of the Negro Writer," which he gave at the Midwest Writers Conference in the spring of 1936—an event covered by Walker for the FWP.[76] On June 13 and 14, the Chicago Writers Group, formerly the John Reed Club, called a conference of Midwest Writers at 63 West Ontario Street. The conference was called for several reasons: "(1) To consider the problems of publication for the Midwest Writer. (2) To combat growing reactionary forces and collectively fight fascist repression through anti-fascist groups; especially those reactionary forces which definitely affect writers."[77] Endorsing this conference, in addition to the Chicago Writers Group, were the League of Arts and Professions of Minneapolis; The Midwest Literary League; Staff of New Writers; Staff of Hinterland, Friends of New Masses, Staff of Signatures; the New Theater Group of Urbana; The Theater Union of Minneapolis; and the American Newspaper Guild, as well as a dozen prominent young writers of the Midwest. During his three years on the WPA in Chicago, Wright would be a member of at least five of these groups of artists and writers. In addition to the John Reed Clubs and the League of American Writers, he was a member of the Midwest Writers Group, which met weekly at night in the Old City Auditorium Building.[78] The conference, in addition to electing various officers, drew up plans for a proposed magazine, *Midwest* and drew up resolutions "of general anti-fascist character and of protective value to working writers and artists of all types." It was moved that the Chicago Writers Group be instructed to call "another conference of all Chicago Writers Groups interested in furthering the broad aims of the June Conference"—it was at this meeting that the SSWG would make its debut. This second conference was called two weeks later at 1418 Lakeshore Drive, and the Continuations Committee of the Midwest Federation of Arts and

Professions was duly elected and organized. Those groups represented at this meeting included: the Chicago Writers Group, the Technical Employees Union, the Chicago Cultural Collective, the Chicago Repertory Group, the SSWG, the Writers Union, the Artists Union, and the Research League.[79]

Attendance at this conference showed the SSWG as a "serious, politically conscious aggregation of young, aspiring, African American writers."[80] Frank Marshall Davis, Edward Bland, Theodore Ward, Marian Minus, Russell Marshall, Robert Davis, and Margaret Walker were regular members of this group organized by Wright in April 1936. Fern Gayden, Dorothy Sutton, Julius Weil, Ann Petry, Chester Himes, Arna Bontemps, Katherine Dunham, Willard Motley—nephew of the aforementioned artist Archibald Motley Jr.—Frank Yerby, Geraldine Brooks, Horace Cayton, Dorothy West, Waters Turpin, Alden Bland, Margaret Danner, and Fenton Johnson were affiliated with the group also. Under the helmsmanship of Wright, the Chicago group formally pursued its interest in social protest and the relation of the African American to his/her folk tradition—a tradition started by Hughes, DuBois, and Locke. They politicized the African American writer's project in the Chicago Black Renaissance's seminal document of literary theory—"Blueprint for Negro Writing." According to Margaret Walker, five or six members of the SSWG contributed to the content of this document: "Wright and myself, and possibly Ted Ward, Ed Bland, Russell Marshall, and Frank Marshall Davis. What Wright did was take ideas and suggestions from four or five drafts by others and rewrite them in definite Marxist terms, incorporating strong black nationalist sentiments and some cogent expressions on techniques and the craft of writing. He published it as his own, and I remember my surprise on seeing the printed piece."[81] Richard Wright combined Hughes's vision and DuBois' political mission in this essay, "Blueprint for Negro Writing."[82] Wright stated emphatically that

> in order to do justice to his subject matter, in order to depict Negro life in all of its manifold and intricate relationships, a deep, informed, and complex consciousness is necessary; a consciousness which draws its strength upon the fluid lore of a great people, and moulds this lore with the concepts that move and direct the forces of history today. Every short story, novel, poem, and play should carry within its lines, implied or explicit, a sense of oppression of the Negro people, the danger of war, of fascism, of the threatened destruction of culture and civilization; and, too, the faith and necessity to build a new world.[83]

In this essay, Wright carefully embraced Hughes's self-affirming declarations and DuBois' political directive, while adding an acute sense of urgency and place. This "complex consciousness" draws its strength from the lore of great people (note Hughes's influence here) and the knowledge of the politics governing the forces of history today—echoing DuBois' propagandistic trend. This awareness compels artists to press themselves down "unknown" paths where "tradition is no longer a guide."[84] When African American writers think they have arrived at something "which smacks of truth, humanity, they should want to test it with others, feel it with a degree of passion and strength that will enable them to communicate it with millions who are groping like themselves."[85] This was a moment to "ask questions, to theorize, to speculate, to wonder out of what materials can a human world be built"; the Bronzeville aesthetic was always a self-reflexive aesthetic.[86]

Resenting the accomodationist habit of pleading with white America for recognition and justice, Wright asserted that African American writers should focus their efforts instead on writing for the black masses about cultural conservatorship, racial advancement, and political protest. Wright believed that black writers were being cast in the role of moral and social leaders and as such they were being called upon to "do no less than create values by which [the] race [was] to struggle, live, and die."[87] To do this effectively, the "Blueprint" stipulates that black writers must assume the proper perspective; that is, they must depict "Negro life in all its manifold and intricate relationships."[88] Bill Mullen terms the "Blueprint" a "call for a revolution in black writing concomitant with a radical critique of class and race oppression in America [that] was meant to kill off both the feudal black literary past and the perceived narrow aestheticism of the Harlem Renaissance."[89] Radically, the "Blueprint" demands that Chicago Black Renaissance writers reject what has been for them their only "black" literary and aesthetic history—the Harlem Renaissance—for a more authentic one. Wright called upon them to learn to view and to present black reality from the vantage point of African Americans in Bronzeville, something that had not been done by previous literary generations.[90]

With the help of WPA funds, the Julius Rosenwald Foundation, and the ever-increasing number of African American–owned and –edited periodicals the Chicago generation of black literati emphatically answered Wright's call/response. In addition to Rosenwald, the WPA gave a start to many black Chicago writers and artists. The WPA not only provided an income during lean times but also offered opportunities for camaraderie in the relationships and affiliations that stemmed from African American writers' and artists' interaction with WPA programs. In Arna Bontemps's estimation, no other writer's project in the country produced such comparable black talent during the Depression. "Chicago," he extolled, "was the center of the second phase of Negro literary awakening" with Harlem being the first.[91] The SSCAC and the SSWG broadened artists' and writers' understanding of black Chicago. Writers and artists were encouraged by the WPA to work in genres they might not have used otherwise, such as reportage, travelogue, and historical narrative. This genre-crossing may have led some WPA writers to further experiment with their own writing. In fact, many black Chicago writers wrote across genres, thereby reaching out to a larger readership. For example, Margaret Walker, the first black poet to win the Yale Prize for Poetry, was a novelist, a children's story writer, and a historical writer. Arna Bontemps wrote adult and juvenile fiction. Frank Marshall Davis, poet and jazz critic, was a sportswriter—all three were members of the SSWG.[92]

There were of course other prominent black writers not affiliated with the WPA or the SSWG who lived in and wrote about Chicago. Knupher mentions Marita O. Bonner and playwright Lorraine Hansberry. Pulitzer Prize–winning poet Gwendolyn Brooks did not get her start with the WPA or the SSWG, yet she drew heavily from the images of Bronzeville and worked with the SSCAC. Brooks, who grew up on the South Side, mixed with the WPA writers but drew from her own connections in the African American community in establishing herself as a preeminent Chicago poet and writer. Her fame would belong to the Chicago Black Renaissance's later decades of writers in the 1940s. Knupher also mentions Black journalists Era Bell Thompson and Thyra Edwards, who did not belong to either group; however, Thompson would become coeditor for the *Negro Digest* and managing editor for *Ebony*. Thyra Edwards, a Chicago social worker involved in the Spanish Civil War, joined popular front organizations while publishing in *Negro Digest* and the "People's Voice." And Margaret Burroughs, influential with the SSCAC, wrote for the Associated Negro Press with Frank Marshall Davis (member of the SSWG).[93]

In essence, Chicago black writers and artists created a cultural and political network during the Chicago Black Renaissance, drawing from the WPA and Chicago's South Side cultural institutions like the South Side Community Art Center and the South Side Writers Group. These cultural institutions created an abundance of cultural activities during the 1930s that would spill into the 1940s: music, dance, theater, painting, sculpture, and writing. These groups of amateurs and professionals were not only talented, producing artists and writers, they were socially conscious, politically aware, and active, civic-minded entrepreneurs. Meetings, exhibit openings, and parties at night and on weekends provided forums for a cross-pollination and exchange of Chicago aesthetic fervor. Walker described these occasions candidly:

> Wright and I occasionally met at studios parties, which were always racially mixed. Sometimes the party originated with the [WPA] project, sometimes with Jewish friends. Sometime[s] people read poetry or stories. The food was always

the same: cold cuts—salami, bologna, sometimes lox or smoked salmon—and pickles, rye bread and pumpernickel, beer and pretzels. I could not drink the beer, but Wright delighted in consuming a great deal, and once he said, "I must have drunk a gallon of beer." These activities stimulated intellectual conversation and artistic creation. In those years Richard Wright developed a craft that gave his daemonic genius a concrete form and produced an immortal body of literature. The explosion of his creative genius coincided with this cultural explosion. . . . I[I]t was my pleasure and privilege to witness these explosions, to come of age, and find my own poetic voice, while I watched in rapt wonder, the amazing community of artists who were rising on the horizon—many, if not most, of them "young, gifted, and black."[94]

Walker's memories pinpoint the arrival of DuBois' "different kind of Youth." Bronzeville's artists were rising. As a backdrop to their ascension, Bronzeville's social ferment, and the Chicago Black Renaissance cultural explosion, an aesthetic ideology of this "different kind of youth," had been born.

The aesthetic formula characterized by the Chicago Black Renaissance found on the canvases of those artists of the South Side Community Art Center and between the pages of the South Side Writers Group articulates a vital political and modern consciousness that would sustain the movement into the 1940s. Following the dictates of the WPA, artists and writers would lend their gazes and pens to their audiences, in a democratizing vein, letting them see the "normal" experience of the black common man. Artists of the Chicago Black Renaissance literally juxtapose the sacred with the profane, street hustlers with businessmen, prostitutes with ministers, merging real-life experiences with the imagination—documenting the African American presence in the American Scene.[95] Motley did this in his paintings, Wright did it in his fiction, and Brooks did it in her poetry. The aesthetic was personal and always political but executed with enough distance to claim objectivity with the African Americans the artists and writers would depict. Motley, Wright, and Brooks could take this approach confidently because of prior aesthetic philosophies that gave them the confidence—even the mandate—to do so. Motley painted, as much as Brooks poetically rendered, a visual narrative of Bronzeville with an immediacy, honesty, and sincerity that DuBois demanded in his criteria for "Negro art." The SSCAC and the SSWG, as producers and defenders of culture, engendered an aesthetic honesty. That consciousness, which set Chicago's Renaissance apart from Harlem's and gave it its greatness, is best captured in a quote from Motley: "I have tried to paint the Negro as I have seen him and as I feel him, in myself without adding or detracting, just being frankly honest."[96]

CHAPTER 3

POLICY, CREATIVITY, AND BRONZEVILLE'S DREAMS

African Americans flocked to Bronzeville, the nation's most prominent black community, between the wars. Chicago's labor shortage lured migrants north where work seemed to be the answer to Southern race problems. This belief in the ethics of work helped some capitalize on the migrant experience by joining in the formal economies of the working and middle class, while others overcame formidable odds to gain a rare foothold among the professional classes. But when the Great Depression began and the Great Migration flooded Chicago's South Side with waves of migrants, once-vital businesses faded as the nation's economy went sour; migrants, as a result, turned toward informal economies of gambling—known as the "policy game" in Chicago's South Side neighborhoods—with hard work, creativity, and artistry that challenged and reinterpreted the ethics of work.

One can attribute the success of policy to the systematic discrimination that blacks faced in seeking legitimate, licit, jobs and the resulting attractiveness of those illegal or marginal paths of mobility that were open to them.[1] A survey of African American employment found increasing opportunities for males during World War I in the meatpacking industry and steel mills; or as porters, janitors, and waiters; or as domestics and laundries for women. Yet a postwar recession led to widespread layoffs of Black workers. Hardship materialized quickly in this economic slowdown, when women could not find work as domestics while men found themselves shut out of employment. The frequency of layoffs and the dangerous and unsanitary working conditions coupled with racial discrimination led Blacks to move between licit and illicit economies. They recognized that they did not have the same opportunities as their white counterparts for more skilled jobs or promotions in major industries and usually were the first to lose jobs during industry layoffs. They also understood the precarious place they held within organized labor.[2] Blacks' troubled and unsuccessful efforts to attain secure positions in Chicago's labor market made alternative options for work an absolute necessity.[3]

Well known is the sociological literature that correlates policy to urban pathology and urban decay. This is not how the game was thought of for those who played it. Yes, the game rose in popularity due to segregation. Yes, their communities were exploited and segregated but these communities were also, as a result, partly self-sufficient. The lack of social services, of financial institutions, and of commercial investment and development, and the ubiquitous political powerlessness of segregated ghettos gave rise to informal "parallel institutions," many of which operated in the gray areas between legitimacy and criminal behavior—but it often depended on who was asking (Fig. 3.1).

In reality, playing policy was not just an escapist entertainment nor was it criminal. It afforded the player a slim hope of relief from grinding poverty. Policy was also a financial institution—one that substituted for "white" organizations that would not provide financial services in poor communities. In this imposed fiscal vacuum "licit" and "illicit" economies and leisure sites moved closer and closer together intermingling to the point of dependency;[4] definitions of respectability therefore became more permeable, exploding gender stratifications but governed still by strict racial boundaries. Chicago's policy men and women, leaders and patrons of the game, capitalized on

Fig. 3.1. "Policy slips litter sidewalk." Edwin Rosskam. 1941. Courtesy of the Library of Congress. LC-USF33-005183-M3 [P&P].

this situation but not without encountering risk and, at times, great cost. This chapter introduces the many spheres of policy: as performance art, as informing black cultural production throughout Bronzeville, and then as a patron and fiscal support of the Chicago Black Renaissance.

Essentially, policy gambling was a type of lottery. In policy gambling bettors placed their money on one or more numbers that they hoped would be among those picked in a drawing of twelve numbers between 1 and 78. A common play was a "gig," a bet on three numbers. If the three numbers were among the twelve drawn, the bettor collected at odds of 100 to 1 or higher. Although the odds favored the policy seller in the long run, on any given day several bettors might select the same winning numbers and thus bankrupt the game. As a result, policy "banks" or "backers" arose to assume the financial risks. For any given banker there might be 100 or more policy sellers (or policy stations) located in neighborhood salons, barbershops, newspaper kiosks, and similar locations. Each policy seller kept a fixed percentage of the money bet and funneled the rest to the banker. In a large syndicate, runners collected from the sellers and carried the betting slips and money to the bank. Once the outcome of the drawing was announced, the banker assembled the winning slips and returned them to the sellers along with the money to pay the winners. The sellers, as a result, earned a steady income without economic risks; bankers assumed the risks in return for the potential profits from thousands of small bets placed through many sellers (Fig. 3.2).[5]

A policy syndicate cultivated a variety of complex relationships with bettors on a daily basis. Therefore, it was a formidable cultural and political machine, wielding powerful influence over the community. And since many of the small neighborhood businesses—including newspaper stands, barbershops, beauty parlors, and saloons—enjoyed a steady income from the sale of policy slips, legitimate businessmen and women were often allies in the protection and promotion of policy gambling. In neighborhoods such as Bronzeville, where policy was immensely popular, policy backers were often a significant resource linked to police, local political and community organizations, the fates of many small and large businesses, and artists' communities and cultural production. The game once bankrolled such prestigious institutions as America's first Black-owned banks—including Jesse Binga's Bank in Bronzeville—insurance companies, private medical practices, arts centers, hotels, and department stores.

Numerous African American communities hosted similar games of chance: Harlem and D.C. had numbers, Pittsburgh had digits, Detroit and Chicago played policy. Harlem's most prolific numbers king was Casper Holstein; his biggest competitor was numbers queen Stephanie St. Croix, a Black Frenchwoman said to have migrated from Marseilles. In 1912, she invested $10,000

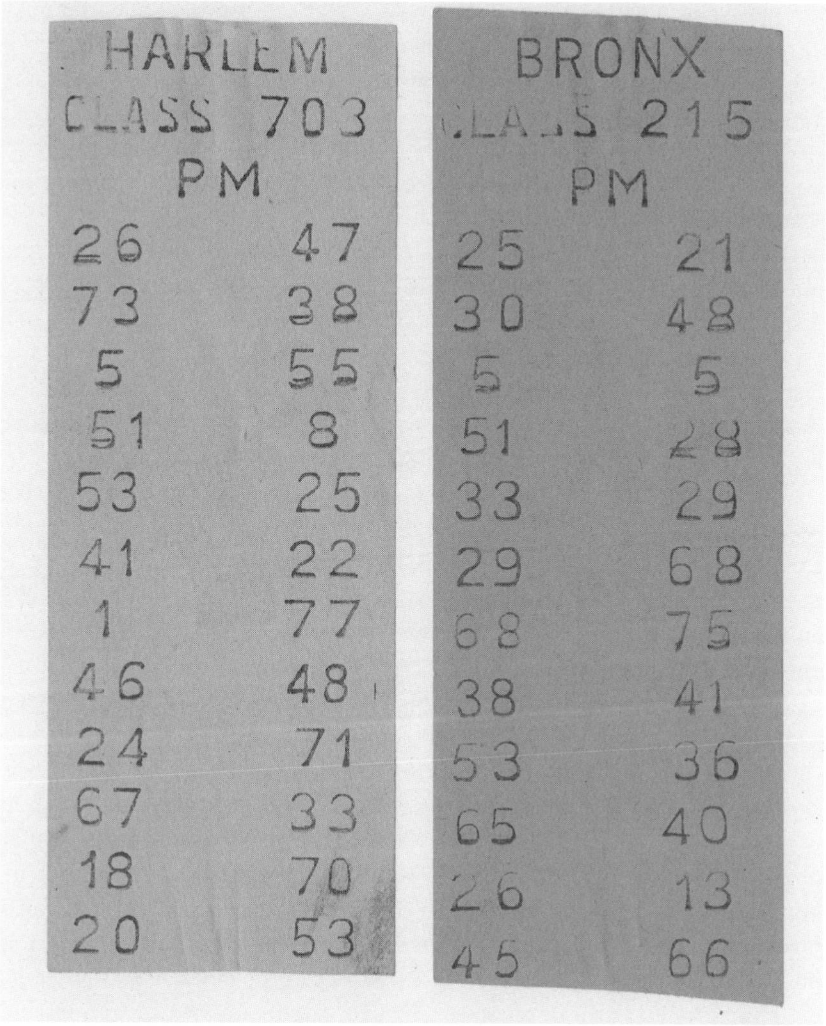

HARLEM CLASS 703 PM		BRONX CLASS 215 PM	
26	47	25	21
73	38	30	48
5	55	5	5
51	8	51	28
53	25	33	29
41	22	29	68
1	77	68	75
46	48	38	41
24	71	53	36
67	33	65	40
18	70	26	13
20	53	45	66

Fig. 3.2. "Policy slips." Digital reproduction: Ernest W. Burgess Papers, Box 37, Folder 5. University of Chicago Special Collections. 1933.

of her own money in a numbers parlor. Within a year she had amassed over $500,000. Chicago's most noted policy kings were John Mushmouth Johnson, Policy Sam Young, and later the Jones brothers;[6] there were far fewer policy queens. Regardless of their sex, Chicago's kings and queens lived lavish lifestyles and were of frequent mention in the press. They drove the finest cars, wore the most expensive clothes, owned summer homes and private airplanes, and vacationed in Europe and Mexico. They invested in Chicago's commercial leisure district of the 1920s at 35th and State Streets,

known as the Stroll, and then later during the 1930s and 1940s, when policy
hit its stride, they continued this trend further south along State Street in
Bronzeville. Businesses such as grocery stores, hotels, Jesse Binga's Bank, the
South Center Department Store—one of the first Black-owned department
stores in the country and part of the South Center Complex at 47th and
South Parkway (the heart of black urban America)—thrived because of the
streams of money flowing in from policy.

Chicago's black policy kings and queens positioned themselves at the
intersection of informal economies and sanctioned economies. They stood
lucratively at this crossroads by promoting a disbelief in the ethics of work
("getting something for nothing") to yield more legitimate, middle-class, and
respectable means of going about labor on the South Side. Thus, with the
steady work of the policy game—be it informal or formal—policy did improve
life in the Black Belt through a symbiotic relationship of vice and virtue.

Sociologists St. Clair Drake and Horace Cayton, in their comprehensive
description of Chicago's Black Belt *Black Metropolis*, published in 1945,
called policy "a cult": "Policy is not only a business—it is also a cult. It
has a hold on its devotees which is stronger than the concrete gains from
an occasional winning would warrant. It has an element of mystery and
anticipation. It has developed an esoteric language. It organizes, to some
extent, the daily lives of its participants. And, as in all cults, it has developed
a group of functionaries and subsidiary businesses dealing in supplies."[7] To
summarize, they deemed policy "an impure commercial enterprise."[8] But a
closer look at the last sentence of the quote—"[policy] has developed a group
of functionaries and subsidiary businesses dealing in supplies"—shows that
despite its overwhelming negative evaluation, the rise of policy revealed its
kings operating at a vital place in an economy traditionally hostile toward
blacks. It is possible to conclude that policy operated at critical levels in
politics, in charity, and in the cultural vibrancy of the Black Belt as a whole.

As mentioned earlier, for many African Americans in Chicago during
World War I, home, civic, and community identities were forged in a commercial leisure district centered at State and 35th Streets. This district
included both the respectable businesses of "Old Settlers" and new sites
of commercial amusement that began to proliferate in cities throughout
America by 1910.[9] Chicago Mayor Edward Dunne simultaneously, and
consciously, orchestrated the Chicago Vice Commission between 1905 and
1910.[10] The term *vice* was widespread in reformist rhetoric at the turn of
the century, and it often encompassed a variety of activities, both legal and
illegal. Under the term, reformers lumped gambling, prostitution, petty theft,
the sale of alcohol from unlicensed distributors, "lewd" dancing, and racial

"mixing."[11] African Americans responded to vice in their neighborhoods by engaging in repeated discussions of respectability and how it served as the foundation for secure homes, sustained civic engagement, and healthy communities in the Black Belt.[12]

How to define respectability became a central concern for Black leaders in large part because of the association made between commercial leisure and illicit activity in the Black Belt. Race leaders, like white reformers, often decried the rise of commercialized leisure for its role in promoting vice.[13] One of the central goals of the National Urban League, both in Chicago and nationwide, was to promote respectability among new migrants; rural southerners were admonished by the Urban League to "act right"—to lower the voice, improve the language, avoid saloons and poolrooms, and attend proper churches.[14] The *Chicago Defender* published lists of dos and don'ts put forward by the League. The don'ts included the following: "Don't use vile language; Don't make yourself a public nuisance; Don't congregate with crowds on the street; Don't encourage gamblers, disreputable women or men to apply their business at any time or place; Don't leave your job when you have a few dollars in your pocket."[15] As blunt as these efforts were, vice went hand in hand with racial segregation, with "licit" and "illicit" economies and leisure sites moving closer and closer together.[16] With formal and informal economies of the Black Belt intermingling to the point of dependency, definitions of respectability became more permeable, exploding rigid class stratifications. This is not to suggest that race leaders promoting respectability accepted the presence of so-called vice or used it as a social leveler in their community. Rather, urban segregation made the sharp lines leaders hoped to draw between licit and illicit economies in the Black Belt more difficult to maintain, particularly with the increasing importance of commercialized leisure in structuring urban life.[17] Chicago's policy kings and queens capitalized on this situation in both fiscal and cultural ways.

By midcentury, Bronzeville's policy royalty were taking in half a million dollars a year.[18] Unlike other cities, where policy created a stream of wealth that ran one direction only: out of Black neighborhoods and into the pockets of white mobsters, in Chicago black policy kings gave back.

Policy became the biggest Black-owned business in the world, with combined annual sales sometimes reaching the $100 million mark and employing tens of thousands of people nationwide. In Bronzeville, policy was a major catalyst by which the Black economy was driven. In 1938, *Time* magazine reported that Bronzeville was the "center of US negro business," and more than a decade later, *Our World Magazine* reported that "windy city negroes have more money, bigger cars and brighter clothes than any other city. . . .

[T]he city which has become famous for the biggest policy wheels, the largest funerals, the flashiest cars and the prettiest women, has built that reputation on one thing, money."[19]

In the vacuum where there were few banks, credit associations, and loan and realty enterprises, policy and numbers gambling emerged. It became a source of capital and ironically a means of savings, a device for personally accumulating some resources. And with the usury industry, policy banks offered the impoverished an alternative institutional system for the savings-investment cycle in the ghetto. These credit services provided to steady policy payers and small retail businesses served as a substitute source for the absence of mainstream banks where lending and loan policies forbade making small loans to impoverished customers or making loans to businesses that could scarcely collateralize their debt.[20]

Aside from supplanting formal economic institutions, policy also blended them or utilized them as facades. It was difficult to draw lines between licit and illicit venues of commercial leisure, in terms of both who frequented these spots and how they were financed.[21] Drake and Cayton reported that policy became so lucrative that some legitimate businessmen turned to it as their major enterprise and used their other business as merely a front. The authors collected data from a variety of professions concluding that policy operated successfully as a proprietor's only business or as their secondary business. One restaurateur reported:

> Two years ago, my business was so bad that I thought I would have to close up. Then I thought of a policy station. I divided the store, and I find that I make more money from the policy than from the lunchroom.[22]

A cigar-store proprietor hoped to open a station soon:

> I have a small turnover—about $15 a day. Money comes pretty slow in the cigarette business, but with a policy station, I ought to do pretty well. Competition has almost forced the Negro out of business.[23]

Another fairly successfully owner of a lunch-stand commented, "work was hard to find, so I thought I would start in business."[24] A friend allowed him to open a restaurant in front of his policy station. A few months later, the friend went out of business and left him both the station and store. He reported: "I kept the station open, putting on a girl to take care of it for me. I was surprised to find that the station earned enough to pay the girl and yet make a profit."[25] In some cases the legitimate business was purely a front, as in the case of a laundryman who told an interviewer: "I just took the laundry business over as a front for my station. I don't really expect to make any money out of it. Yet I may start up a hand laundry. I am just an agent for a white laundry now and the percentage don't amount to much."[26] It was often to a legitimate businessman's advantage to rent out the rear of his store to a policy station, thereby reducing his overhead. In a selected area of the Black Belt, policy stations were fronted with shoeshine parlors, candy stores, barbershops, cigar stores, beauty parlors, or delicatessens.[27]

The policy kings and queens invested a portion of their take in legitimate businesses as well. Taverns, shoe stores, food marts, and real estate businesses were among the enterprises based on what Drake and Cayton called an "unorthodox form of primitive accumulation."[28] However, "many ministers, civic leaders, and politicians," wrote the authors, "have eschewed any discussion of policy, purely on the ground that the game is a business, employing many people, a game that gave some reality to the hope of erecting an independent economy within the black belt."[29] About 20 percent of the largest African American business enterprises, and those most conscious of the value of public good will, were owned by policy people.[30]

Leading policy kings Eddie Jones and his brothers operated most of Chicago's policy wheels. The Joneses invested their policy earnings in legitimate businesses, purchasing a Ben Franklin Store, 436 East 47th Street, four hotels, a food market, and several apartment buildings. Bankers, businessmen, and politicians from all walks lined up to do business with the Jones brothers. Al Monroe, columnist for the *Chicago Defender*, reported, "General opinion through Chicago was that the Jones brothers could furnish the answer to any problem—political, business, or professional . . . parents of graduates would look to the Jones brothers to put in a good word with prospective employers on their kid's behalf."[31] Certainly, policy kings and queens were sought-after advisors and cultural icons.

Even though policy gambling was defined as illegal, specifically with the 1905 antipolicy Act, passed in the wake of policy king John Mushmouth Johnson's unparalleled success,[32] it was important in structuring economic relations in Black neighborhoods, where participation in the formal economy often was tenuous and unstable. Policy, as an organized parallel institution to legitimate economies, was quite a viable option for those who perceived the social institutions aligned against them when opportunities to get ahead legitimately through a combination of hard work, sacrifice, and merit were constricted or blocked because of their race, religion, or social status.[33] Policy then became an institutional means as a way of amassing wealth and resources that constitute the ingredients of social mobility and status.[34] Therefore, the distinction between formal and informal economies in Black urban communities was ambiguous because the two were dependent on one another for creating employment and stimulating economic exchange. These connections attest to the fluid boundaries between respectability and vice in the Black Belt but also its integration into the lifeblood of the community. Policy then was an innovative response to social contingencies and realities that defined the Black Belt.[35] A community defined by, as scholar Robin Bachin wrote, respectable and "illicit" elements of cultural life in the Black Belt rubbing up against one another.[36] Chicago's policy kings and queens capitalized on this friction and brought positivity, racial pride, and prosperity to the Black Belt during a time of deep economic despair and racial hostility.

Policy served as passage for many newly arrived migrants toward a better education and fostered incredible class mobility. Together, only in Bronzeville, race and vice facilitated success; it was not despite their color that African American policy kings and queens, such as John Mushmouth Johnson, got into Bronzeville's highest social circles, but because of it. Specific links between the world of policy gambling and the arts can be made with the story of Mushmouth, banker Jesse Binga, his wife Eudora Johnson Binga, and their nephew and famed poet Fenton Johnson. Eudora was the sister of John "Mushmouth" Johnson, the city's first gambling and policy king, who owned a major State Street casino as well as the upscale Frontenac Club on 22nd Street. The family home, financed by Mushmouth's fortune, where he, Eudora, their sister Cecilia, and their mother Ellen lived, was at 5830 South Wabash. As wife of Jesse Binga and inheritor of Mushmouth's fortune, the House of Binga was based partly on the fortune that Mushmouth derived from gambling."[37] Mrs. Johnson was a well-known philanthropist of many causes in Bronzeville, including the arts.[38] Fenton, born in 1888 to a well-known clubwoman and railroad porter/bail bondsman, studied at Northwestern and the University of Chicago, met all of Black Chicago's elite, and was well known by his peers. He wrote news articles and features for the *Defender* and had plays and musical reviews performed by the Pekin Stock Company. The Pekin's owner, Robert Motts, was a former employee of Fenton's well-known uncle—Mushmouth Johnson.[39]

Mushmouth kept policy gaming alive when Policy Sam, Chicago's first policy king, withdrew from the game after the antipolicy law of 1905. In 1931 the syndicate was formed to resist threats from outside influences of the Mafia and the law. Binga's fortune came from John Mushmouth's fortune. It's ironic that Binga's bank, a legitimate business, turned illegitimate. In 1908 Binga founded a private bank and with the great influx of Negroes during the migration, it prospered. He married the sister of "Mushmouth" Johnson,[40] notorious gambler-politician, and when "Mushmouth" died much of his fortune went into the bank. In 1920, his bank shifted from a private bank to a state bank. On July 31, 1930, the state examiner closed the House of Binga—"insufficient cash and frozen assets." He was arrested on March 5, 1931, on a charge of embezzlement. He was paroled in 1940 to the custody of a Catholic priest. Afterward, for a brief time, he became a janitor.[41]

But in the minds of Bronzevillians, Binga, Mushmouth, and policy men like him, such as the Jones brothers, were not criminals but victims of the white man's system.[42] Respectable people in Bronzeville defended policy on the basis of the achievements of men such at the Jones brothers. Ironically, a few months after the prison gates opened to release Binga, they closed on one of the Jones boys, who reputedly took the rap for the family's alleged collective evasion of income-tax payments. But to Bronzeville, pondering the fate of both, neither Binga nor the Jones boys were criminal; this estimation should extend to the game of policy as a whole. For instance, Drake and Cayton quote one legitimate businessman who commented, "I'm glad to see our group go into business enterprises no matter where the money comes from."[43] One female tavern owner did not know how to explain it but commented "the people who have opened the best business are those who have made the money from policy." They also quote an informant who tried to visualize the effects of stopping policy, "If the heat were turned on, 5,000 people would be unemployed and business in general would be crippled, especially taverns and even groceries, shoe stores, and many other business enterprises who depend on the buying power of the South Side."[44] It was the underworld of policy gambling that stabilized the city's black economy and social world, especially during the Depression.[45]

The wives, husbands, and children of policy men and women echoed these sentiments when they said policy was a "realization of a dream."[46] Less numerous than policy kings, some women took it upon themselves to take part in the game instead of being party to the fiscal success of their brothers, husbands, or lovers. Women's involvement in policy spans several decades. During the 1940s and 1950s, when policy was quite successful, Bronzeville's policy kings and queens were targeted in raids by the police force, perhaps encouraged by white neighborhoods that did not want the game or upwardly mobile African Americans expanding into their neighborhoods. The policy queens of 1940s Bronzeville were Irene Coleman, Leslie Williams, and Anne Roane; Coleman and Williams were the owners of the Belmont and Old Reliable Policy Wheels, formerly owned by Coleman's father, Buddy Coleman. Roan was a partner in the Second Ward–based Alabama/Georgia, Jackpot, and Whirlaway Wheels with Matt Bivins.[47] Coleman, Williams, and Roane were indicted along with twenty-three policy kings in the "Big Conspiracy Trial" of 1942. In the aftermath of the trial, all of the kings' clubs reopened.[48] Roan would eventually join forces with Ed Jones, of the Jones brothers, not for policy revenue, but in a different venture. They opened a milk delivery business: Hawthorn Milk Store.[49]

The most famous queen of Chicago's policy game was Florine Reynolds Irving Stephens, the former wife of James D. Irving, who was once hailed as the undisputed mid-twentieth-century "King of Policy" until he was sent to the federal penitentiary on income-tax evasion charges. Stephens married Irving in 1937 when he was a cabdriver and divorced ten years later. The divorce settlement included a $250/week income, a cash settlement, and one of Irving's many policy wheels—the Boulevard-Avenue wheel that reportedly made her $25,000/week.[50] Irving, released from the penitentiary in 1959, was furious at Stephens. She had taken the opportunity during his absence to branch out and take over several wheels that had been controlled by Irving.[51] Stephens employed sixty runners who distributed betting slips in drugstores, newsstands, liquor stores, beauty parlors, and other establishments in the area where the wheels operated. A July 17, 1960, *Chicago Daily Tribune* article reported Stephens to be the "operator of the largest policy wheels on the Southside" as well as "a great fan of mink coats and diamonds."[52] A 1961 *Chicago Daily Tribune* article quoted detectives saying "that the Spaulding-Silver-Dunlap wheel, which is only one of the wheels owned by Mrs. Stephens . . . nets $14,000 a day in income for her, totaling up to more than five million dollars annually. . . . [T]he wheel operates seven days a week, 52 weeks a year."[53] Stephens met her demise in late 1961 at forty years old when she was arrested November 30 at the home of her son James Irving Jr., at 7539 Indiana Avenue by four detectives of the organized crime division's gambling detail under Sergeant Clark Gordon.[54]

Of the sixty runners Stephens employed, one can assume that there were women who held the post. In an interview conducted for his dissertation at Northwestern University, Lewis Caldwell interviewed a former policy writer who stated that in 1928 there were eight hundred writers working for her boss, and about half of them were women.[55] The same *Chicago Daily Tribune* article on February 23, 1964, that reported on Stephen's earnings from the Boulevard-Avenue wheel also reported that despite orders to district commanders to crack down on vice and gambling policy was running wide open.[56] The reporter followed scores of gamblers entering an alley door at 6312 St. Lawrence Avenue and found women counting large stacks of money while men counted policy slips. For many women who could scarcely make it as domestic laborers, maids, or laundresses, policy was both a lucrative and respectable means of employment. Drake and Cayton interviewed several female policy writers/runners and players and one stated: "Policy is a godsend. Girls could make $20/week. They couldn't make that in a laundry or a kitchen."[57] Caldwell's interview illustrates the rise of the game in Chicago and the relief it offered from harsh domestic work:

I left Oklahoma with my two children, two and three years old, in 1921 after saving money from my maid's job. My husband was glad to get rid of us. Two days after being in Chicago I got a dishwashing job in a north side restaurant. In 1925 a doctor told me to stop that work because the soap was injuring my hands. I had to do something in order to feed my children, so got a job writing policy. I was given instruction for a week before I got a book. In less than a month I was writing $20 a day, and keeping five for my share. From then until 1930 I made good money but had to stop because my feet began swelling. I'm forty-five years old and have lived in four states but that's the best job I ever had.[58]

Wives of syndicate men called policy a "realization of a dream" while employees of the game called it "a godsend" or "the best job [they] ever had." These women show that policy opened avenues to them that may not have been available otherwise. But the policy queens and female numbers runners are the exceptions to this narrative, not the rule; far more common were the men and women who used what money they could to place bets on the various wheels owned and operated by the Johnson family, or wheels owned by Stephens, Roan, Coleman, or Williams. It is to their stories we turn next.

Drake and Cayton quote a policy king who said the game was supported in the main "by the small change of poverty-laden workers, housewives, prostitutes, and gambling-house flunkies who were lured by the 180-to-1 dividends."[59] The research of sociologist Ernest W. Burgess included lists of "characters" he found at a variety of wheels and stations in Bronzeville.[60] Many of the patrons of the game in his research were women, middle-aged, some on relief, while others stopped to place bets after a hard day's work.[61] Lewis Caldwell's study also attempted to give portrait to those placing 350,000 bets daily on policy. For a period of four months—January through April, 1937—five investigators for the Old Age Assistance Division of the Cook County Bureau of Public Welfare attempted, for the purposes of his study, to determine what percentages of their clients, or members of their families, bet on policy.[62] Those homes visited were in the area bounded by Federal Street–West, Cottage Grove Avenue–East, 26th-Street–North, and 44th Street–South. Five hundred homes composed the sample. In four hundred of those homes, 80 percent, evidence of the policy game was found. No efforts to conceal the drawings were encountered; policy stations were found in the front rooms and storefronts of business sections in adjacent neighborhoods; usually a barbeque pit, beauty parlor, eatshop, confectionary, or barbershop occupied a part of each station. Nor were efforts to conceal these locations made either, as prominent signs in the window or doors read "We write all books."[63] By patient observation, Caldwell stated, he found that a majority of the patrons of these locations were women. He attributed this to the "fact that the men are working during the day and remain content to allow their wives to make their bets. At least four instances were encountered, however, where the wife was playing policy without knowledge or consent of her spouse."[64] He cited a conversation he had with one elderly player of the game: "I had lived in Chicago for four years when I began playing policy in 1930," she began. "At the laundry where I worked, the girls had played for years, but I never gave the game a thought 'til one night I dreamt of my mother who had been dead for thirty years. At work I mentioned the dream to Jessie, and she made me play a quarter on the 'dead mother' row. Well, sir, as I'm living this minute, the gig fell out and I won $25. That started me off. My luck got so good, and since I was bothered with rheumatism I quit the laundry."[65] Residents of Bronzeville's lack of effort to conceal participation in the policy game as writers, runners, and patrons illustrates African Americans' belief that the game, to borrow from Drake and Cayton, was "on the level."[66]

Even though gambling was defined as illegal, it was important in structuring economic relations in Black neighborhoods, where participation in the formal economy was tenuous and unstable—or plain backbreaking. Policy, then, was viewed as, and existed as, quite a viable option for the overwhelming amount of women who confronted a profound lack of opportunities to get ahead legitimately through hard work and sacrifice. Bronzeville was a community defined by respectable and "illicit" elements of cultural life coexisting and at times conflicting with one another.[67] Chicago's policy men and women capitalized on this friction and captured unheard-of possibilities.

Policy afforded migrants relief from the grind of poverty and the rigidity of gender rules; it also gave migrants a moment to imagine themselves beyond the harsh conditions of Bronzeville. Policy has a creative element akin to the creativity and imagination of authors and artists of the Chicago Black Renaissance. The creativity of art and literature is synonymous with the creativity of gambling or the ability of patrons to see themselves beyond the scope of poverty—a fictive imagining of oneself outside of one's current context—hearkening a similar consciousness to the protagonists of Gwendolyn Brooks's *A Street in Bronzeville*, who aspire to send a dream "up through onion fumes" or travel beyond "the front yard."[68] Blacks of Bronzeville did this through policy. The transformative elements of literature are evident in the transformative potential of winning at policy. There are also tangible links (not dreams or wishes or hopes of pulling the right numbers) between policy and the world of African American cultural production. Chicago Black Renaissance luminary Langston Hughes wrote about it, and Fenton Johnson, poet and nephew of Mushmouth Johnson, lived it; Archibald Motley painted scenes of vice in the South Side; and many more authors, artists, and musicians make mention of it. But the literature of policy is the game's dream books, where authors or African American diviners wrote the script of black urbanism through visions captured while Bronzeville slept. Policy's theatrical script is the language of gigs, saddles, and horses; its costumes are upper-class silks and satins, middle-class tweeds, the working poor's burlap, and the lower-class' holed and soiled mittens; its stage directions send policy runners left and right and wheels spinning twice a day—drawings in the morning and the evening. Policy's financial patrons, analogous to the Chicago Black Renaissance's Julius Rosenwalds, are its kings and queens. The hungry audience to consume this literature is a primed Bronzeville populace inspired by New Negro consciousness.[69]

Davarian Baldwin lends a useful theoretical lens when he writes, from his fantastic study of Chicago's South Side, *Chicago's New Negroes*, "The way policy gambling continued older southern and diasporic traditions of black gaming made it both a cultural and economic institution in the North by serving as another popular art form in the city."[70] Amid low-status employment in the formal economy, the predominantly white ownership of African American businesses in African American neighborhoods throughout the early to mid–twentieth century, and the inspiration of social movements, the world of illegal policy gambling (now legalized as state lottery), leisure, and recreation served as the centerpiece of the Black Metropolis.[71] Chicago's black gamblers and entrepreneurs took advantage of the consolidation of the city's vice on the South Side to make the area a mecca for cultural innovation.[72] The fact that leisure activities became the cultural and economic foundation of the Black Metropolis serves as a commentary on the power of black consumer culture and the profound exclusion of black professionals from the mainstream world of labor, leisure, and political influence. Studies of Chicago's black policy gaming make clear that the creative excitement of black entertainment, emergence of black gambling syndicates, and rise of black politics were closely interrelated and had a broad impact.[73]

Policy bankers underwrote an important urban culture of theaters, dance halls, and athletic and traditional business enterprises. Many reformers argued that gambling deluded working people into wasting their money on a long-shot dream, and city officials made attempts to thwart its corrupting effects. For sure, Baldwin states, policy was a blend of exploitation and enterprise, both capitalizing on the dire economic conditions of black residents and circulating money back into the black community. However, he continues, many migrants also saw direct parallels between their bets and the investments whites placed in the stock market, except policy did not discriminate. Moreover, he concludes, policy provided a relatively higher rate of return while becoming an avenue toward race advancement, especially in the discriminatory job market of the 1930s.[74]

Even indirectly, policy provided both the physical and conceptual space where Chicago's New Negroes would work out many of the cultural styles, forms, and institutions that were initially critiqued and are now celebrated within black communities. Baldwin writes, "the new settler possibilities offered by the blurring lines between labor and leisure served as the catalyst for a different set of New Negro "popular arts" and institutions that both paralleled and even funded cultural production within the famed Harlem Renaissance";[75] for the purposes of this project I highlight the same for Chicago—Bronzeville specifically. Policy's modern canvas for the creation of ideas was situated directly within and not in evasion of twentieth-century socioeconomic realities. In many cases, Baldwin stresses, the consumer marketplace of the Stroll and then Bronzeville was one of the only sites where New Negroes could buy and sell culture, dreams, and products of self-transformation and create both personal and communal desires (read imaginings) for a different Black Metropolis and a different world.[76] Baldwin's different world is revealed in one example, through policy's dream books and the imaginative world of gaming.

According to historian Ann Fabian, American dream books were a continuation of a long tradition of popular knowledge, a sort of vernacular divination that offered keys to the unknown future;[77] but they also say something about the present. Dreams and their interpretation serve a literary device to "read" or discern race relations and life in the urban north.[78] American dream books offered a number of alternative interpretations of life in Bronzeville while they undergird the Chicago Black Renaissance's aesthetic.

Dream books were often printed as cheap pamphlets by popular publishers in Chicago, New York, and Baltimore. American divination was written in the language of African American popular culture. The web of metaphor, which connected the baffling present of the dream to its realization in the future, was spun by the conjurers and seers who had once interpreted life for fellow slaves. Obviously dream books were marketed to urban, literate (largely northern) audiences, among whom they may well have competed not only with rational explanation but also with storefront fortunetellers. However, by naming "Old Aunt Dinah," "Old Aunt Madge," "The Gypsy Witch," and "Arabs Professor Abdullah," and, in the 1920s, "Professor Uriah Konje" as fictional authors, argues Fabian, publishers based expertise on folk wisdom derived from slave communities or on exotic knowledge increasingly lost to city dwellers. They called upon the interpreters, the wise figures of Africa and the Orient, who were privy to knowledge invisible to modern men and women. Although the interpretations they advanced may have been arbitrary, superficial, and invented quite recently, authors themselves were figures who embodied traditional principles of interpretation.[79]

To the nineteenth-century urban, white, middle class, dream books were trivial souvenirs and provided parlor entertainment. Numbers are presented as curious asides, and dreams are read as keys to courtship, finding lost objects, and assurances of wealth and well being (like fortune cookies). But, Fabian stresses, one must not ignore the ways middle-class play is filtered through African American seers. The presence of these seers is evidence of an African American hand in northern popular culture and of the survival of folk beliefs that persists in a Chicago Black Renaissance aesthetic wedding place and artistry. Christopher Reed articulates this relationship in a term he develops in his study of Black Chicago, something he terms the "concept of Black Metropolis": the desire of African Americans to have dominion "over space and culture because it satisfied their cultural needs to experience a glimpse or taste of home every day of their lives. In a world where they were denied so much because of racism and impoverishment, the means, abilities, and resources to satisfy their dreams gained even greater currency."[80] Thus, the figures who presided over the language of dreams and northern migrant experience served as arbiters of "the dream of black metropolis." As such mirrors of African American desire, dream books are as reflective of an African American aesthetic as Archibald Motley's genre paintings of the same era and locale.[81]

According to Fabian, as early as the middle of the nineteenth century players read dream books to arrive at a number to play, to arrive at the coordinates to plot themselves in the economic landscape, and not for the science of interpretation.[82] Exactly how dreams came to signify certain numbers is a subject dream books never address. They describe in detail theories of dreams and dream interpretation, but calculations of numerical equivalents remained the product of ancient traditions and mysterious arts. Dream books—of which "Aunt Sally's Policy Players Dream Book" is by far the best-known—link dream images (e.g., dream of a cook or dream of a locomotive) to divinatory meanings (e.g., "you will receive a letter" or "beware a strange man"), and they also give numbers for betting (e.g., 5-14-50 or 65-41-55). In a typical numbers book, the dream images are listed in alphabetical order, with one, two, three, or four numbers beside each item, specifically designed for the convenience of those who bet on policy. "A dream"—asserted the "Policy Player's Lucky Number Dream Book"—"is a motion or fiction of the soul, signifying good or evil to come, and it depended on the character or class as to whether it may signify its true meaning or directly the contrary."[83]

There are a number of different dream books on sale. The authors of these dream books are largely unknown to modern players, but among the most prolific were Herbert Gladstone Parris, who wrote under the pseudonyms Professor Konje, Professor Uriah Konje, and Professor De Herbert; Madame Fu Futtam (Dorothy Hamid, 1905–1985), a candle-shopkeeper in New York, who taught spiritual and occult work as well as giving dream interpretations and lottery luck numbers to her clientele; Black Herman (Benjamin Rucker, 1892–1934), a stage magician and a root doctor as well; and Rajah Rabo (Carl Z. Talbot, 1890–1974), whose "Pick 'Em Dream Book" gave prophetic information in addition to numbers.[84]

Interpreting a dream ran as such: Player A dreams, the night before, that she sees her dead mother. In the dream book that's the "dead mother row," and is interpreted as 12-27-29. Player A will not rest until she has put a quarter or half-dollar in the three drawings and in two or three of the popular books. She is likely to invest several dollars on the gig. But before she becomes discouraged and gives up, she will have another dream about her sweetheart (30-47-72), and the player jumps to this row.[85] A few more specimens are: WHITE POLICEMAN—if you dream of meeting up with a white policeman, play numbers 28-35-67; COFFIN—if you dream of a coffin, which signifies that you will soon be married and own a house of your own, play numbers 9-49-50; TOMBS—if you dream of being among the tombs, which denotes a speedy marriage, play numbers 7-8-31; TUMMY—if you dream that one's tummy is great and large, which predicts a fair and large estate, play 10-11-22; GIN—If you dream of gin, which denotes pleasure and disappointment in life, play numbers 8-16-42; POLICY OFFICE—if you dream of a policy office, which foretells riches, play numbers 4-11-44. The latter is the favorite of all numbers.[86]

Policy players' dream books acknowledge African American subjectivity. They often comment directly on race, frequently reversing the power relations of the waking world.[87] Some African Americans during the early twentieth century believed that "supernatural traditions were integral" to helping them deal and overcome limited employment and economic hardship, and race, class, and gender discrimination.[88] Historian LaShawn Harris argues that black female mediums provided their customers with a sense of autonomy and empowerment over their public and private lives.[89] Most black women mediums, especially those who were working-class, did not leave personal papers or records that documented their public and private lives.[90] Dream books then, become primary sources detailing the dreams and realities of black urban experience. Historian Victoria Wolcott posits, "Although the informal economy is usually gendered in the popular imagination as a male world of danger, bravado, violence, and exploitation, illegal activities that involved monetary exchanges also employed women."[91] African American mediumship was nearly exclusively the realm of women. African American female mediums were known for selling "lucky numbers" to policy customers. Numbers players believed that mediums were critical to selecting winning numbers. "The five most popular dream books in 1938 and 1939 were *The Three Witches, The Gypsy Witch, The Japanese Fate, Aunt Dell's,* and *Aunt Sally's.*"[92]

African Americans used dream books and spiritualists for the "translation of personal experiences and public occurrences into numerical expressions,"[93] and they did that through female translators such as Madame Williams. Listed as "Your Friend and Adviser," Williams advertised special meetings every Wednesday, Friday, and Sunday evening and had "advised thousands in their personal problems with complete satisfaction." The Madame offered "advice on all affairs of life, love, health, domestic and financial conditions." She advertised LUCKY NUMBERS—11 HITS IN 3 DAYS. She made no charge, but lifted a silver offering announced as twenty-five cents! There were several hundred such advisers in Bronzeville.[94]

Mediums distributed lucky numbers to policy players in a variety of ways. Policy customers received lucky numbers through private consultations, from dream books, on street corners, and by attending religious services at storefront churches. Dream books were part of the commercialization of mediumship and supernaturalism. They served as guides to interpreting and understanding dreams, superstitions, and symbols and were used to pick winning policy numbers. Some sold for thirty-five cents a copy and could be purchased at various women's candle shops or at newsstands or stationary stores.

Astronumerologist Professor Edward Lowe sold his gigs ranging in price from ten cents to three dollars, the latter guaranteed or money back. He asserted that he got his "gift" from his mother, that he studied the science of numbers and the zodiac, which helped him write several dream books; Adam and Eve Roots, Policy Player's Oil for 50 cents, Genuine Live Lodestone, and the Lucky Oil of Mystery were all displayed outside his store. Definitely, there is a material culture world of policy given Drake and Cayton's impressive detailing of luck oils, jinx-removal candles, and sprays.[95]

Dream books took random events and transformed them into a discernible language. This language of numbers bettors was a lexicon and a fiction for the South Side. It took time for writers to learn the numbers of his neighborhood gigs—akin to sociologists or anthropologists getting to know their surroundings. Legislators doubted that such random events led to financial decisions. This manner of reordering random events continued to astonish the commissioners, but it suggests that the search for calculations of certainty and order so charismatic of the late-nineteenth-century business community and its bureaucracy had equally able practitioners who operated in a different mode. Like businessmen, policy players arrived at calculations, at figures that were to provide a base for action, but figures for numbers bettors were not keys to an ever more rationalized and plotted universe. They were just figures, random, irrational figures, and their equivalents were in the unquantifiable substance of dreams, not in the accumulation of profits.[96] Much like authors and poets.

A guide to the pattern hidden in such accidental happenings and their numerical equivalents could be found in dream books. "There is dream books," J. Lawrence Carney, the policy writer, explained to the investigators, "'Common Sally,' and 'Three Witches,' and 'Wheel of Fortune'; now these books have every word in the dictionary, I guess, and they will have the lucky."[97] Although witnesses asserted that there was no system in the play of policy, the dream books provided a system for interpreting the random events of the word and more important the means of ordering and acting on the chaos of that segregated world. The actions impoverished dreaming policy bettors took were economic actions, even if they involved the expense of a single penny. It is appropriate that dreams—the least controlled and least predictable site of human imagining—led straight to the economy, a region that remained for the poor the least predictable site of human expression. Dream books literally contained the knowledge or information that made play and survival in the urban north possible.[98]

With the counsel of dream books and the "services" of numbers writers, even if poor bettors were not the most active participants in the market culture in which they lived, they were among its most innovative interpreters.[99] To bet on dreams and hunches against very long odds was not simply a traditional response to a closed economy but was the means of opening the closed economy to the play of the imagination—play based on a distinct vision of human nature and its expression in the market. Policy players made dreams and the inner imaginative worlds of the African Americans public. The men and women discussing their visions exchanged dreams, transforming the most private of imaginative forms into communal property. They all became interpreters and authors of black urban experience; furthermore, to borrow from Michael Denning, they became laborers of culture.[100]

Right from the start, historians Shane and Graham White attest, artists and authors working in a variety of genres recognized the centrality of numbers and policy to an urban black culture now being transformed by the Great Migration and used it as a vehicle for ruminating about African American identity.[101] Gambling, policy, and numbers were grist for the mills of many writers associated with the Illinois Writers Project; blues singers who recorded in the 1920s and 1930s; and playwrights, novelists, poets, and filmmakers that made Bronzeville famous for African American cultural production.

One such cultural endeavor, the Illinois Writers Project, covered policy thoroughly and creatively. The Illinois Writers Project, based in downtown Chicago, distinguished itself as one of the most accomplished state offices of the Federal Writers' Project and the Writers' Program that succeeded it. These programs were part of a larger national effort from 1935 to 1943 to employ artists and writers who might otherwise have been unable to work during the Great Depression. The Illinois office, directed by Northwestern University professor John T. Frederick, included Nelson Algren, Richard Wright, Jack Conroy, Willard Motley, Frank Yerby, Saul Bellow, Margaret Walker, Arna Bontemps, Sam Ross, and Louis "Studs" Terkel. Its official publications included a massive guide to Illinois and smaller guides to localities, as well as studies of subjects ranging from baseball to industry and including policy gaming.[102]

Policy enjoyed a lengthy discussion in the IWP under the "Negro in Illinois" title. Mathilde Bunton authored "Policy: Negro Business," in which she offers a comprehensive discussion of the game: its walking writers, wheels, and policy's syndication in 1931.[103] Herman Clayton offers a similar discussion in his October 1, 1940, piece "Negro in Illinois: The Game Policy." In his piece, he details the construction of the policy wheel: "a collapsible wheel, which includes a small barrel mounted on bearings, is generally used. In a few of the places the drawings are made from baskets. Seventy-eight small rubber capsules, or one for each number, each containing a two-by-two stripe of rubberized fabric upon which the respective numbers appear in red, are thrown together in the receptacle for each drawing."[104]

IWP writer Andrew G. Paschal took the description another step further in his contribution "Policy: Negroes' Number Game," describing the next step in drawing numbers: twelve numbers are drawn in the presences of witnesses, and then stamped in a column along the lengthwise margin of a piece of paper. The numbers are rewrapped and then placed back in the keg. Again twelve numbers are drawn and stamped along the other margin of the slip of paper, which completes the drawing for one "book." Each wheel has several books; some of the popular names of the books are: "Black-Gold," "Goldfield," "Wall Street," "Royal Pal," "Northshore," "North-South," "East-West," "Rio Grande," "Harlem," "Bronx," "Wisconsin," and "Red Devil." The names, which generally suggest mystery and money, and seemingly drawn from every conceivable source, are stamped at the top of the slip along with numbers identifying wheel and station, and the notation, "A.M.," "P.M.," or "Midnight," to denote the time of drawing.[105]

IWP writers were granted unprecedented access to Chicago's leading policy kings. Herman Clayton interviewed several of the Jones brothers, as did Chauncey Spencer.[106] Spencer asked George Jones bold questions regarding his investments, his reputation as a policy king, and any connections that the Jones brothers' famed Ben Franklin Store might have. In his interview with Jones he asked, "I have seen you in the office of the bookie, and drawing that place also was an interest of yours and your brothers wasn't it?" *Jones*: "In a way, yes it was." *Int.*: "You say it was, have you no interest in it now?" *Jones*: "I did not say anything." *Int.*: "Are you interested in politics or are your connections in any of your business ventures political?" *Jones*: "Not at all, everything that we have entered has been on our own with no political backing in any form." *Int.*: "Well, I know that gambling is illegal here and bookies, policy stations, etc. are not in accord with the law." *Jones*: "The public is going to gamble some way regardless law or no law. And this place you are talking about is like others all over the city the police etc. know nothing of it. Questions like this I do not know anything about so I can't give answers. Look around the store, over our goods. I am going to have to go."[107]

The IWP records also show writers' access to spiritualists. Mathilde Bunton interviewed Mr. "Professor" Edward H. Lowe in 1941.[108] Bunton was able to inventory Lowe's Incense Book Store, which consisted of incense, herbs, dream books, roots, candles, and lucky oils and powders (his stock was at least sixteen different oils and over ten different powders). Bunton closed her exchange with Lowe with the following advertisement tacked on his shop's wall: "SPECIAL TO NUMBER PLAYERS: Are your dreams unlucky to you? Do the Gigs you get from your dreams split out? Do others CATCH on your dreams when you fail to play them? Do you have trouble remembering your dreams? If so, you should read the 70th Psalm and use MYSTIC DREAM INCENSE $.15 – $.25."[109]

In 1940, the IWP published *Cavalcade of the American Negro*, a sweeping history of black contributions to all phases of American life from 1865 to 1940. The book was edited by Arna Bontemps and illustrated by Adrian Troy, of the Illinois Writers and Art Projects, respectively, and was one of the more important contributions to the American Negro Exposition/ Diamond Jubilee Exposition held in Chicago in 1940. The book includes a useful description of all the exhibits at the exposition. The exposition and other programs celebrated the emancipation of the American Negro and his achievements over seventy-five years since the conclusion of the Civil War in 1865. The advantageous location and spaciousness of the Chicago Coliseum were two of many factors allowing for a most successful exposition. The Coliseum was filled with exhibitions from every state in the Union, from several Caribbean islands, and from Liberia in Africa. The large black population of Chicago and from throughout the Mississippi region swelled the attendance at the popular event.[110]

The American Negro Exposition of 1940 marked the seventy-fifth anniversary of emancipation. Staged as a celebration of African American progress and achievement, Chicago's "Diamond Jubilee" exhibition included displays from federal agencies, cities and states, black newspapers, black colleges, churches, fraternal organizations, and a myriad of other groups—a total of ninety-two installations. There were also art and book exhibits, murals, and dioramas. Bands and choirs performed, as did famous black entertainers. Visitors could also attend one of several performances specially staged for the exhibition, including *The Cavalcade of the Negro Theater*, a review of African American music, written by Langston Hughes and Arna Bontemps, and the *Chimes of Normandy*, an operetta performed by the Federal Theatre Project.

Claude Barnett, founder of the Associated Negro Press (ANP), was one of the Exposition's main organizers. Officially, he was in charge of the federal government exhibits and art exhibitions, but he had his hand in nearly everything else as well.[111]

The Illinois Writers Project also afforded writers time to work on their own. Wright, for instance, worked on the landmark novel, *Native Son*. Algren wrote his breakthrough novel, *Never Come Morning*, while employed by the project. Writers on the project also influenced one another. Conroy, Algren, and other established figures advised novices like Terkel and Walker (and intimidated Bellow, who remembers that he "rather looked up to" the veterans, who "rather looked down on" him). Several African American writers on the project staff participated in the South Side Writers Group, which extended the momentum of the Harlem Renaissance of the 1920s, as Bontemps put it, "without finger bowls but with increased power."[112] In Chicago, the WPA was instrumental in spawning the South Side Community Art Center, which opened in 1941 and played a central role in the development of African American designers in Chicago. Today it is the only art center out of approximately one hundred established by the WPA that has survived. In the 1940s and 1950s, the Art Center was a place where African American artists, young and old, could take classes, show their work, and meet for discussions. Although the Art Center began as a WPA-sponsored project, it redefined itself after the WPA ended and became a place whose programs were no longer shaped by government policies or programs.[113]

Most of the African American designers who came up in the 1940s and 1950s had some involvement with the Center, either as students, administrators, or participants in the many discussions about art that were held there. The Art Center was probably the most important place where black artists and designers could meet each other and was surely responsible for some of the networking that developed among the few black professionals in the graphic arts. One of the artists who was central to the Center's activities was William McBride, who was an art promoter more than an artist or designer but he did have a strong sense of style and produced important graphic works for the Center's Artists and Models Balls, which were attended with high pomp and circumstance by Bronzeville socialites, including many policy kings and queens.[114]

Policy was also on the minds of African American playwrights. Plays such as Wallace Thurman and William Jourdan Rapp's *Harlem: A Melodrama of Negro Life in Harlem* (1928) and the musical *Policy Kings* (1932) featured numbers as a prominent part of Harlem life. Langston Hughes portrayed the game in *Little Ham* (1935). He wrote about policy in his work for the *Chicago Defender*, mentioning it in a June 11, 1949, article when he was a visiting scholar at downtown's International Home.[115] He dreams of policy—a mark of his creativity. Playwright Georgia Johnson, in *Starting Point* (1938), likewise wrote plays that were centered on the numbers.[116]

Novelists, too, recognized numbers and policy gambling as resources for their fiction. Carl Van Vechten made the Bolito king—a thinly veiled depiction of Casper Holstein, credited by Shane White and Graham White as the inventor of numbers—an important character in *Nigger Heaven* (1926); Rinehart, one of the major figures in Ralph Ellison's *Invisible Man* (1952), was identified by others as a Harlem preacher, pimp, and numbers runner.[117] Also in the literary realm, Richard Wright's day-in-the-life novel set on Chicago's South Side, *Lawd Today!* (1935), leveled a trenchant critique of the American Dream while providing a description of the game.[118]

Several black writers have based entire novels on numbers or policy. The aforementioned sociologist Lewis Caldwell was born in 1905 Chicago, an Eagle Scout and graduate of Englewood High School (*Chicago Tribune* obituary, October 3, 1993), and he completed his master's thesis at Northwestern University entitled "The Policy Game in Chicago." Employed as a probation officer at the Cook County Juvenile Court in 1941, he used his knowledge of Chicago's black underworld to write *The Policy King* (1945), a novel that laid bare the workings of policy on the South Side following the fortunes of the fictional Marshall family. New Vistas Publishing House (publisher of *New Vistas Magazine*) published the manuscript. Caldwell's Joe Marshall, son of a Negro minister on Chicago's South Side, is driven from home at seventeen after disgracing the family by serving six months in the state reformatory. Seeing few alternatives for himself, Joe joins a gambling syndicate, and in spite of his youth begins his phenomenal rise to king of policy gambling in Chicago. Jerry and Helen, his younger brother and sister, look with disdain on Joe's career, but welcome the money that he provides for their support as they attend college and seek the respectability that he has been denied. Factual and convincing in his approach, Caldwell recreates many facets of Negro life. Joe and Jerry accurately represent the Negro of the street and the bar, while Jerry in his college years represents the black intellectual seeking his place in a white-dominated society, and Helen, as a social aid worker, tries desperately to alleviate the terrible suffering of the thousands of poverty-stricken Negroes on Chicago's welfare rolls. *The Policy King* is a striking family portrait depicting some of the good and some of the bad in growing up black in 1920s Chicago. From 1967–1979, Caldwell served in the Illinois House of Representatives, where he would oppose the introduction of the State Monopoly Lottery on the ground that lotteries would quickly kill off policy and, as it did, would undercut entrepreneurship in minority communities. Julian Mayfield's novel *The Hit* (1957) traced one day in Hubert Cooley's obsessive search for a way out of Harlem by winning the numbers. Robert Pharr's *Book of Numbers* (1969) set in 1935, detailed the travails of Dave Green as he introduced numbers for the first time to a southern town. But probably the best-known today of these novels is Louise Meriwether's *Daddy Was a Number Runner* (1970), set in Harlem in the 1930s—a book that has proved to be enormously popular with adolescent readers.[119]

Poets found policy a fruitful source as well. Frank Marshall Davis's *47th Street* is his fourth book of poetry, a chronicle of African American life on the South Side. In his title poem he mentions a policy writer. *Sundays of Satin-Legs Smith* by Gwendolyn Brooks explores winnings from policy on display in Smith's actions and pursuits.

Much the same interest in the numbers has permeated the black film industry. Films such as *Dark Manhattan* (1937) and *Policy Man* (1938) feature the game. No contemporary reviews of *Policy Man* have been located; however, *Motion Picture Herald* release charts lists this film as having been released by Sack Amusement Enterprises on July 1, 1938, with a running time of sixty-one minutes. According to modern sources, this was a Creative Cinema Corp. production, with a cast including Ann Harleman, Henri Wessell, Jimmy Baskette, Ethel Moses, Count Basie and his Orchestra, and The Plantation Club Chorus. Films like *Moon Over Harlem* (1939) are known to only a few film aficionados today, but when first released they were popular in theaters in the black areas of northern cities, largely because they featured all-black casts and depicted through their portrayals of numbers in Harlem and policy in Chicago one version of what it meant to be black, urban, and sophisticated.[120]

Clearly, Baldwin asserts, more traditional arts and letters were not removed from or rising above the messiness of the consumer marketplace but were aesthetically inspired and institutionally funded by the Bronzeville's commercial world. The "high art" visual and literary products along with the low testify to the impact of urban migrant and mass consumer culture on the overlapping frequencies of black life in the city.[121]

The proliferation of policy in the arts and the plethora of actual policy stations beneath the facades of legitimate African American business institutions show a shifting in the notions of what type of arts and business served as symbols of control, stability, and respectability in Bronzeville, and what would be its authentic aesthetic. Policy certainly gave form to the "dream of Black Metropolis," its authors, artists, and "Race Men and Women."

A quote from Duke Ellington evidences the respect from the community the policy men and women received:

> The Southside was together. It was a real us-for-we, we-for-us community. It was a community with 12 Negro Millionaires. No hungry Negroes, no complaining Negroes, no crying Negroes, and no Uncle Toms. It was a community of men and women who were respected, people of great dignity—doctors, lawyers, Policy operators, boot blacks, barbers, beauticians, bartenders, saloon keepers, night clerks, club owners, cab drivers, stock yard workers, owners of after-hours joints, bootleggers—everything and everybody, but no junkies.[122]

Ranked in the community among doctors and lawyers, policy kings and queens were able to wield some control over community institutions. Some of the kings and queens assumed philanthropic roles, making donations to churches, providing scholarships to promising students, and helping to stimulate general social and economic developments. They supported food drives, clothing drives, and much more. Oral Historian Timuel Black commented, "if they knew you, you wouldn't be standin' in no bread line."[123] They backed groups such as the Wabash YMCA and the *Chicago Defender* Charities, and were among the first financial backers of the first-ever Bronzeville Parade, Bud Billiken Picnic, and later the Bud Billiken Parade. As mentioned earlier, many of the policy kings and their associates were founding members of the South Side Community Arts Center, America's oldest cultural institution of its kind, an offshoot of the WPA Federal Arts Project, officially dedicated on May 8, 1941, by First Lady Eleanor Roosevelt.[124] It is because of events such as this that history must look to policy kings and queens as race heroes and see the game as a patron of the Chicago Black Renaissance.

CHAPTER 4

Two Bronzeville Autobiographies

Q: (George Stavros)

Are your characters literally true to your experience or do you set out to change experience?

A: (Gwendolyn Brooks)

Some of them are, are invented, some of them are very real people. The people in the little poem called "The Vacant Lot" really existed and really did those things. For example: "Mrs. Coley's three flat brick / Isn't here any more. / All done with seeing her fat little form / Burst out of the basement door." Really happened! That lot is still vacant on the street where I was raised. (My mother still lives on the street.) "Matthew Cole" is based on a man who roomed with my husband's aunt. And I remember him so well, I feel [it] really came through in the poem. "The Murder" really happened except for the fact that I said the boy's mother was gossiping down the street. She was working. (I guess I did her an injustice there.) "Obituary for a Living Lady" is based on a person I knew very well.[1]

Gwendolyn Brooks, a lifelong Bronzeville resident and the first African American to win the Pulitzer Prize, showed an abiding commitment to the people of Bronzeville in this 1969 interview with *Contemporary Literature*; this commitment made her poetry and fiction so powerful for the duration of her literary career. The people of Bronzeville are her chief inspiration for the works spanning her lifetime from her first publication in 1945, *A Street in Bronzeville*, to her famed poetry during the Black Arts Movement of the 1960s. The people of Bronzeville assist her in evoking a great feeling of place in her work; she's quoted as saying "I start with the people. For instance, Maud Martha goes to the Regal Theater, which is almost dead now, but had a great history in Chicago. She looks at the people; she looks at the star; she looks at the people coming out of the theater. But . . . suffice it to say that I don't start with the landmarks."[2] The city itself, with its people's despair, defeats and small victories, and teeming human diversity, yielded subjects enough to inspire her creative imagination as well as many other authors, poets, and visual artists of the Renaissance period.[3] As one of the primary authors of the Chicago Black Renaissance, Brooks, along with other Chicago artists and literati, distinguished a self-consciousness of what it meant to be writing in Bronzeville concomitant with a consciousness of the significance of that place and its people to her writing. Bronzeville's authors evidence an awareness of this relationship between place, their life stories, and craft; this understanding had a lasting impact on African Americans' racial self-distinction.

Brooks traversed various Bronzeville addresses, as this chapter will track, with a different sense of ease than that of other writers and artists of the Chicago Black Renaissance, especially Richard Wright. Both Wright and Brooks, at various points of their lives, up until Brooks's death in 2000, lived in the heart of Bronzeville. Certainly additional authors,' artists,' and musicians' lives warrant similar examination during this vibrant period—Margaret Walker, Archibald Motley, Langston Hughes, Frank Yerby, and Lorraine Hansberry to name a few. As individuals with deep and abiding connections to Bronzeville, their lives, too, evidence a profound relationship between place and craft.

Gwendolyn Brooks is vital to any understanding of the Chicago Black Renaissance. Her fiction is so important because she was deeply immersed in Bronzeville's geography. The reason why any of Brooks is useful after *A Street in Bronzeville* published in 1945 is that her setting remains the South Side of Chicago. There are few moments later in her selected poems when she dealt with material outside of Bronzeville, such as Little Rock, Arkansas, or when she wrote about the 1955 Emmett Till lynching[4]—but she did it in the guise of Chicago; her characters were always Bronzeville mothers. Her poetry reminds readers of the Black Belt; whatever she wrote it was always about the people living there, and all she was doing was looking out the window, asking the people outside her door to just "live." Her genius, however, elevated them above the literal. To this end, her art captured the beauty of blackness as seen in the expressions and daily activities of Bronzeville's people. She searched the souls of black folks, registering in her supremely successful realism—friend Margaret Walker called her poetry socially conscious and documentary at its core[5]—the unique qualities she found.

Surely there was much anxiety, intra- and interracial anxiety, to be had by authors migrating into Bronzeville at the time, as Blacks entering unknown black and white spaces. Margaret Walker noted this anxiety when she went to meetings of the South Side Writers Group, and Archibald Motley noted it as well as he came in and out of Bronzeville to paint "Negroes as [he] saw them." Both relate a feeling of not belonging there. One can track a similar anxiety throughout Wright's *Black Boy (American Hunger)*. This chapter argues that these anxieties helped produce a multiplicity of aesthetic discourses and styles that made the Chicago Black Renaissance so vibrant. This vibrancy erupts, to draw a comment from Adam Green's *Selling the Race: Culture, Community, and Black Chicago, 1940–1955*, from an "alternate vision of black life in Chicago as vital and unresolved process, rather than dreams deferred or betrayed. . . . [They invite readers] to see the city as a site of creativity, rather than constraint: a space of imagination as much [as] one of brute fact."[6] The lived experiences of literary figures such as Brooks and Wright and their fictional characters become windows into the worlds that produced them.

Turning to the primary spearheaders of the movement, this chapter has as its focus the literary genesis and intertwining of two Bronzeville lives—those of Richard Wright and Gwendolyn Brooks. From Richard Wright's autobiography *Black Boy (American Hunger)* and Gwendolyn Brooks's sonnet "The Anniad," the bulk of Pulitzer Prize–winning *Annie Allen*, along with some help from her autobiography *Report from Part I*, emerge two radically different portrayals of African Americans living in Bronzeville as well as two radically different modes of aestheticism. But as radically different as they are, both Brooks's and Wright's narrative and aesthetic choices are fueled by a profoundly personal understanding of urban space.

Wright and Brooks fought against an impetus to frame or situate black cultural production through outside categories. In the past, African American works' reliability or ability to be recognized rested upon an aesthetic assignment to various categories such as naturalism, realism, ghetto pastoral, etc; this omitted artists' and authors' own understanding, lived experience, and navigation of their racial realities and aesthetic categories. Wright and Brooks presented *Black Boy* and *Annie Allen* through many categories (not merely aesthetic categories): genre, migrant status, locality; whether they stay or leave Chicago; and finally, most importantly, what their characters' worlds look like in terms of race and place. This demonstrates how a focus on race and urban space was a concerted artistic effort to articulate a certain kind of literary realism.

To develop a sound geographic and literary methodology, this chapter tracks Wright's and Brooks's travels through Bronzeville with a fine level of specificity—mentioning their addresses, including vivid descriptions of their homes from their nonfiction and fiction, while making reference to Bronzeville's streets and landmarks whenever possible. Thus this chapter falls back on the original impetus of this book: an examination of the strange work that place and race do to the reading and study of African American cultural production.

The art institutions, settlement houses, and migration from the South and other places in the Midwest collectively make sense when one turns to Brooks's story and Wright's ten years of living in Chicago and his complex relationship with it after his departure. This is what the Chicago Black Renaissance was all about: various artists standing together with the help of these institutions and patronage and throwing their rock into the pile. There is anxiety about the toss of their "home" into the pile: belonging to or fitting into this truly interdisciplinary moment of cultural production.[7] This action was significant for its recognition that as artists and authors they were "a part of" not relegated to being "apart from," this moment of artistic fervor in Black Chicago. Alain Locke extended this beyond 47th and South Parkway adding that this would indicate that black people were being considered significant to the country as a whole. Here was a small crack in the wall of racism, a fissure that was worth trying to widen.[8] Alain Locke felt that the black artist had even more to gain than other American artists from the desire to create an art independent from outside influences and rooted in themes of the American scene.[9] Locke stressed that an art that adequately reflected America must of course include the "American Negro": "He can teach us to see ourselves not necessarily as other[s] see us but as we see."[10] Each book, each poem, and each painting became a weapon against old conceptions of an America without "the Negro." Thus, the aesthetic climate, as the world prepared for World War II and recovered from the Depression, popularized imagery derived from indigenous American sources. The climate that created the "socially inclined" artist also met the needs of black citizens, artists and nonartists alike, who not only wanted to express their "Americanness"—through multiple aesthetic manifestations—but were impatient to help effect social change.

Wright was less than optimistic that urban America or America at all could meet these needs. Correspondence between Wright and his friend Claude Barnett, founder of the Associated Negro Press, showed this disappointment; Wright expressed to Barnett that African American writers "sit too close to the fireside," while white writers such as Ernest Hemingway head to Europe for more material, exploration, intellectual stimulation.[11] In 1946, *Atlantic Monthly* articles tracked Wright, "breaking with US" and moving to Paris.[12] He wrote to Barnett, "Paris soothed his heart"; eventually Wright died there never again returning to the United States.[13] It was clear that Wright's experience of grabbing "that rock" and tossing it into the "pile," showed that for African Americans the Promised Land in America was nowhere.[14] *Black Boy (American Hunger)* permits readers to grasp afresh why Wright's life as a wronged human being was so powerful a stimulus for creative work. His autobiography is designed to illuminate how obscene was denial of access to full participation in the democratic process by law, custom, and the practice of race.[15]

Black Boy (American Hunger) nicely blends the meaning, the challenge, and the significance of being black and male in America. Published in 1945, *Black Boy* is Wright's story of the journey from innocence to experience in the Jim Crow South. *American Hunger*, published posthumously in 1977, exposes the North's transformation by the urban environment into clear ideas about the pervasive constrictions placed on authentic human freedom in the North as well as the South. As he inspected the dirty laundry of race, oppression, and class in the North through the second half of his autobiography, Wright exposed the deepest ironies/fraud of racism in America—providing a charge to authors in Chicago and throughout the world.[16]

Wright's early experiences in the North were variations, within a bleak setting, of what had happened to him in the South.[17] Migration to the North was accepted as an essential prelude to his people's enjoying the full blessings of liberty and citizenship; Wright's story of his life up to his leaving Memphis for Chicago reinforced belief that the South was a socially unreconstructed region where blacks who asserted their basic human rights invited retribution or death and that his decision to migrate north would only bring better. It is interesting to track Wright's living accommodations and professions as he moved from southern migrant to what many termed *the* African American writer of the twentieth century. It shows how, like Brooks, his fictive influences and subject matter were, more often than not, the spaces and places of Bronzeville. But Wright, unlike Brooks, would abandon Chicago as his permanent residence early on in the Chicago Black Renaissance with a move to Harlem in 1937—before his autobiography was even published.

Richard Wright was born on a plantation near Natchez, Mississippi, on September 4, 1908. His father, Nathaniel, was an illiterate sharecropper and his mother, Ella Wilson, was a well-educated schoolteacher. The family's extreme poverty forced them to move to Memphis when Wright was six years old. Soon after, his father left the family for another woman and his mother was forced to work as a cook in order to support the family. Wright briefly stayed in an orphanage during this period as well. His mother became ill while living in Memphis, so the family moved to Jackson, Mississippi, and lived with Ella's mother.

Wright's grandmother, a devout Seventh Day Adventist, enrolled him in a Seventh Day Adventist school near Jackson at the age of twelve. He also attended a local public school for a few years. In the spring of 1924 the *Southern Register*, a local black newspaper, printed his first story, "The Voodoo of Hell's Half Acre." From 1925 to 1927, he worked several menial jobs in

Jackson and Memphis. During this time he continued writing and discovered the works of H. L. Mencken, Theodore Dreiser, and Sinclair Lewis.

Wright left Memphis for Chicago in 1927 with his Aunt Maggie, who hoped to open a beauty salon, and they moved into a South Side rooming house. Wright worked as a delivery boy in a delicatessen, and then as a dishwasher. He found Chicago stimulating and less racially oppressive than the South, but was often dismayed by the pace and disarray of urban life. He passed the written examination for the postal service in the spring of 1928, and then in the fall he failed the postal service medical examination required for a permanent position because of chronic undernourishment. He returned to washing dishes and undertook a crash diet to increase his weight. He passed the physical examination and was hired by the Central Park Office at Clark Street and Jackson Boulevard as a substitute clerk and mail sorter. He moved with his family to four rooms at 4831 Vincennes Avenue—deep in Bronzeville. "Aunt Maggie had now rented an apartment in which I shared a rear room. My mother and brother came and all three of us slept in that one room; there was no window, just four walls and a door."[18] Within the relative comfort of this new home, Wright began to write and read regularly while attending meetings of a local black literary group, but he felt distanced from its middle-class members.

In 1932, Wright sold insurance policies door-to-door and then worked as a street-cleaner where he grew quite familiar with the streets of Bronzeville. At this point he moved from Vincennes Avenue to a slum apartment: "We moved into a tiny, dingy, two room den in whose kitchen a wall bed fitted snugly into a corner near the stove. The place was alive with vermin and the smell of cooking hung in the air day and night."[19] Wright was increasingly unable to sell policies to blacks impoverished by the Depression. In 1933, he was recruited by fellow post office worker Abraham Aaron to join the newly formed Chicago branch of the John Reed Club, a national literary organization sponsored by the Communist Party. Soon he was elected executive secretary of the Chicago John Reed Clubs and organized a successful lecture series that allowed him to meet a variety of intellectuals. The next year, Wright joined the Community Party, and enjoyed publications in Left Front, Anvil, and New Masses. At a time when he was rubbing shoulders with Nelson Algren, Margaret Walker, and Saul Bellow,[20] he and his family moved to an apartment at 4804 St. Lawrence Avenue, near the railroad tracks, while he worked at Michael Reese Hospital caring for animals used in medical research, which he referenced in his autobiography. The hospital laid him off, and the family, with Wright as its sole support, moved to 3743 Indiana Avenue. Wright attempted to navigate this painful reality and found work with the Federal Writers' Project (part of the WPA) to help research the history of Illinois and the "Negro in Chicago" for the Illinois volume in the American Guide Series.[21] Other notable writers also found employment on the project in literary centers across the country, including Saul Bellow, Nelson Algren, Margaret Walker, Lionel Able, Maxwell Bodenheim, and Ralph Ellison. These writers, however, comprised a small minority of FWP employees; one 1938 survey indicated that of the 4,500 workers, only 82 were considered "recognized writers" and 97 had held "important posts."[22] In April 1936, Wright took a leading role in the South Side Writers Group[23] and the Midwest Writers Congress. Later in 1937, Wright broke with the Communist Party in Chicago, basically over the question of his freedom as a writer. His brother found a job with the WPA and assumed some responsibility for the support of the family. This alleviated some of the strain on Wright, and he moved to New York City to pursue a career as a writer. By mid-June, he lived in a furnished room in the Douglas Hotel at 809 St. Nicholas Avenue in Harlem. He would never again make Chicago his permanent residence, but scholars Robert A. Bone and Richard Courage stress that he remained closely connected with Black Chicago's cultural scene. He served as patron of an art exhibition to help Bronzeville artists secure representation by New York galleries, assisted the editors of *Negro Story* to launch their journal, and helped Gwendolyn Brooks secure her first contract.[24] Longtime friend Horace Cayton recalled that, until Wright moved to Paris in 1947, they "were in constant contact, either by letter or his visiting me in Chicago or my going to New York."[25] Although he never moved back, his presence, albeit brief, would make a lasting impact on the writers of the Chicago Black Renaissance and African American writers to come.

Wright experienced his American jeremiad as an exercise in *lack* or physical and emotional devastation; he experienced this lack literally in his belly and figuratively in his heart. His journey stood as tragic witness to African Americans' collective as well as the individualized realities of racial movement from childhood to manhood through particular times and places. Hunger for a home and belonging defined his journey so much that he was on the verge of self-destruction and suffering. But this thirst for home, for solace, would be unfulfilled throughout the entirety of his childhood and arguably into his adulthood. At an early age his mother became the symbol of this suffering:

> My mother's suffering grew into a symbol in my mind, gathering to itself all the poverty, the ignorance, the helplessness; the painful, baffling, hunger-ridden days and hours; the restless moving, the futile seeking, the uncertainty, the fear, the dread; the meaningless pain and the endless suffering. Her life set the emotional tone of my life, colored the men and women I was to meet in the future, conditioned my relation to events that had not yet happened, determined my attitude to situations and circumstances I had yet to face. A somberness of spirit

that I was never to lose settled over me during the slow years of my mother's unrelieved suffering, a somberness that was to make me stand apart and look upon excessive joy with suspicion, that was to make me self-conscious, that was [to] make me keep forever on the move, as though to escape a nameless fate seeking to overtake me.[26]

At first he coped with this world of suffering through fantasy:

My imaginings, of course, had no objective value whatever. My spontaneous fantasies lived in my mind because I felt completely helpless in the face of this threat that might come upon me at any time, and because there did not exist to my knowledge any possible course of action which could have saved me if I had ever been confronted with a white mob. My fantasies were a moral bulwark that enabled me to feel I was keeping my emotional integrity whole, a support that enabled my personality to limp through days lived under the threat of violence."[27]

But Wright was to remain skeptical of everything while seeking everything, tolerant of all and yet critical.[28] His would be an insatiable hunger for answers to "questions that could help nobody, that could only keep alive in me that enthralling sense of wonder and awe in the face of the drama of human feeling which is hidden by the external drama of life."[29] This environment, first southern then northern, deafened and stifled the young Wright. As a child he felt emotionally cast out of the world, had been made to live outside the normal processes of life, had been conditioned in feeling *against* something daily, had become accustomed to living on the side of those who watched and waited.[30] He wrote, "I was a non-man, something that knew vaguely that it was human but felt that it was not."[31] Friend and biographer, Margaret Walker summarized these feelings this way: "Through Wright's rendering of his own character, readers gain that Wright is the wanderer, he is the alienated, the perpetual fugitive, the dual-minded or ambivalent, the adventurer; and he wishes, moreover, to be the rogue, the picaro, the rascal, above all the rebel. He is seeking most of all to find and know himself—his true identity."[32] *Black Boy* literally throbs with the passionate expression of this seeking. It is a passionate tale of a young boy who lived through hell and agony, through trauma after trauma, who escaped into books and continually sought to know the meaning of his life amid the dehumanizing effects of southern and then northern racism.[33]

In his journey throughout the South he wondered at those—both black and white—he saw surrounding him. He observed their attempts at living and tried to emulate what seemed at first very serene. He wrote, "I would sit listening for hours, wondering how on earth they could laugh so freely, trying to grasp the miracle that gave their debased lives the semblance of a human existence."[34] Or "often, when I was perplexed, I longed to be like the smiling, lazy, forgetful black boys in the noisy hotel locker rooms, with no torrential conflicts to resolve. Many times I grew weary of the secret burden I carried and longed to cast it down, either in action or resignation. But I was not made to be a resigned man and I had only a limited choice of actions, and I was afraid of all of them."[35]

Wright clearly had no home in his southern rock. The only meaningful thing of life came with his conviction that "the meaning of living came only when one was struggling to wring a meaning out of meaningless suffering."[36] This consciousness plagued him throughout his travels in the South and was bleakly reinforced when he arrived in the North. But before he found the North to be similar to the South, he approached his move to the Chicago environment with some hope: "I was slowly beginning to comprehend the meaning of my environment; a sense of direction was beginning to emerge from the conditions of my life. I began to feel something more powerful that I could express. My speech and manner changed. My cynicism slid from me. I grew open and questioning. I wanted to know."[37] He sought to "strike a deal," with this environment: "Having no claims upon others, I bent the way the wind blew, rendering unto my environment that which was my environment's, and rendering unto myself that which I felt was mine."[38] He sought forgiveness from this harsh urban setting: "Hungry for insight into my own life and the lives about me, knowing my fiercely indrawn nature, I sought to fulfill more than my share of all obligations and responsibilities, as though offering libations of forgiveness to my environment."[39] One excerpt from the latter portion of the book finds Wright openly and honestly displaying this hunger: Wright went to a relief station for the first time in his life to pick up free food for his family. Surely this, he must have thought, would stop the hunger pangs or at least admit something to the universe: "When I reached the relief station, I felt that I was making a public confession of my hunger."[40] But ultimately this would not quell his hunger, his desire for a new life free from the fetters of racism, or even recognition of the racial realities of this life. He demanded honesty from the Black Belt: "I wanted somebody to know that out of that vast sea of ignorance in the Black Belt there was at least one person who knew the game for what it was."[41]

But Chicago had not nor would it ever, for Wright, deliver on its promise.

Slowly I began to forge in the depths of my mind a mechanism that repressed all the dreams and desires that Chicago's streets, the newspapers, the movies were evoking in me. I was going through a second childhood; a new sense of the limit of the possible was being born in me. What could I dream that had the barest possibility of coming true? I could think of nothing. And, slowly, it was upon exactly that nothingness that my mind began to dwell, that constant sense of wanting without having, of being hated without reason. A dim notion of what life meant to a Negro in America was coming to consciousness in me, not in terms of external events, lynching, Jim Crowism, and the endless brutalities, but in terms of crossed-up feeling, of psyche pain. I sensed that Negro life was a sprawling land of unconscious suffering, and there were but few Negroes who knew the meaning of their lives, who could tell their story.[42]

Wright asked himself, "Well, what had I got out of living in the city? What had I got out of living in the South? What had I got out of living in America?" He replied, as he paced the floor, "knowing that all I possessed were words and dim knowledge that my country had shown me no examples of how to live a human life. All my life I had been full of a hunger for a new way to live."[43] He thought Chicago would be the environment that had the most potential for showing him a new way to live. That Chicago held the most promise for him assigning a home to a rock. But Chicago offered him only more bleakness: "Whenever I thought of the essential bleakness of black life in America, I knew that Negroes had never been allowed to catch the full spirit of Western civilization, that they lived somehow in it but not of it. And when I brooded upon the cultural barrenness of black life, I wondered if clean, positive tenderness, love, honor, loyalty, and the capacity to remember were native with man. I asked if these human qualities were not fostered, won, struggled, and suffered for, preserved in ritual from one generation to another."[44] Wright could not find a home in "dat rock"— southern or northern. He could, for the remainder of his life, rely only on his words—that source of alternate consciousness—to guide him through the paths of inexpressible darkness that wandered his soul. "I would hurl words into this darkness and wait for an echo, and if an echo sounded, no matter how faintly, I would send other words to tell, to march, to fight, to create a sense of the hunger for life that gnaws in us all, to keep alive in our hearts a sense of the inexpressibly human."[45] Subsequent writers in Chicago, members of the South Side Writers Group and young poets such as Brooks, would heed this call and demand such honesty in their fiction—something that inexorably made the Chicago Black Renaissance unique.

Wright lived in Chicago for only a decade. He arrived almost a man; in Chicago he would mature. In his Introduction to *Black Metropolis*, he wrote, "I, in common with the authors, St. Clair Drake and Horace R. Cayton, feel personally identified with the material in this book. All three of us have lived some of our most formative years in Chicago. . . . Drake and Cayton, like me, were not born there; all three of us migrated to Chicago to seek freedom, life. . . . There in that great iron city, we caught whispers of the meanings that life could have." Wright's Chicago years were his maturation years. As much as he left his mark on the Chicago Black Renaissance, Chicago left its impression on him. He became part of a rich cultural, social, and intellectual life in Chicago. As this book shows, it was political, intellectual, and richly artistic, but in Chicago Wright found no sustenance. Yet we must look to him, despite his melancholy, as part and parcel of that flourishing, serving as prime contributor to and foundation of the Chicago Black Renaissance.

Wright believed that artistic portrayal of reality meant intensifying the real until it was "more real than the real"; he did so by turning to the particularities of urban space as a way to work out his own brand of literary realism.[46] And at first one can get caught up in the sensational and explosive incidents in *Black Boy (American Hunger)*. Margaret Walker, however, urged readers to use caution: "it is the method, not the message, that creates for us a baffled and strange impression of this book."[47] This is not a book of purely factual and verifiable incidents—although one can tie events throughout the book to specific places in Bronzeville. They are truth as Wright chose to render it. *Black Boy (American Hunger)* is an ingenious blending of fact and fiction; how much it contains of each one can never be sure, but it is because of this method of poetic realism[48] that this piece of work rises above mere literary forms.[49]

Gwendolyn Brooks's greatness rests on a similar axis of fiction and fact. Critic George Kent describes her poetry prior to 1967 as "work that was conditioned to the times and the people."[50] In other words, poetry that leapt from her pages brought forth ideas, definitions, images, reflections, forms, colors, etc., that were molded over distances of many years and many different Chicago addresses—her poetry notebook started at the age of eleven—as a result of and as a reaction to the American reality (whether it be a meadow of lilies or a real knockdown alley fight).[51] Prefacers to her autobiography, *Report from Part One*, cite the following among Brooks's greatest influences: World War II,[52] the work of Langston Hughes and Richard Wright, the South Side of Chicago where she lived until her death, Inez Cunningham Stark at the South Side Community Art Center (Brooks walked off with four poetry prizes between 1943 and 1945 at Midwestern Writers Conferences at Northwestern University), the appearance of poems in the *Chicago Defender* and *Poetry Magazine*, working with the NAACP's young people's group, appearance in *Mademoiselle Magazine* as one of the "Ten Women of the Year" in 1945, grants from the American Academy of Arts and Letters and Guggenheim Fellowships, and other publications in major magazines that published "American" poetry.[53]

Brooks was conceived in Chicago but born in Topeka, Kansas, to David and Keziah Brooks. David, born in Oklahoma, attended Fisk University, hoping to prepare for a medical education, but was unable to stay more than a year. Early in the century, he came to Chicago and was one of the 2 percent of the population that blacks comprised up to 1910. He went into the service area as a porter with the McKinley Music Publishing Company on East 55th Street, a job he would hold for thirty years. In 1914 he accompanied his friend Berry Thompson to the home of Thompson's friend Gertrude Wims at 4747 South State Street, where he met Keziah Wims. They were married in July 1916 at the home of Keziah's parents, in Topeka.

The new Brooks family took a series of residences in Chicago. They roomed at 4142 South Evans until Keziah became pregnant with Gwendolyn and she briefly returned to her mother's in Topeka. Shortly after Gwendolyn's birth in Topeka on Thursday June 7, 1917, Keziah and David took an apartment at 5626 South Lake Park Avenue, Chicago, participating in a migration accelerated by labor opportunities during World War I.[54] The family took afternoon walks to Jackson Park, "where we played and occasionally ate lunch."[55] Led about the second floor Hyde Park apartment by members of the family, Gwendolyn was not allowed to crawl: "Walked around chairs and was led around the apartment by members of the family when I was strong enough."[56] Sixteen months later, Gwendolyn's brother, Raymond, was born: "had no playmates before my brother arrived. He was born when I was sixteen months old";[57] the family was complete.

The family lived at 56th and Lake Park Avenue only briefly until they found a lifelong home, when Brooks was four, in a changing neighborhood at 4332 South Champlain. The Brooks family was the second black family on the block. The neighborhood was secured institutionally for blacks, since they had purchased the Carter Temple Church a few months before. South Champlain was a short street cut off from the main traffic and marked by family homes with large front porches, well-kept lawns, beautiful trees, and clean streets: "Life was more enjoyable for we had playmates, front and back yards, porch, hammock, a sandbox located in the back yard near a huge snowball bush and the chance to make all the snowmen we desired."[58] Keziah, Gwendolyn, and Raymond—"*never* my father"—regularly attended the church and were participants in its various functions. "We . . . trotted off to Sunday School. Carter Temple Colored Methodist Episcopal Church was at the northwest corner of our block."[59]

Biographer George Kent described the Chicago Brookses as among those Horace Cayton and St. Clair Drake called the "respectables,"[60] people not of self-conscious class, color, educational, or aristocratic distinctions but somewhere in the middle, the good-looking people determined to live within a firm moral ordering. The Brookses belonged to what historian Christopher Robert Reed describes as "a small *refined* element of culturally assimilated African Americans . . . with an expanding *respectable* segment composed of churchgoing, laboring folk, dominating the mass of black society numerically. They 'best typified black Chicago.' They were church affiliated, morally upright, but less culturally anchored in the dominant white world both because of less interest in that group and its high culture and because of a lack of socialization, or educational training, about its supposedly superior values. They felt comfort in their enjoyment of what St. Clair Drake referred to as an Afro-American subculture."[61]

Other biographies and autobiographies of Chicago Black Renaissance artists, authors, and musicians have confirmed the existence of the various Chicagoes: the extreme American Dream striving of Katherine Dunham's father in Glen Ellyn and environs; the ostensibly assimilated family of Willard Motley (nephew of painter Archibald Motley Jr.) growing up among whites in the West 60th Street area; the hard-pressed, disintegration migrant families of Richard Wright's *Black Boy (American Hunger)*.[62] Brooks, a first generation Chicagoan, experienced a band of order that her parents had not. She reaped the benefits of her parents' hunger for this order. Both having been through a refining fire before coming to Chicago, her father struggled through the terrors of Southern racism in Oklahoma, her mother migrated to Chicago after struggling to attain an education as a concert pianist in Kansas—they were eager to provide tradition and order for their children.[63]

Home, for Brooks meant "a quick-walking, careful Duty-Loving mother, who played the piano, made fudge, made cocoa and prune whip and apricot pie, drew tidy cows and trees and expert houses with chimneys and chimney smoke, who helped her children with arithmetic homework, and who sang."[64] Home meant

> my father, with kind eyes, songs, and tense recitations for my brother and myself. . . . He had those rich Artistic Abilities, but he had more. He could fix anything that broke or stopped. He could build long-lasting fires in the ancient furnace below. He could paint the house, inside and out, and could whitewash the basement. He could spread the American Flag in wide loud magic across the front of our house on the Fourth of July and Decoration Day. He could chuckle. . . . It was gentle, it was warmly happy, it was heavyish but not hard. It was secure, and seemed to us an assistant to the Power that registered with his children.[65]

Wrapped in these warm blankets of security, as a little girl Brooks "dreamed freely, often on the top step of the back porch—morning, noon, sunset, deep twilight."[66]

There was an awareness in Brooks, at a young age, of the tension between the refuge of her home and an external order of things that conditioned her South Champlain existence. She related this through a story about her mother preparing for a Christmas meal: "Fruitcakes were made about a week before Christmas. We didn't care what the recipe books said. We liked having all the Christmas joy as close together as possible. Mama went downtown, as a rule, for the very freshest supplies, for then, as now, distributors sent their *worst* materials to 'the colored neighborhood.'"[67] Brooks also felt this awareness in her contact with less sheltered children throughout her youth, a contact that placed its mark upon her personality and art.[68]

After graduating from Englewood High School, Brooks published a poem in the *Chicago Defender*, and some seventy-five more pieces during the next four years. While writing for the *Defender* she studied at Wilson Junior College and became involved in the NAACP Youth Council, the Community Art Center organizing committee, and a group called the Cre-Lit Club. Here she met Margaret Burroughs and her future husband Henry Blakely. In 1939 Gwendolyn married Blakely. They met through a friend who told Blakely that he would find a "girl who wrote" at the NAACP Youth Council.[69] He, as a "fella who wrote," was eager to meet Brooks. He stood, "all dignified, in the door, there at the YWCA on 46th and (then) South Park"—a block away from the Savoy Complex. Brooks was "sitting with painter Margaret Taylor Goss, now Mrs. Charles Burroughs . . . [and] observed immediately 'There is the man I am going to marry.' Margaret yelled, 'Hey, boy, this girl wants to meet you.'"[70] Bone and Courage stress that the road from the Cre-Lit Club to her first collection, *A Street in Bronzeville*, led through these experiences and relationships.[71]

In facing the raw economics and brutally discriminatory housing of Chicago,[72] the newlyweds struggled. Brooks and Blakely went through a series of one-room kitchenette apartments. Brooks observed as she relates the details of this early married life that "it is not true that the poor are never 'happy,'"[73] but she remembered feeling bleak when taken to her honeymoon home, the kitchenette apartment in the Tyson on 43rd and South Park, after the nice little wedding in her parents' living room. But she recalled company, reading, and mutual reading in subsequent housing: in the room at Mrs. Sapp's and in the kitchenette at 6424 Champlain, where their son was suddenly born; and in the damp garage apartment at 5412 Indiana, where their son contracted bronchopneumonia; and in the kitchenette at 623 East 63rd Street (where, "when the mice came out of the front radiator 'in droves,' my husband, then a National Guardsman, was able to 'HUP two three four, HUP two three four,' while I stood, perilously, shrieking on a chair of very skimpy make.")[74] Six hundred and twenty-three East 63rd Street Brooks labeled her "most exciting kitchenette."[75] It was right on the corner, the corner of 63rd and Champlain, above a real estate agency. She wrote, "If you wanted a poem, you had only to look out of a window. There was material always, walking or running, fighting or screaming or singing."[76] Brooks did an interview much later in life where she was asked if she were disturbed by this environment, to which she replied, "In my twenties when I wrote a good deal of my better-known poetry I lived on 63rd Street—at 623 East 63rd Street—and there was a good deal of life in the raw all about. You might feel that this would be disturbing, but it was not. It contributed to my writing progress. I wrote about what I saw and heard in the street. I lived in a small second-floor apartment at the corner, and I could look first on one side and then on the other. There was my material."[77] She recalled receiving the letter from publisher Harper and Brothers at this address accepting *A Street in Bronzeville* for publication, after which she "ran into the community bathrooms, locked the door, and gasped through the gold of a firm acceptance."[78]

These raw, realistic, no-nonsense confrontations combined with the stream of contacts from the Chicago Black Renaissance, such as Inez Cunningham's poetry class at the South Side Community Art Center, the Abraham Lincoln Center, the George Cleveland Hall Branch Library, the National Negro Congress, the South Side Writers Group, Parkway Community House, and the Illinois Writers Project—during which Brooks met and collaborated with Wright, Davis, Walker, Bontemps, and Motley—continued to push Brooks's artistic sensibility further toward sophistication and poetic realism.[79] Brooks couched this commitment to realism within her ambition to create a complexity of form equal to her responses to life in the city. Brooks's work, like that of Langston Hughes, always touched at some level on the problems of blacks in America. The landscape in which she explored these problems had always been Chicago—she fully and comfortably immersed herself personally and fictionally in Black Chicago. Chicago was her cultural base. lee explained this as a process of self definition—defining one's self from a historically and culturally—and geographically—accurate base and following through on that in your work.[80] Her personal poetic credo articulated this: "think of how many fascinating human documents there would be now, if all the great poets had written of what happened to them personally—and of the thoughts that occurred to them, no matter how ugly, . . . fantastic, . . . seemingly ridiculous!"[81] Brooks defined herself by a Chicago landscape; identified with a race of people; identified with all the cultural, religious, political advantages or disadvantages that were associated with that race of people, whether she accepted them or not. This was part of her aesthetic strategy: to answer the question of how blacks defined themselves in light of personal and, most importantly for this project, Chicago landscape. This is something inadequately answered by previous Renaissance movements and an omission the Chicago Black Renaissance sought to rectify.

Wright's review of Brooks's poetry reflected this concern. Along with her letter of acceptance, Elizabeth Lawrence, Brooks's *A Street in Bronzeville* editor, sent Brooks a letter of evaluation that Harpers had sought from Wright. This was a more direct contact with Wright than Brooks had had before he moved

from Chicago to New York.[82] Wright's letter of response to the poems was
addressed to his own Harper editor, Edward C. Aswell: "Thanks for letting
me read Gwendolyn Brooks' poems. They are hard and real, right out of the
central core of Black Belt Negro life in urban areas. I hope she can keep on
saying what she is saying in many poems."[83] Wright registered the full impact
of Brooks's poems by stating their orbit around the core of African American
life at the time—Bronzeville. He also recognized her poetic genius grounded
in her ability to render dealing with the depressing realities of Bronzeville's
kitchenettes where he and Brooks had both lived. Brooks possessed a credible
accuracy when it came to rendering such details. Wright remarked at the way
Brooks "takes hold of reality as it is and renders it faithfully. There is not so
much an exhibiting of Negro life to whites in these poems as there is an honest human reaction to the pain that lurks so colorfully in the Black Belt."[84]
Brooks's street credibility made her a "real poet; she knows what to say and
how to say it. I'd say that she ought to be helped at all costs. America needs a
voice like hers and anything that can be done to help her to bring out a good
volume should be done."[85] Kent stressed that these letters evidence Wright,
as the leader of the 1930s Renaissance, exerting a strong influence upon the
basis of acceptance accorded a work of the 1940s.[86]

Brooks's thrust after the publication of A Street was focused on two
projected works: "American Family Brown," renamed Maud Martha and
published in 1953, and the collection of poems Annie Allen. After being
rejected by Harper in October 1947, "American Family Brown" was set
aside for the time being, and Annie Allen saw publication first.[87] As lines
from Annie Allen—and Maud Martha, covered in more depth in the next
chapter—indicate, Brooks was still deeply involved with black life, black
pain, black spirits, and Black Chicago.[88] Her commitment to Chicago, such a
specific locale, did not preclude her appeal to all Americans, black or white.
The popularity of Annie Allen confirmed this. This marked a transition point
in the Chicago Black Renaissance as its artistic produce embarked upon
larger audiences.[89] Literary critic don l. lee wrote, "If A Street paved the
way, Annie Allen opened the door."[90] Annie Allen (1949) ran away with the
Pulitzer Prize—making Brooks the first black person to receive the honor.
After winning the Pulitzer, Black Chicago now belonged to everybody and
the best poet in America—black or white—delivered it to them.[91]

Annie Allen further developed the resources and approaches present in
A Street. The poems of A Street offer a full realistic surface and make use
of the conventions and techniques of poetic realism. Annie Allen's subject
matter is the same—people and their life stories appear in plots sharply out-
lined, presenting easily recognized issues and places from daily Bronzeville
existence—but Annie Allen comments upon the human condition beyond

the poems' striking realism. A good deal beyond realistic, representative, or pictorial functions were already to be found in *A Street*. Brooks modified the realistic image on some occasions by merely attaching to it a striking descriptive term ("crowding darkness") or by combining a gesture with it ("could a dream send up through onion fumes / Its white and violet"). The imagery system of *Annie Allen* moves still further away from this style into the symbolic ranges of its functions. This imagery system got richer as Brooks inserted more of herself into her poetry. In *Annie Allen* Brooks explored minutely the complex rhythms of existence and made coherent the psychology of a young woman similar to herself experiencing the world in a similar fashion. She maintained a distance between her reader and her character throughout the book, while simultaneously exploring intimately the inwardness of a young thoughtful black women's experience. It expresses in her a growing global sensibility to the surface of her writing; *Annie Allen* is not as localized as *A Street* or *Maud Martha*. But, as Kent stressed, the work's "strong autobiographical overtones . . . [puts] into order deep and obsessive personal drives and confusions."[92] In *Annie Allen* she continues with local particularities—as poems such as "children of the poor" or "I love those little booths at Benvenuti's," or "Beverly Hills Chicago," evidence—but bought to the universal that which was particular.[93] Brooks explored this range to its fullest in *Annie Allen*'s longest poem: "The Anniad."

"The Anniad" is close in style to *A Street*'s "The Sundays of Satin-Legs Smith." "The Anniad," like the rest of *Annie Allen*, is the story of Annie Allen—a young newlywed, whose experience forces her to accept disillusionment and the narrowness of the areas in which life's small satisfactions can be seized.[94] She matures by moving from the epic universe of her dreams to the more prosaic one in which her best-laid plans often go astray.[95] The poem is a continuation of the life of the woman in *A Street*'s "the kitchenette." "The Anniad" extends this character throughout street life in Bronzeville. The character is the same tired heroine moving between a dream world and her vulnerable kitchenette apartment existence. The dream and the flesh-and-blood woman proved the romantic and the realist, a binary that defines the poem throughout. Annie is optimistically "Prosperous and ocean-eyed / Who shall rub her secrets out / And behold the hinted bride."[96] Following this are images of the poem in which Annie realizes she has to negotiate that which she has inherited:

> Think of thaumaturgic lass
> Looking in her looking glass
> At the unembroidered brown;
> Printing bastard roses there;

Then emotionally aware
Of the black and boisterous hair,
Taming all that anger down.[97]

This binary of romantic and realist is a description that runs throughout Brooks's larger body of work. Her description of Maud Martha maintains this binary through the juxtaposition of her protagonist's preference of meadow lilies to dandelions:

> She would have liked a lotus, or China asters or the Japanese Iris, or meadow lilies—yes, she would have liked meadow lilies, because the very word meadow made her breathe more deeply, and either fling her arms, depending on who was by, rapturously up to whatever was watching in the sky. But dandelions were what she chiefly saw. Yellow jewels for everyday, studding the patched green dress of her back yard. She liked their demure prettiness second to their everydayness; for in that latter quality she thought she saw a picture of herself, and it was comforting to find that what was common could also be a flower.[98]

Brooks warmly and affectionately remembered the process of creating *Annie Allen* and the pleasure it afforded, although it was "labored, a poem that's very interested in the mysteries and magic of technique."[99] Closely textured was "every stanza in that poem; each one was worked on and revised, tenderly cared for. More so than anything else I've written, and it is not a wild success; some of it just doesn't come off. But it was enjoyable."[100] I think this poem harbored so much meaning for Brooks because she invested in it such a great amount of herself, her youth, and her connectedness with its setting. It, along with *A Street in Bronzeville* and then *Maud Martha*, suggests characters who take tough-minded looks at the difficulties of life, meet them courageously, and reveal in the process richly reflective minds. Life is to be fought for and unchangeable conditions rigorously faced. The trials of Bronzeville life for her female protagonists allow them to feel out their capacities and to assert themselves as both dreamers and real-life figures of urban structures. Although Annie's dream of happiness is, in the end, shattered, the images of the last stanza suggest that she salvaged something from her experiences:

> Stroking swallows from the sweat
> Fingering faint violet.
> Hugging
> gold and Sunday sun.
> Kissing in her kitchenette
> The minuets of memory.[101]

Throughout their tenuous walks on these fine lines of real life and fantasy, her characters reveal humor, courage, anger, and reflection—responses to the external conditions affecting their fates and submission to the idea that their dreams may not be fully realized in this life unfolding the crucial impact of racial conflict and situation. Brooks "wished to prove to others (by implication, not by shouting) and to such among themselves as have yet to discover it, that they are merely human beings not exotics."[102]

Annie Allen shows Brooks's relationship between her poetic concern and geographic commitment to Chicago and how this relationship then yields a cultural product. The Chicago Black Renaissance is not her only moment—her poetics stem across periodizations enhancing her poetic legacy. She supersedes those poets from Harlem because she is the only one who actually gets bridged over to the Black Arts Movement. But this book's most important point of emphasis is that while Brooks bridged these movements, her subject matter did not shift from Bronzeville. In so many ways her narratives, her poems, her imagery, and her own personal story would have been different if she had written them anywhere else. This forces the question as to whether there is a Chicago Black Renaissance without Brooks. There may have been a flourishing but one hesitates to put such an emphasis on it being a Chicago Renaissance. Brooks herself and her fiction are so embedded in this geography it is indeed a strange thing to divorce her from Chicago and the Renaissance from her success.

In "Blueprint for Negro Writing," Wright and members of the South Side Writers Group wrote, "no theory can take the place of life."[103] The stress here is on life rather than an apparatus for understanding—a most articulate iteration of the Chicago Black Renaissance's aesthetic. To understand the Chicago Black Renaissance, then, is to understand the lives within it; *the* life to which one should refer for understanding is most surely that of Gwendolyn Brooks. She experienced the hardships of migration, grew up during the Great Depression, experienced discrimination by restrictive racial covenants and segregation, and exhibited a cautious optimism with World War II—all hallmarks of the Chicago Black Renaissance. Her life and work reflected a profound commitment to Chicago—most importantly Bronzeville. Settling almost exclusively in Bronzeville's kitchenettes to its garage apartments, she lived a Black Belt life. She enjoyed the hustle and bustle of 47th and South Parkway, the Bud Billiken Parades; she spent nights at the South Side Community Art Center in classes with the explosive talent of Margaret Walker; she threw parties in her kitchenette apartment for Langston Hughes; she sat on her front porch and watched Bronzeville's stars—little aware that she was one of them. She possessed a remarkable power of portraiture and an ability to go through Chicago with wide open eyes and artistically move the reader into its realities.[104] Wright was right when he wrote in a review of *A Street*: "This is the real thing. So is Miss Brooks."[105]

CHAPTER 5

KITCHENETTES

As Black Chicagoans and the most prominent figures of the Chicago Black Renaissance, Richard Wright and Gwendolyn Brooks stood at the forefront of this vibrant movement in Windy City life. They stand as literary models of the Chicago Black Renaissance, a movement, Adam Green stresses, that engendered a unique cultural consciousness and fostered ideas of racial identity that remain influential today.[1] Brooks and Wright created work that involved complex and compelling debates on the future of their identities— identities paused at the precarious intersection of domestic and transnational politics, modernity, urbanism, segregation, and cosmopolitanism. These intersections contributed to the massive migration of African Americans from the South to northern cities, revealing the creation of "a city within a city" in Chicago following the Depression, as Bronzeville became the capital of Black America.[2] The migrants' (Wright a migrant from Mississippi and Brooks, as an infant, a migrant from Kansas) heritage encompassed slavery, virtual serfdom after emancipation within the agricultural system of the South, and wage slavery in unskilled industrial and service jobs for those who migrated North over successive generations.

From these urban spaces, specifically the kitchenette apartment, sprang interesting and poignant conversations on the tensions of black modern life and consciousness. Wright described the kitchenette as migrants' first contact with "the brutal logic of jobs," the northern "world of things," and "the beginning of living on a new and terrifying plane of consciousness" in the cramped and deteriorating "kitchenette" apartments sequestered "beyond the business belt, a transition area where a sooty conglomeration of factories and mills belches smoke that stains our clothes and lungs."[3] The rickety frame dwellings, sprawled along the railroad tracks, "bespeak a way of life at an opposite pole from that of the quiet and well-groomed orderliness of middle-class neighborhoods."[4] Unscrupulous landlords subdivided buildings into the tiniest possible apartments and, as impoverished newcomers who could afford no better, black migrants were forced to cope with overpriced, substandard housing as best they could. Kitchenette apartments, as these units were called, were essentially old houses or larger apartments, long since abandoned by Chicago's wealthy whites, converted into multiple apartments, each installed with a communal restroom, small gas stove, and one small sink. Subject to the desire of Northern landlords, or what Wright termed "Bosses of the Buildings," African American migrants soon found themselves entangled in the games of price gouging: "The Bosses of the Building rent these kitchenettes to us at the rate of, say, $6 a week. Hence, the same apartment for which white people—who can get jobs anywhere and who receive higher wages than we do—pay $50 a month is rented to us for $42 a week!"[5] Wright continued, "the kitchenette is the author of the glad tidings that new suckers are in town, ready to be cheated, plundered, and put in their places."[6]

Such spatial realities set black life and its coherency apart from all others. Thus, this life and its relationship to all those rituals and institutions by which society orders its center remained estranged, orphaned, or in Brooks's own words, "unpredictable, ambivalent, and adventitious."[7] Brooks and Wright carried these threads throughout their fictions. They problematized notions of gender, locality, nationhood, belonging, and difference. Brooks's and Wright's characters, certainly, were no strangers to these feelings of difference. The Chicago Black Renaissance stood as an artistic and cultural exercise in mining coherence from these emotions. Brooks's and Wright's fictions figured forth a "new expressive world,"[8] in locational or geographic terms that investigated Bronzeville's metalevels of space, place, and time. This chapter illuminates African American artists' struggle against traditional dynamics of Afro-American creativity as a project of cultural production and geography. Toward this end, it puts into dialogue Wright's 1941 photographic essay *12 Million Black Voices* and selections from his novel *The Outsider* with Brooks's 1945 collection of poetry *A Street in Bronzeville* and selections from her only novel, published in 1953, *Maud Martha*. Brooks's and Wright's narratives rested on an axis of place and on assertions of racial identity and consciousness. Together their work investigated place and gender, a consciousness of the gendered spaces of Chicago's flats, alleyways, blocks, and one-room kitchenette apartments. These are the prescriptive elements of their fictions: how to impose coherence, how to impose and set boundaries, how to give place and craft image upon a population bound to the urban landscape but placeless in a racist society.[9] Their texts have very clear spatial sensibilities that do the work of articulating a fine and unique Bronzeville literary aesthetic.

Houston Baker, in *Workings of the Spirit: The Poetics of Afro-American Women's Writing*, drew from a scene in Wright's *Native Son* to explain black Chicagoans' "bound yet placeless" circumstance:

> Bigger and his friend Gus meet on a South Side Chicago street. Leaning against a building, comforting themselves in sunshine warmer than their kitchenette apartments, their attention is suddenly drawn upward. An acrobatic skywriter is spelling out the bold, commercial message: USE SPEED GASOLINE. Bigger gazes in childlike wonder and says, "Looks like a little bird. Gus responds, "Them white boys sure can fly." Bigger continues, "I *could* fly a plane if I had the chance." Gus promptly responds, "If you wasn't black and if you had some money and if they'd let you go to that aviation school, you *could* fly a plane." [10]

The skywriter in Wright's novel suggests the enormous confinement of black life; it is not a disruption of place but a signifier implying black placelessness. It has the effect of making African American geographies into placeless places. Why placeless? Because Bigger's South Side lacks the quality of place as it is traditionally defined. For a place to be recognized by one as actually PLACE, as a personally valued locale, one must set and maintain the boundaries. If one, like Bigger, is constituted and maintained by and within boundaries of a dominating authority, then one is not a setter of place but a prisoner of another's desire. Under the displacing impress of authority even what one calls and, perhaps, feels is one's own place is, from the perspective of human agency, placeless. Bigger Thomas, as well as the other characters in the literature of the Chicago Renaissance, occupy authorized boundaries and are therefore insecure in their worlds but maximally secured or incarcerated by interlocking, institutional arrangements of power. [11]

Black life's rites of coherence, enacted after the displacements of slavery, migration, and urban segregation, performed in the area where the radical uncertainties of existence festered most densely and most acutely—the physical surfaces of Chicago's South Side. Wright and Brooks offer a virtual tour of this life at street level; often one can imagine their characters brushing past one another on the streets. This is a technique first introduced by W. E. B. DuBois in his famed study *The Philadelphia Negro* and used by Drake and Cayton in *Black Metropolis*. Consider, for instance, this famous passage from their book:

> Stand in the center of the Black Belt—at Chicago's 47th Street and South Parkway. Around you swirls a continuous eddy of faces—black, brown, olive, yellow and white. Soon you will realize that this is not "just another neighborhood" of Midwest Metropolis. . . . In the nearby drugstore colored clerks are bustling about (they are seldom seen in other neighborhoods). In most of the other stores, too, there are colored salespeople, although a white proprietor

or manager looms in the offing. In the offices around you, colored doctors, dentists, and lawyers go about their duties. And a brown-skinned policeman saunters along swinging his club and glaring sternly at the urchins who dodge in and out among the shoppers.[12]

Here, the sense of vibrant human community and space, the array of sturdy public institutions—a variegated professional and merchant class, an alert office of the law—evoke a captivating sense of functionality in the central black district of Bronzeville.[13]

The fiction of Wright and Brooks, however, profoundly challenged the functionality and autonomy of this "city within a city" functioning "well, on its own terms, and of its own accord."[14] In Wright's view, the forces of slavery and segregation left the personalities of modern black folk numbed, partially deformed, and half-articulate: "Three hundred years are a long time for millions of folk like us to be held in such subjection, so long a time that perhaps scores of years will have to pass before we shall be able to express what this slavery has done to us, for our personalities are still numb from its long shocks; and, as the numbness leaves our souls, we shall yet have to feel and give utterance to the full pain we shall inherit."[15] As a result, the African American immigrants explored in Wright's as well as poet and cultural activist Brooks's fiction existed between two "vastly different plains of reality."[16] One was determined by material conditions and bound by immediate circumstances, its truths dependent upon surface appearances and direct perceptions; the other determined by the internal, intangible, expansive possibilities of consciousness.[17] As a consequence, migration to the city and its unkept promise of freedom left African Americans on Chicago's South Side suspended between two planes of existence—but bound inside the kitchenette apartment. For Wright, the kitchenette apartment meant race in Chicago was hell, but for Brooks this gendered space allowed her to engage the realities of mobility and constraint in ways that Wright would only see as the "feminization" of the race. Further analysis of their treatment of the kitchenettes will help readers see why they offer such different treatments of the same space.[18]

Wright engaged in the kitchenette project first with the photographic image and then with text. Responding to the massive migration of African Americans from the South to Northern cities, *12 Million Black Voices*, authored by Wright with Edwin Rosskam as director of photography, gives visibility to the socioeconomic injustices that perpetuated the existence of the black underclass of Northern cities in the early twentieth century. Wright's poetic text coupled with the Rosskam photographs present the South Side's misery and struggle, a neighborhood whose "humble folk" swam in the depths of poverty and despair.[19] Wright and Rosskam captured this marooning in their photographs and prose of the South Side's kitchenette buildings, its sidewalks, alleys, and subways.

In his Introduction to *Black Metropolis: A Study of Negro Life in a Northern City* (1945), the sociological investigation authored by St. Clair Drake and Horace Cayton, Wright identified Chicago as the American place that most powerfully encompasses this suspension. As sociologists of the Chicago School, Drake and Cayton saw the city of Chicago as a laboratory for the scientific investigation of the social, economic, and historical forces that create and perpetuate economically desolated and isolated urban communities. Originally, theirs was a project designed to study the problem of "juvenile delinquency on Chicago's South Side"; soon this problem ultimately became subordinated to the "larger problem of description and analysis of the structure and organization of the Negro community, both internally, and in relation to the metropolis of which it is a part."[20] On the one hand, Chicago was the quintessential "self-conscious" and "known" city;[21] on the other, it was the place where the contemporary facts of African American experience take "their starkest form [and] crudest manifestation."[22] Wright stressed, "there is an open and raw beauty about that city that seems either to kill or endow one with the spirit of life. I felt those extremes of possibility, death and hope, while I lived half hungry and afraid in a city to which I had fled . . . to tell my story."[23] For Wright, the segregated urban landscape forced a masculine economics of self-preservation, in a material sense, as a prerequisite to the acquisition of self-consciousness or knowing one's "story." The results of migration and urban segregation show African Americans marooned between these planes of disembodied existence, between their material and metaphysical selves. Wright's brilliant blend of text and image evidenced a discrepancy or a discontinuity between what African American migrants thought and what they were living. Wright and Rosskam came to the conclusion that this incongruence caused a suspending effect to occur: where black bodies were frozen in the spaces of the photograph and caught between lines of poetry—as each aesthetic medium oscillated around the image of the kitchenette.

For Brooks, as she focused on the feminine connotations of this space, the realities of kitchenette life could not afford—not even for a moment—African Americans the luxury of "knowing one's story" or the acquisition of consciousness. For the purposes of this study, the kitchenette building, then, was the locus of urban segregation; the kitchenette was the material embodiment of the suspending conditions of segregation in the mid-twentieth-century American city—specifically Chicago, Illinois. Wright and Brooks converged in their focus on the space of the black, urban, feminine kitchenette—a woman's domestic space. Their spatial insights and conclusions, however, are vastly different because of the way each author genders the space; for Wright it's damnable, for Brooks, as the analysis will show, possibilities emerge from the problematic kitchenette.

Viking Press published *12 Million Black Voices* in 1941, one year after Wright's novel *Native Son* provoked national attention toward race matters.[24] The book's "photo-direction" is credited to Edwin Rosskam, a German immigrant who studied painting at the Philadelphia Academy of Fine Arts and who took the position of picture editor with the Farm Security Administration in 1938. As Rosskam later explained it, the collaboration with Richard Wright followed the working principle that "whatever would normally be description is a picture. And whatever is abstraction or concept is written."[25] Exposition in *12 Million Black Voices* was written entirely by Wright; the choice and format of photographs, by masters such as Russell Lee, Dorthea Lange, and Jack Delanao, was principally Rosskam's. The book's limited number of captions consists of phrases that Rosskam extracted from Wright's accompanying prose. Aside from four news agency photographs and two personal photographs (one taken by Wright and one by Rosskam's wife Louise), the book's other eighty-two images all came from FSA files.[26]

12 Million Black Voices provides a powerful commentary on three centuries of oppression. It begins with an account of the slave trade and follows the course of slavery to the point of the Civil War, when the inevitability of industrialization made slaves and the "inheritors of slavery" seem "children of a devilish aberration, descendants of an interval of nightmare in history, fledglings of a period of amnesia."[27] Wright detailed the sharecrop system, African American life in the South, and the Great Migration. Throughout Wright expressed his view of black migration out of the South, a journey he himself experienced. This bittersweet migration often traded the harsh, rural repression of the South for the overcrowded, anonymous ghettos of the North. He began his third chapter, "Death on the City Pavements," with one of the book's few statistics: "From 1890 to 1920, more than two million of us left the land."[28] The steady influx to the city brought about serious complications. Maren Stange, author of *Bronzeville: Black Chicago in Pictures 1941–1943*, provides startling demographic data piecing together Chicago's migration story: as African Americans had continued the northward migration begun in the teens, becoming more urban than rural by the 1960s, Chicago absorbed wave after wave of newcomers. The Depression years saw a 20 percent increase in the city's black population, who lived for the most part mercilessly overcrowded. Population density was 70,000 per square mile on the South Side; the death rate exceeded the birthrate by 2 percent. The war years, a moment of renewed migration,

saw some 60,000 more new arrivals between 1942 and 1944, swelling the
black population to 337,000, one-tenth of the city's total and double what it
had been before World War II. Buildings abandoned and condemned in the
1930s were reinhabited during the war years as the Black Belt remained, in
Richard Wright's words, "an undigested lump in Chicago's melting pot."[29]

Wright and Rosskam accompanied prose with a stark photograph of
several kitchenette buildings perilously sitting in the foreground of over
twenty smokestacks, which emit white billows of smoke clouding the
city's faint horizon line. A few visible bodies, along with several automobiles, traverse a thin steel bridge serving as the sole barrier separating
the industrial from residential spaces. A single visible face occupies the
photograph—a small black child, with hands gently rested on his or her
windowsill, gazes out the third- or fourth-floor window of the kitchenette
apartment closest to the camera's lens. The child squints as the sun glares
off the kitchenette's dry, dilapidated siding. Its windows hang wide open,
combing the stale humid air for a faint breeze, as the heat scorches the
worn wooden roofs of the apartment building—what Wright termed "Our
death sentence without a trial" (Fig. 5.1).[30]

The juxtaposition of the overcrowded city landscape with the solidarity
of the lone visible face exacerbates Wright's sense of African Americans
being "put in their places."[31] As if to acquire some respite from the interior
goings-on of the kitchenette, the child flees to the window, but instead of
catching a brief moment of freedom from the overcrowded space of kitchenette life, the child finds a densely packed city landscape from which he or
she cannot escape. Home, for our weary window-gazer, is thinly separated
from work; the apartment building rests "just beyond the factory areas,
behind the railroad tracks, near the river banks, under the viaducts, by the
steel and iron mills, on the edge of the coal and lumber yards."[32] This child
sought refuge from the overcrowded interiors of "crowded barn-like rooms,
in rotting buildings where once dwelt native whites of a century ago," only
to find his or her respite, a gaze from a window, assaulted by clouded and
hazy skies, dilapidated buildings, and dozens of smoke stacks.[33] There is no
space in this photograph, but the image clearly articulates a definite place
and function for the African American migrant in this dismal cityscape. Every inch of the photograph is overcrowded: factory buildings, smokestacks,
or apartment buildings dominate the frame. Every inch of the kitchenette
bears the trace of these urban elements and moreover a colorline that runs
deep into both the kitchenette and its inhabitants' compositions. Such is
the case for our small window-gazer. Segregation in Pittsburgh—where
Rothstein took the photograph—and on Chicago's South Side afforded no

Fig. 5.1. "Slums Pittsburgh, Pennsylvania." July 1938. Arthur Rothstein. Farm Security
Administration–Office of War Information Photograph Collection. Courtesy of the
Library of Congress. LC-USF33-002819-M3 (black and white film nitrate negative).

respite for this small child burdened with crying babies, chores, or simply the hot stifling heat of the kitchenette apartment.

"Sometimes five or six of us live in a one-room kitchenette, a place where simple folk such as we should never be held captive."[34] Home, for these simple folk, was a place where emotions waged war: "one part of our feelings tells us that it is good to be in the city, that we have a chance at life here, that we need but turn a corner to become a stranger, that we no longer need bow and dodge at the sight of the Lords of the Land [plantation owners]. Another part of our feelings tells us that, in terms of worry and strain, the cost of living in the kitchenettes is too high, that the city heaps too much responsibility on us and gives too little security in turn."[35] Wright captured the pace of the kitchenette's congestion, its desolation, and psychological ruin in fifteen sentences or "verses" poised carefully between seven stunning images of women, children, and, very infrequently, men crammed inside these dark and dismal living spaces. For example, the third verse, "The kitchenette, with its filth and foul air, with its one toilet for thirty or more tenants, kills our black babies so fast that in many cities twice as many of them die as white babies," rests beneath a photograph of a seatless toilet crammed in the corner of a room, shards of porcelain and splinters of wood surround its base, plaster peels off a wall anchored by a stack of wood resting near the toilet's amputated seat (Fig. 5.2).

It seems only natural that verse three is followed by verse four's delineation of the medical perils of the space: "The kitchenette is the seed bed for scarlet fever, dysentery, typhoid, tuberculosis, gonorrhea, syphilis, pneumonia, and malnutrition."[36] Most disturbing, however, is the fact that these verses straddle a photograph of three small children nestled peacefully under a quilt on top of a dirty mattress (Fig. 5.3).

The mattress, sheetless and without pillows, lies crudely on a concrete floor, a hamper full of laundry resides in the corner near an exhausted child's shoes—strewn absentmindedly on his way to bed. Verse five follows this mélange of image and verse: "The kitchenette scatters death so widely among us that our death rate exceeds our birth rate, and if it were not for the trains and autos bringing us daily into the city from the plantations, we black folks who dwell in northern cities would die out entirely over the course of a few years."[37] Here, Wright gave no indication that this cycle will end. In each "verse" the kitchenette acts: it "poisons," "scatters," "blights," "jams," "fills," "piles," "reaches out," and "funnels." The photograph unmasks the actor while the text reveals its crimes: Wright identified the feminine domestic kitchenette as criminal and its inhabitants as its victims. The crimes of the

Fig. 5.2. "Toilet in the basement of an apartment house rented to Negroes. Chicago, Illinois." April 1941. Russell Lee. Farm Security Administration–Office of War Information Photograph Collection. Courtesy of the Library of Congress. LC-USF34-038617-D [P&P].

Fig. 5.3. "Negro children asleep. South Side of Chicago, Illinois." April 1941. Russell Lee. Farm Security Administration–Office of War Information Photograph Collection. Courtesy of the Library of Congress. LC-USF34-038820-D (black and white film nitrate negative).

kitchenette, "our prison, our death sentence without a trial, the new form of mob violence that assaults not only the individual, but all of us, in its ceaseless attacks," do not issue a call for justice by Chicago's forgotten—no one is willing to listen: the kitchenette is the "funnel through which our pulverized lives flow to ruin and death on the city pavements, at a profit."[38]

According to Stange, author of *Bronzeville: Black Chicago in Pictures*, the chosen images in the photo-essay, she stresses, were meant to represent features of northern urban life in general, and cropped to exclude sky, horizon, or recognizable landmarks.[39] The images are printed quite dark so that cityscapes or images of walled-in spaces and backgrounds read as gray or gray-black tones—as a result they are overwhelmingly grim. Stange also stresses that Rosskam extended all images to the edges of the page, rather than setting the pictures off with a white border. She points to two photographs specifically employing this technique. The first photograph, captioned "Negro Housing," taken by Russell Lee, April 1941, shows a three-story kitchenette building flanked to the left by a neighboring kitchenette apartment building and to the right by a brick church with worship times boldly printed on its front door. In the foreground, a makeshift fence separates camera from subject: three tall steel or wood posts adjoined by strands of crudely affixed steel rods comprise the boundary. The fence continues off the page along with the buildings. Viewers cannot see the edge of the church building or the far left wall of the kitchenette apartments. This never-ending fence lines a narrow dirt path traversing the picture from side to side continuing, one is to guess, along down the street; a stroll down the path, viewers could guess, would provide a never-ending cycle of similar scenes (Fig. 5.4).

The final photograph, "Street scene under the elevated," is attributed to Rosskam and pictures four African American children bundled up in their winter clothes. They play under the elevated section of the subway, which Chicagoans call simply "the elevated" (Fig. 5.5).[40] A four- or even five-story (viewers are left to question) kitchenette building flanks the children to their right as its stairs wind to the top of the photograph. The elevated juts, violently, across the photograph's middle, shooting from the scene's hazy horizon in the back left corner out over the four children, dwarfing them in the process, only to quickly recede off the top right corner of the page. Viewers see neither the elevated's beginning nor its end. Stange posits that this suggestion of indefinite extension, rather than specific containment, in the images implies the dialectics of placelessness and boundedness—both of which call to mind Wright's dislocating planes of diasporic reality or consciousness.[41] Wright's text, emphasizing the kitchenette as the migrant's death sentence, with Rosskam's and collaborators' use of full-page bleed

Fig. 5.4. "Chicago, Illinois. Scene in Negro section." April 1941. Russell Lee. Farm Security Administration–Office of War Information Photograph Collection. Courtesy of the Library of Congress. LC-USF34-038720-D (black and white film negative).

techniques emphasizing the unprotected and overly cramped nature of the kitchenette's urban landscape, reiterate the inadequacies of the feminine sphere. The kitchenette as home, as security, is a failure; relegating the race to this space emasculates it, becomes its "death sentence." The kitchenette's inability to serve as a protective space against the harsh physical and sub-conscious realities of Chicago's migration story damns African American men and women to a dilapidated unsustaining hearth.

In 1945, four years after the publication of *12 Million Black Voices*, Gwendolyn Brooks's examination of an unknown street in Bronzeville appeared.[42] In a series of poems she explored both the hope and hopelessness of a people caught in the maelstrom of urban migration and segregation. The power of this collection of poems, such as "The Mother," "Kitchenette Building," "A Song in the Front Yard," "The Ballad of Chocolate Mabbie," "Sadie and Maud," and "Ballad of Pearl May Lee," resides in their concern with women's social issues such as abortion, poverty, the limitations of class restrictions, restrictive gender roles, and lynching. Similar to Wright's photo-essay, *A Street in Bronzeville* presents material concerned not with a talented tenth, but poetic renderings of the people she observed from

Fig. 5.5. "Children playing under the elevated on the southside of Chicago." April 1941. Russell Lee. Farm Security Administration–Office of War Information Photograph Collection. Courtesy of the Library of Congress. LC-USF34-038601-D (black and white film negative).

her kitchenette apartment navigating the city's South Side ghetto. Brooks's Chicago was not one of the elite, not the city of spectacular boulevards and buildings.[43] This was a city of black streets and back alleys, of kitchenettes and vacant lots. Brooks wrote: "If you wanted a poem, you had only to look out a window. There was material always, walking or running, fighting or screaming or singing."[44]

Brooks's Bronzeville was symbolic of the impersonality of the overcrowded ghetto ignored by those caught in the activities of their own lives[45]—as a result she offered a different lens through which to explore the material world's relation to or inspiration for consciousness. Her first poem in *A Street in Bronzeville*, "The Kitchenette," finds her looking through a window from Bronzeville's streets to the dark, dim, interiors of its kitchenettes. This poem is set literally and figuratively next door in Brooks's overcrowded and subdivided cityscape:

> We are things of dry hours and the involuntary plan,
> Grayed in, and gray. "Dream" makes a giddy sound, not strong
> Like "rent," "feeding a wife," "satisfying a man."

But could a dream send up through onion fumes
Its white and violet, fight with fried potatoes
And yesterday's garbage ripening in the hall,
Flutter, or sing an aria down these rooms

Even if we were willing to let it in,
Had time to warm it, keep it very clean,
Anticipate a message, let it begin?

We wonder. But not well! not for a minute!
Since Number Five is out of the bathroom now,
We think of lukewarm water, hope to get in it.[46]

She sought, through poems such as this, to explore the feminine lived-in spaces of urban segregation. Few realized that existing behind the facades of the multitude of kitchenette buildings were ordinary people leading ordinary lives and, at the surface, the poem seems to suggest that these people were not daring to dream their dreams. The kitchenette, as a product of segregation, isolated Chicago's forgotten women psychologically and physically from the rest of the city.

Brooks, however, possessed a tenacious and lucid vision that permitted her to observe her people in a particular setting that articulated recognition of the relationship between place and life.[47] Her characters, many of them unnamed women, were urban figures that existed in an environment that did not care about them. That many of them lived in a kitchenette building where dreams "fight with fried potatoes / And yesterday's garbage ripening in the hall" adds to a general sense that these women were bound by their immediate circumstances at the expense of their dreams. This poem follows a character's stream of consciousness, verse by verse. Readers move with a tired narrator, perhaps while she scrubs her concrete floors: from fact—dry hours, to fantasy—fluttering dreams singing arias, back to fact—lukewarm bathwater and dripping children. Brooks captured in this short sketch the "misery of place."[48] The suffering inside the kitchenette is irrefutable evidence that the rituals that should give meaning and substance to human lives cannot compete with the daily struggle to survive.[49] In the kitchenette, a dream, "even if we were willing to let it in, had time to warm it, keep it very clean," is fleeting—"we wonder / But not well! not for a minute!" As a consequence that is where Brooks ended her poem and where her character rested her thoughts: "we think of lukewarm water, hope to get in it." The issue here in this gendered poem is more than mere survival; meaning is found in the mundane—taking baths, caring for one's children, cooking dinner—this contrasts with the dominant observations by sociologists and damning observations of Wright made on this feminine space. Brooks's people are challenged, certainly, when they seek to project their identities beyond the harsh realities of their environment—an environment that does not care about them yet strictly defines them; but she gives her female characters an alternate ending, a grace moving beyond mere survival to possibility.

Brooks's work delineated lines of caste, race, gender, and class difference on the South Side in a manner providing a critical feminine dimension to the photographs and poetics of Wright's photo-essay. Brooks's passionate portraiture of women inhabiting their domestic space carved room for their solace and security amid the urban crisis of segregation. The diverse nature of Brooks's characters enabled her to reveal the many facets, complexities, and paradoxes of the urban black experience. Although their worlds were drab and ordinary, they went about their daily lives not only managing to survive but to survive with grace.[50] There is an acceptance of the realities of life, no matter how unpleasant—therein lie her characters' power. It was Brooks's aim, then, to show that the struggle to survive *is* the meaningful ritual, or that thing that imbues rituals with meaning. Brooks did not romanticize life inside the kitchenette. Clearly aware of its ugliness and oppression, she chose to defy it with grace, allowing her characters to live as best they can.[51] The miracle she did present is the very fact that her people—in spite of everything—could exist from day to day.

Brooks captured this grace, most poignantly, in her poem "The Mother." The poem portrays the difficult and intimate conversations between a mother and her aborted children. Brooks explored, through a series of magnificently thoughtful and provoking verses, a mother's feelings of anxiety, guilt, impotence, and anguish. Literary critic Beverly Guy-Sheftall points out that Brooks, in the appendix of her autobiography, later referred to this mother as "hardly your crowned and praised and 'customary' Mother; but a Mother not unfamiliar, who decides that *she* rather than her World, will kill her children."[52] Although she realizes that she has shielded her unborn babies from the harsh realities of the life they would have lived as residents of the kitchenette, the mother admits she has stolen from them whatever joys they might have been able to experience:

> if I sinned, if I seized
> Your luck
> And your lives from your unfinished reach,
> If I stole your births and your names,

Your straight baby tears and your games,
Your stilted or lovely loves, your tumults, your marriages, aches,
and your deaths,
If I poisoned the beginnings of your breaths,
Believe that even in my deliberateness I was not deliberate.[53]

Throughout the poem, one has the feeling that if circumstances were different, if she had been able to provide for these children, they would have been allowed to live. Ironically, Guy-Sheftall stresses, "it was her deep concern for them as well as her own situation, which caused her to have the abortions."[54]

Believe me, I loved you all.
Believe me, I knew you, though faintly, and I loved, I
loved you.
All.[55]

She knew what life would have brought them and her own fate:

You will never neglect or beat
Them, silence or buy with a sweet.
You will never wind up the sucking-thumb
Or scuttle off ghosts that come.
You will never leave them, controlling your luscious
sigh,
Return for a snack of them, with gobbling mother-eye.[56]

In this powerfully succinct and sincere poem, Brooks afforded her female character a moment of agency. This agency, however, comes at a deep emotional price; the mother suffers psychologically: she struggles with the responsibility for the death of her children in a world where her existence is bound by her sex and race. She takes full responsibility for her actions: "Though why should I whine? Whine that the crime was other than mine?" all the while conscious of her own powerlessness: "Believe me that even in my deliberateness I was not deliberate." Born into the world that would have killed them, born into homes unable to provide them with the protection they need, the world of kitchenette apartments, where "twice as many" black babies "die as white babies,"[57] where "black mothers sit, deserted, with their children about their knees,"[58] where "crimes against women and children" happen commonplace,[59] both Wright and Brooks agreed, this is no place for a child. The mother, in this case, does the best she can; Brooks's "mother" took away the boundedness and the placelessness of the ghetto by refusing to birth any more victims into the tangled world of urban segregation. This is evidence that Bronzeville's migrants could, at a cost, project their identities beyond the harshness of place—testaments to their resilience.

An obvious difference between Brooks and Wright is the greater amount of attention she devoted to the experiences of females. For example, in her poem "A Song in the Front Yard," the female voice finds itself in combat against the confines of space. The narrator, a girl, stayed in the front yard her whole life and now wants "a peek at the back," or "to go in the back yard now / And maybe down the alley" or "strut down the streets."[60] Brooks crafted a poetics of enclosure juxtaposed against the openness of the dangerous places of urban life. Her narrator pivots between the front yard and the inside of her house, where her mother calls her in at a "quarter to nine," where she has stayed all her life, with rough and untended backyards, winding alleyways, and public streets. She wants to play in the backyard "where the charity children play," "do wonderful things," "have wonderful fun," where children do not have to go in at a quarter to nine.[61] This salacious backyard is "rough and untended," teeming with hungry weeds and seemingly unending in that it has no back gate—George, one of the charity children, sold it. But along with these freedoms come her mother's moralists and heeding warnings that charity children such as Johnnie Mae will "grow up to be a bad woman," or that "George'll be taken to jail soon or late."[62] The narrator concludes that this would be fine; that she would like to be a bad woman, dress like one, "wear the brave stockings of night-black lace / And strut down the streets with paint on [her] face."[63] In this juxtaposition between the safety and boredom of the enclosed spaces—the front yard and house—and the enticing expanse of the backyard that leads to alleyways and streets, Brooks remapped safety to the black matriarchal home—spaces in which women can control their children—placing danger and moral disdain beginning with untended open backyards, that lead to alleyways, that take young girls and boys to lives of crime and sexual promiscuity on Chicago's city streets. But Brooks left readers with an interesting twist at the end of this poem, in that the unsafe city streets are exactly where a little girl wants to be—she wants to strut the street with paint on her face. The young girl wants the life her mother does not warn her against—she thinks it would be just "fine."[64]

The heroes and heroines of Wright and Brooks are uprooted and orphaned from any sort of sanctuary or protective patronage. Affiliation with protective philanthropic institutions, communities, families, or chivalric male companions usually turns sour, leaving them stranded and isolated, with little hope of redemption or prospective acceptance into any collective shelter. The fates of these modern uprooted protagonists would seem to spell out an "essential sadness [that] can never be surmounted" that Said ultimately attributes to the condition of exile.[65] I believe, however, that Wright and Brooks coped with racial exile and confinement in their crafting of an "aesthetics of impermanence."[66] They developed characters that have fallen out of synchrony with normative white American culture and its "myths" of belonging. Their literature articulated African Americans' sense of homelessness or impermanence—their living at once within and out-of-sync with white normative frameworks of aesthetics, modernity, urbanism, cosmopolitanism—echoing questions W. E. B. DuBois asks in the closing chapter of *The Souls of Black Folk*, "Your country? How came it yours?"[67] And "Why did God make me an outcast and a stranger in mine own house?"[68] This aesthetic of nonsynchronicity or impermanence challenges the ideologies of belonging or nationality. Brooks and Wright, then, crafted an aesthetic that restructured notions of ethnic and national identities to include paradigms of nationhood and definitions of African American identity marked by the mutilations of American racism.

Wright crafted his epically tragic figures as one of the few African American authors wealthy enough at the time to traverse the globe. Despite this literary success, Wright was not totally satisfied even after becoming the great African American writer, since the color of his skin still imposed limits on him. His climb up the social ladder had only caused him to confront the racial problem on a larger scale. He realized he would never enjoy all his rights as an American citizen, and that not all the readers of his country were ready to consider him a full-fledged author—thus in 1946 he left the United States for Paris, where he would eventually die of a heart attack in 1960. In his essay, "I Choose Exile," written six years after his arrival in Paris, Wright found himself imbued "with a new sense of social confidence" concluding, "the sharp contrast between French and American attitudes demonstrated that it was barbarousness that incited so militant a racism in white Americans."[69]

Wright published *The Outsider* thirteen years after his famous novel, *Native Son*. Written from Paris but set in Chicago and Harlem, *The Outsider* opts for an individual and very masculine struggle against white racism—highlighting Wright's personal, existential struggle as an alienated black intellectual. *The Outsider* has African American "Cross Damon" for its hero; his is the story of a mail sorter on the night shift in a south Chicago post office. Cross is consumed with despair, guilt, shame, and self-loathing, trying to anesthetize his overpowering sense of the drudgery of city life imprisoning him with whiskey and women. When Cross has the chance to let another man's body be mistaken for his in a subway wreck he never hesitates. He flees all personal responsibility, feeling no obligations toward his wife, children, mistress, or mother. And to make good his escape he murders his best friend.[70]

Wright juxtaposed this violence against Cross's presentation as a meditative, introspective man, addicted to self-analysis and philosophical speculation. Cross arrives at these intersections of self-reflection because he is, regardless of his new identity via the subway wreck, an outsider in American society. The realities of this racism, as he lives them daily, lead him to the conviction that existence was senseless, that society had no moral claims on him, that there were no divine or traditional laws that applied to him. Cross believes that life is an incomprehensible disaster and human beings are "nothing in particular." So, if no ideas were necessary to justify his acts, he could kill impulsively to satisfy a passing whim or for his own convenience. Cross's dilemma in his story is that "each act of his consciousness sought to drag him back to what he wanted to flee"[71]—his body, or more importantly, his skin. Cross's real concern lies in his awareness of "his body as an alien and despised object over which he had no power, a burden that was always cheating him of the fruits of his thoughts."[72] Each episode following the subway wreck allows Cross, to a certain degree, the opportunity to start from scratch—at first he enjoys the newness of anonymity but eventually he finds he cannot overcome what becomes *the* insurmountable obstacle, more so than any other urban element—the color of his skin. Racism, grafted onto the physical surfaces of Chicago's imprisonment, follows him relentlessly as the plot twists and turns, finding its conclusion with his dying words from prison, "I wanted to be free. . . . To feel what I was worth. . . . What living meant to me. . . . I loved life too . . . much."[73] But that life, defined by American racism, functions, as Said states, as a kind of orphaning sadness where dwelling is impossible. His family and the monotony of the South Side of Chicago are problematic; they do not function as sources of resilience or beauty because they are irreparably mutilated by racism.

Brooks's only novel *Maud Martha* (1953) finds its characters navigating the same streets of Chicago's Black Belt: Washington Park, Cottage Grove, 47th Street, and State Street. This is very different from Wright's setting, which was always more macrolevel: his characters existed merely in the South Side. Brooks's characters traverse named streets, eat at known diners, visit popular theaters and ballrooms; her poetry functions on a distinctly microcosmic level helping to illustrate the importance of setting and geographic landscape. And yet, as Barbara Christian asserts, her work does not sacrifice the harshness of setting to the inner realities of her characters, who may be hampered by the environment but are not completely made of or by it.[74] Her protagonists exist in process, flowing in and out of themselves and their worlds around them—locally, globally, and epically manifested. Brooks elucidated this process through her fiction's unwavering devotion to the present, its ability to sense, perceive, and translate her characters' perceptions into precise words. These words are not dramatic. There are few grand topics in her works; instead her themes are commonplace and therefore great. And always the tone is understated, dramatic because it is muted.[75]

Maud Martha's story is of a young married African American woman experiencing the impact of racism in her daily life as Brooks subtly wove it throughout the stories and streets of Bronzeville. As Maud Martha navigates this racism, she attempts to know herself, exhausted by the seeming trivia of the commonplace yet finding truths through continuously experiencing everyday life. Maud Martha is an ordinary woman; she is neither an aspiring lady nor necessarily a doomed heroic beauty. The novel is a revelation of her thoughts and her reflections on her limited world. Brooks showed her traversing her small Bronzeville world, her relation to other people and her physical environment. For example, in a chapter entitled "The Kitchenette," Maud and Paul move into their first home:

> Paul, after two or three weeks, told her sheepishly that kitchenettes were not so bad. Theirs seemed "cute and cozy" enough, he declared, and for his part, he went on, he was ready to "camp right down" until the time came to build." . . . [T]he Owner would not allow the furniture to be disturbed. Tenants moved too often. It was not worth the Owner's financial while to make changes, or to allow tenants to make them . . . having to be satisfied with the place as it was—[was] not the only annoyance that had to be reckoned with. She was becoming aware of an oddness in color and sound and smell about her, the color and sound and smell of the kitchenette building. The color was gray, and the smell and sound had taken on a suggestion of the proprietors of color, and impressed one as gray, too. The sobbings, the frustrations, the small hates, the large and ugly hates, the little pushing-through love, the boredom, that came to her from behind those walls (some of them beaver-board) via speech and scream and sigh—all these were gray. And the smells of various types of sweat, and of bathing and bodily functions (the bathroom was always in use, someone was always in the bathroom) and of fresh or stale love-making, which rushed in thick fumes to your nostrils as you walked down the hall, or down the stairs—these were *gray*.
> There was a whole lot of grayness here.[76]

The kitchenette serves as the basis for the world she knows and imagines. The grayness begins to consume her, nearly all of her until one day she encounters a mouse she had been hunting for three weeks: "There. She had it at last. . . . It shook its little self, as best it could, in the trap. Its bright black eyes contained no appeal—the little creature seemed to understand that there was no hope of mercy from the eternal enemy, no hope of reprieve or postponement—but a fine small dignity."[77] Maud Martha wonders what the little mouse might be thinking—she imagines that it has similar worries as herself if she were near death: "that there was not enough food in its larder," housework "would be left undone," or that "Bobby's education was now at an end."[78] Maud Martha could not bear its little black eyes, she urges, "go home to your children," "to your wife or husband." Suddenly, with this act of mercy, this "small fine dignity," Maud Martha extends herself beyond the harshness of her kitchenette apartment:

> [S]he was conscious of a new cleanness in her. A wide air walked in her. A life had blundered its way into her power and it had been hers to preserve or destroy. She had not destroyed. In the center of that simple restraint was—creation. She had created a piece of life. It was wonderful. "Why," she thought, as her height doubled, "why I'm good! I am *good*." She ironed her aprons. Her back was straight. Her eyes were mild, and soft with godlike loving-kindness.[79]

Maud Martha spares the mouse even as the author of its fate, for she sets and maintains the boundaries over the mouse. It echoes Baker's commentary that for a place to be recognized by one as actually PLACE, as a personally valued locale, one must set and maintain the boundaries. Instead of imprisoning the mouse, as Maud Martha herself finds it inside her gray kitchenette apartment, she sets it free. In this short episode, Brooks recorded the impact of city life but reduced its power in Maud Martha's ability to extend beyond the harshness of the kitchenette apartment to act mercifully. Brooks did not hold the city completely responsible for what happens to people; its effects are still tragic, but the city was simply an existing force with which people must cope.

Maud Martha muses on this life:

> On the whole, she felt life was more comedy than tragedy. . . . The truth was, if you got a good Tragedy out of a lifetime, one good ripping tragedy, thorough, unridiculous, bottom-scraping, *not* the issue of human stupidity, you were doing, she thought, very well, you were doing well.[80]

Maud Martha, then, is a woman caught in the existential dilemma familiar to Cross Damon. But Brooks replaced the intense drama of Damon's story with a careful rendering of the ordinary, careful rending to the rituals, the patterns of the particular, where racism, Barbara Christian interprets, is experienced in sharp nibbles rather than the screams of a subway wreck.[81]

Brooks juxtaposed making do to small significant dreams.[82] Maud Martha helps to transform her own world through her thoughts and imaginings. Maud Martha's sensitivities to her situation become her. For example, Maud

Martha has come to work as a maid at the home of a rich white couple, the Burns-Coopers:

> [S]o these people looked at her. As though she were a child, a ridiculous one, and one that ought to be given a little shaking, except that shaking was not quite the thing, would not quite do. One held up one's finger (if one did anything), cocked one's head, was arch. As in the old song one hinted, "Tut, tut! now now! Come come!" Metal rose, all built, in one's eye.
>
> I'll never come back, Maud Martha assured herself when she hung up her apron at eight in the evening. She knew Mrs. Burns-Cooper would be puzzled. The wages were very good. Indeed, what could be said in explanation?
>
> Why, one was a human being. One wore clean nightgowns. One loved one's baby. One drank cocoa by the fire—or the gas range—come the evening, in the wintertime.[83]

This passage evidences the human, physical, local correlative of Cross's dilemma in *The Outsider*. Maud Martha's response to the Burns-Coopers' "now nows" are tangibles: clean nightgowns, cocoas, and fireplaces prove her household is just as good as theirs. Brooks did not romanticize her life as a maid, or as a wife fighting with mice in her small, dingy, kitchenette apartment. Clearly aware of racism's ugliness and oppression, Brooks empowered Maud Martha with defiance through grace—she allowed her to live the best life she could with tangible clean nightgowns, loved babies, and cocoa. Maud Martha's resilience illustrates the many facets, complexities, and paradoxes of the female urban black experience. Although her world may be drab and ordinary, Maud Martha goes about her daily life accepting her plight and somehow managing to survive. There is a celebration of the realities of life, no matter how unpleasant—therein lies Maud Martha's power.

Maud Martha does not attempt to overcome these realities through a didactic plot. Rather than faking her death in a subway wreck, Maud Martha takes hold of the resources she does have and uses them for self affirmation. It appears that Brooks's character sees this process through, more clearly, in the simple—that which already exists and has sustaining value. Maud Martha finds her advantage in the everyday, the already, the present, whereas Cross Damon lunges, unsuccessfully, toward affirmation through fabrication and evasion, through an identity he crafts for himself. The trouble with Cross Damon is that his journey must end. He could not change his self—that which he could not escape—his existence as a black man is not a negotiable point of resistance.

Gwendolyn Brooks's subtle and nuanced observations of racial struggle in *Maud Martha* measured African Americans' resistance to racial exile through the triumph of simplicity. Her feminine and localized challenge labored to defy the representation of African Americans as a socially problematic group without resources to shape American culture and history actively. She instead showed how displacement, poverty, racial subordination, and racial exile in modern mass culture are not necessarily mutilating forces—as they figure in Cross's fate. Instead she celebrated this life—a life out of sync with white culture—evoking a sweet sense of contentment, a soothing victory of the simple.

Wright and Brooks essentially viewed a particular place, such as the kitchenette apartment building on Chicago's South Side, as symbolic not only of black ghettos across the country, but also of the isolation wrought by urban segregation and the unkept promises of migration. Their photographs, text, and poetry recorded, commemorated, and interrogated the struggles, styles, and structures of black urban life in segregated America.[84] In rising above the specificity of locale and through their thoughtful examination of the inner recesses—physically and psychologically—of tortured human souls, Brooks and Wright demonstrated the inadequacies of the kitchenette as a place to gain immunity from the racial insults of everyday life.[85] Inside the kitchenette, the new home between the margins of slavery and segregation, black consciousness surrendered to material actuality. As a result, Wright felt African Americans were "not allowed to react to life with an honest and frontal vision."[86] Brooks would reach different conclusions. Both Wright and Brooks explored these dialectics of placelessness and boundedness through their visual and poetic imaginations. Wright's, however, was a different project in terms of both location and gender—his locational project was far larger and riddled with despair and his gendered project was decidedly masculine, where the kitchenette as feminine space was damning the race. Location served Brooks as a promise. A Street's specificity was distinctly microcosmic, and her characters were, more often than not, female; Brooks's artistry and advocacy apportioned the women of Bronzeville more agency than Wright's photographs or The Outsider's lead protagonist, Cross Damon. Brooks alleviated the strain of Bronzeville's desolation by affording the mothers and daughters of Bronzeville grace and beauty within their daily struggle to survive. Within the beauty of the commonplace and the specificity of locale, Brooks allowed readers to see and feel the effects of racism and capture the struggle to survive against grayness and hate.

CONCLUSION

Bronzeville's writers, gamblers, musicians, artists, and businessmen and businesswomen revolutionized their fields. The neighborhood produced the most famous African American male and female writers of that time—Richard Wright and Gwendolyn Brooks. Chicago's musicians revolutionized musical performance, dance halls, big-band music, jazz, and bebop. Visual artists made their impact alongside technological developments in radio, newspaper and magazine publishing, and athletics. This book is by no means an exhaustive account of all the remarkable innovators and producers of black culture; never could it be. Lest this study paint too rosy a portrait of Bronzeville, the remarkable cultural output from the Chicago Black Renaissance was backbreaking work exacerbated by an unforgiving and consuming, to use Richard Wright's words, urban environment. Chicago's artists, authors, entrepreneurs, and athletes navigated the precarious postmigration metropolis and capitalized through unswerving determination and fortitude—because they had to. This study has as its aim, like the artists, institutions, and authors it covered, a course of authentic representation of the period that echoes the aestheticism binding the movement: that life be presented from the lived realities of Bronzeville. By maintaining this course, set to a compass of unforgiving realism, this serves as a portrayal of Bronzeville's good and bad artists, entrepreneurs, and authors who exerted control over their communities for a brief period of time but left a profound legacy.

The Chicago Black Renaissance's momentum wound down in the latter portion of the 1950s; this decline ran simultaneously to the neighborhood's struggle with the pressures of segregation and economic disparity—that moment when the unforgiving streets that once provided fonts of material for writers and artists became damnable; in addition, the rise of hysterical McCarthyism and a significant aesthetic shift added to the artistic disintegration. All of these reasons were enough for many artists and authors to relocate, thus putting an end to the Renaissance period.

The disintegration of the Chicago Black Renaissance runs parallel to the urban disintegration of Bronzeville, which started happening in the early 1960s. A key element in that disintegration was the demolition of thousands of homes and apartments to make way for the wall of high-rise public housing—dozens of buildings along the west side of State Street.[1] This was a victory for many white city residents and elites who had, since the Great Migration, worked to contain Blacks within the borders of Bronzeville and deliberately stripped the neighborhood of its resources. Unscrupulous real-estate practices, landlord negligence, and dismissal by city authorities gave it a reputation for vice, social disorganization, and declining property values. In the postwar era, the same elements worked together with national urban policies to define Bronzeville as an economic and social wasteland. Since the beginning of the twentieth century the development of the neighborhood had been shaped by white elites' efforts to contain Black residents and Black elites' accommodation to those efforts.[2] Adam Green tells us that Black Chicago faced a sobering future after 1955, the hyperreality of arrested campaigns for justice, jobless ghettos, and lost youth that by now seems as much the stuff of local legend as the optimism of migrant masses first arriving here. Black Chicago, he concludes, became a land of trial and even tragedy as much as it was a land of hope.[3] And because of this many simply got up and left.

While racial hostilities shaped its original outlines, after World War II, where this study stops, urban renewal, industrial collapse, and public housing programs (despite the ongoing efforts and victories of public housing activists) were the biggest factors in neighborhood development and the exodus of the black middle and working class. These state-sponsored strategies not only helped confine poorer Blacks to the neighborhood, but they packed the neighborhood with low-income public housing residents while displacing homes and businesses. Postwar urban renewal programs in 1948, after restrictive racial covenants were outlawed by the Supreme Court in 1947, did not help the situation. The resulting white flight and subsequent African American population boom contributed to the concentration of poverty in Bronzeville or Douglas/Grand Boulevard. In their epilogue, "Bronzeville 1961," Drake and Cayton state that "the Negro population of Chicago doubled between 1950 and 1960."[4] Because of inadequate relocation strategies, urban renewal advocates made the construction of public housing central to their plans. African American elite would capitalize on the expanded and, to some extent, "captive" Black Belt market: captive, Drake and Cayton relate, because the business center of Bronzeville shifted two miles southward as the community grew in size—from 47th Street to 63rd Street—close to the rising housing developments.[5] In attempting to house residents dislocated by the construction of public housing complexes, the Chicago Housing Authority was forced to violate its own admission rules, housing people and families who did not meet income requirements. From 1950 to 1954, more than half of all public housing units constructed were allocated directly to families displaced by government building programs. Thus, by the time the projects were finished, Bronzeville was home to the largest concentration of public housing in the country, which stood in a four-mile procession along Chicago's State Street, south of the city's central business district. Each project (five in all) grew successively more intimidating and imposing in scale, climaxing with the massive Robert Taylor Homes: twenty-eight identical, sixteen-story high-rises, containing over forty-four hundred apartments. Named after the Chicago Housing Authority's first African American chairman, the Robert Taylor Homes opened in 1962 as the largest single public housing project in the country, housing twenty-seven thousand people when fully occupied, more than twenty-thousand of them children, and nearly all of them African American.[6]

These decisions left a troubling legacy; by 1990, the Prairie Avenue Courts, Dearborn Homes, Ida B. Wells projects, Stateway Gardens, and Robert Taylor Homes made up half of the community's housing units.[7] The exodus of wealthy, middle-class and working-class African Americans, the collapse of the working-class industrial base, together with the construction of thousands of high-rise public housing apartments and their mismanagement, left Bronzeville a slum of deep and unrelenting poverty, one of the poorest communities in the nation. Once a landscape dotted with vibrant theaters, dance halls, department stores, banks, funeral homes, and community institutions, by 1990 its landscape was dominated by vacant lots, acres and acres of desolate urban prairie.[8] According to longtime political activist and Bronzeville resident, Timuel Black, "There's not enough there to give the aura of what was—physically, culturally, and socially."[9] Without these once vital community institutions, that vibrant and bustling intersection at 47th and South Parkway, the epicenter of social vitality of what was the arts scene, dissipated.

The Chicago Black Renaissance also found stunting during the McCarthyism era of the 1950s. Richard Wright found his first success as a writer with the Communist Party's John Reed Club, which he joined upon arrival in 1932. So much had changed by the year 1950, not only Richard Wright's relationship with the Communist Party individually, but the country's estimation of the Comrades in red. In the late 1940s the Cold War displaced the wartime Soviet-American alliance, and its domestic repercussions fractured the labor-liberal-Left coalition of the New Deal years. The Federal Art Project and the Federal Writers' Project were already casualties of the mobilization of resources for World War II. By 1950, the projects associated with the FAP were long gone, and numerous artists and intellectuals left Chicago. As the "iron curtain" fell across the continent of Europe the curtain fell on most relationships and resources that once served as fonts of cultural expression for African Americans in Bronzeville. To make matters worse, the House Committee on Un-American Activities (HUAC) quickly started its investigations, and many a Bronzeville writer, actor, and musician was targeted. Bone and Courage write "as a major center of radical influence, Black Chicago was deeply affected." Frank Marshall Davis fled to Hawai'i; Margaret Burroughs was summoned to an interview at the Chicago Board of Educators headquarters and questioned about her political associations and subsequently took a one-year sabbatical in Mexico.[10]

With regard to changes in aesthetic styling, Bone and Courage's *Muse in Bronzeville* (one of the few scholarly books to do so) notes that Bronzeville's avant-garde had their own individual passions and motives for discarding old established forms and exploring what they perceived as the most innovative, productive, and challenging possibilities in their artistic genres[11]— indeed this is the reason why there was a Renaissance in Bronzeville in the first place. Bronzeville's artists and authors found the legacy of aestheticism left by Harlem deeply dissatisfying. At the beginning of the Chicago Black Renaissance what was new and innovative was that which presented realities and life in the form of aesthetics honed by the South Side Writers Group's "blueprint." Its days were numbered. Bone and Courage characterize a 1950s aestheticism distinguished not by place or location but by broader opportunities in the literary marketplace and expanding aesthetic possibilities beyond black writers' felt need to defend their own humanity.[12] They quote Brooks's brief essay in *Phylon*, "Poets Who Are Negroes," which highlighted the exigencies of craft: "The Negro poet[s]' most urgent duty, at present, is to polish his technique, his way of presenting truths and his beauties."[13] Bone and Courage point out that her statement was emblematic of a shift from emphasis on content to emphasis on form—from a "perspective" (to use a key term in Wright's "Blueprint for Negro Writing") in which words and place are meant to be deployed as weapons to move the Negro masses in the struggle against injustice to a perspective in which words are meant to be enjoyed like gemlike artifacts by knowledgeable players in a game of language. This is a fine and interesting analysis by Bone and Courage but it detracts from one of the sustaining legacies of the Chicago Black Renaissance, as evidenced by Gwendolyn Brooks's decision to remain a resident of Bronzeville forever and for her work to do the same. Her style enjoyed many shifts and manifestations throughout her career, evidencing the remarkable adaptability and ingenuity of her writing craft, but what remained the same was her unswerving devotion to perspective—a Bronzeville perspective.

Legacy and a Current State of Affairs

Bronzeville's current boundaries are 26th Street to the north, 51st Street to the south, Cottage Grove Avenue to the east, and the Dan Ryan Expressway to the west. Today, Bronzeville is 90 percent African American and its redevelopment is associated with the influx of the black middle class.[14] While many developing inner-city areas experience an influx of white residents, Harlem and Bronzeville are transforming without drastic racial changeover; they are experiencing "black gentrification." Instead of middle-class whites, middle-income blacks are returning to these communities. This movement followed some initiatives from the city and its institutions and victories by public housing activists. For example, the city moved the police headquarters from its downtown location to the center of Bronzeville. The Illinois Institute of Technology, a large university in the neighborhood, declared it would proceed with a multimillion dollar campus renovation and expansion. And finally the city made good on its promise to destroy all of the community's high-rise public housing and replace it with mixed-income housing developments. At the same time several upscale bed and breakfasts and coffeehouses opened. Many private, market-rental buildings converted to condominium units, and banking institutions not only began to make loans in the area but were also opening new commercial businesses. The generation that abandoned this community is returning.[15] Problems still surround the community. Class strife, crime, neighborhood displacement, and poverty persist as visible markers of the work that is yet to be done; but these successes concomitant with the legacy of the Chicago Black Renaissance create hope for a future informed by the arts.

Two institutions stand as inheritors of this legacy as well as sustaining forces of this legacy: the DuSable Museum of African Art and the South Side Community Art Center. Both institutions survived the rough early 1960s. Together they created a small black cultural corridor along Michigan Avenue. The DuSable Museum of African American History is devoted to the history, art, and culture of the African diaspora. Through the years the museum has functioned as a nerve center for political fundraisers, community festivals (including Chicago's Nigerian festival), and social and civic events serving the black community. The museum and its founder, Margaret Burroughs, rose to national prominence, and its model has been replicated in other cities around the country, including Boston, Los Angeles, and Philadelphia. DuSable's archival holdings preserve the Chicago Black Renaissance. These include twentieth-century artifacts, and archival materials such as the letters, photographs, and memorabilia of sociologist St. Clair Drake. The significant African American art collection includes work by Charles White, Archibald Motley Jr., Charles Sebree, and Marion Perkins (all of whom studied at the South Side Community Art Center), and numerous works from the WPA period.[16]

The South Side Community Art Center, still in existence today, also maintains the legacy of the Chicago Black Renaissance. I discovered this from a personal visit on a cold and sunny February day along South Michigan Avenue; despite its surroundings' decay, the SSCAC explodes with children nearly every afternoon. I walked up the Art Center's stairs, a beautiful brownstone mansion formerly owned by Charles Comiskey; I dodged energetic young smiling faces to my left and right. These young children seven or eight years old had recently been dismissed from a class and were teeming out of the building onto the street. Along with art classes, lectures, and forums, the SSCAC offers art tours for community residents, art patrons, collectors, students, and tourists that are interested in learning about and acquiring art by African Americans.[17] Programs such as this show that the Renaissance legacy is alive and well along the South Side.

The next face I met on my way up the stairs was one of a young man welcoming me to "take a look around." As I walked through the first-floor gallery and then up to the second floor of classrooms and seminar rooms, I felt the significance of this place; the building's past, present, and future pulsed through me. After perusing through some literature in the front hall, the young man invited me to come back anytime, saying "we'll still be here." I was comforted by his last statement and thought to myself, "yes, you will."

In *Black Metropolis*, Drake and Cayton state, "understand Chicago's Black Belt and you will understand the Black Belts of a dozen large American cities."[18] More recent studies of Bronzeville continue to stress the importance of these communities as critical black icons; there is much at stake in understanding the troubling mixture of vibrancy and decay of these historic African American communities.[19] It is tempting, simple, and easy to view the first half of the twentieth century as encompassing the rise and fall of Black community—tempting, but misguided.[20] The experience of Bronzeville's residents during this period was not one of unmitigated triumph followed by unfortunate demise; instead it was a contradictory blend of expansion, progress, and stagnation.[21] From 1910 to 1950 neighborhood residents produced and witnessed a remarkable growth in cultural, economic, and political institutions designed to serve their growing needs. Thus, the history of the neighborhood is an uncomfortable and conflicting mixture of opportunity and subjugation. But does this minimize the import and legacy of the Chicago Black Renaissance? No, it speaks to a rich complexity.[22] Our goal when reconstructing the past should be complexity instead of false nostalgia. But does complexity mean one should surrender the narrative of all the good of the Chicago Black Renaissance—the Regal Theater, the South Side Community Art Center, the Savoy Ballroom, the South Center Department Store, the Stroll's vibrant and exciting neighborhood—to all of the bad—accommodationism, exploitation, or death in the city's kitchenette apartments and then in its housing projects? Adam Green asks, "what do we miss when we view Black Chicago's history through such a rueful and fatalistic lens,"[23] while others ask what we miss when we do not. Dilemmas persist; Green concludes: "the story remains to be told . . . out of reach from any conclusion."[24] Such comments help *Along the Street*'s cause; we must come to terms with the *actual* existing economic, political, and cultural relations of the period as well as any ambiguities that follow.[25]

These points bring me to the original impetus of *Along the Streets of Bronzeville*: filling a void in African American cultural arts scholarship while delineating new modes of artistic thought and aestheticism that rely on a uniquely Bronzeville perspective. To reiterate this point and illuminate the necessity of realism toward understanding the complex circumstances of black cultural production and its epistemology, it will be useful to take a chronological leap forward from Chicago at mid–twentieth century to the Black Arts Movement of the 1960s. Rebecca Sklaroff notes that seminal cultural figures of the 1930s and 1940s, who sought out what they believed to be more authentic representations of African Americans, advocating for control over the promotion of racial imagery and aspiring to create self-defined notions of blackness independent of white influence, influenced this next generation of artists, authors, and activists. Yet, while an older generation of African American writers and artists deeply influenced the cultural nationalism manifest in the Black Arts Movement, Sklaroff attributes also a historical distinctiveness to the movement through a quote from Larry Neal. Neal critiques Harlem saying that "it failed to take root, to link itself concretely to the struggles of that community, to become its voice and spirit. Implicit in the black arts movement is the idea that black people, however dispersed, constitute a *nation* within the belly of white America."[26] That the Black Arts Movement did this is true, but that its artists were the first is questionable. Chicago's artists had been doing this since 1937; Chicago's African American artists and authors shared a common question, a common theme, and a common politics—that their art should always present black reality from the vantage point of African Americans in Bronzeville.

Radically, Richard Wright's "Blueprint," demands that Chicago Black Renaissance writers reject what has been for them their only "black" literary and aesthetic history—the Harlem Renaissance—for a more authentic one. Wright called upon them to learn to view and to present black reality from the vantage point of African Americans in Bronzeville—its good and bad, its arias and rotting garbage. This is the lesson to be learned from the Chicago Black Renaissance and what sets it apart from all others. Its legacy is a configuration of subjectivity and identity that retheorizes the relationship between artistry and place so that one resists the misguided impulse to view the African American urban experience during the first half of the twentieth century as something it was not. The aesthetic formula characterized by the Chicago Black Renaissance forces a perspective that disallows overdetermined narratives of hope and/or despair.

Found on the canvases of those artists of the South Side Community Art Center and between the pages of the South Side Writers Group, the Chicago Black Renaissance articulates a vital political and modern consciousness. Its aesthetic was personal and always political but executed with distance to claim objectivity with the African Americans the artists and writers would depict. Motley, Wright, and Brooks could take this approach confidently because of prior aesthetic philosophies that gave them the confidence—even the mandate—to do so. Motley painted, as much as Brooks poetically rendered, a visual narrative of Bronzeville with an immediacy, honesty, and sincerity that DuBois demanded in his criteria for "Negro art," or Alain Locke suggested when he wrote that the black artist had even more to gain than other American artists from the desire to create an art independent from outside influences and rooted in themes of the American scene.[27]

Wright wrote in his blueprint that "Negro life may be approached from a thousand angles, with no limit to technical and stylistic freedom."[28] The word about Bronzeville is getting out; whether it is in the neighborhood itself, scholarly anthologies on the Renaissance, or artists and residents offering retrospective accounts, angles are being pursued and, yes, Wright, the possibilities are endless.

NOTES

PREFACE

1. Gates Jr. and McKay, eds., "Gwendolyn Brooks," 1577.
2. Brooks, "Interviews: Summer, 1967," 136.
3. Ibid., 72.
4. Motley, "Negro Art in Chicago," 19.
5. Bone, "Richard Wright," 446–468.
6. Floyd Jr., *Power of Black Music*, 187.
7. Bone stressed that a successful intellectual recognition, theorizing, and recovery of this movement as a conceptual category involves its inclusion within the larger historical narrative of America's literary canon. Frequently, anthologies rush from the Harlem Renaissance to the Black Arts Movement within the context of the Civil Rights Era with a passing, piecemeal mention of African American artists whose work mostly revolved around World War II—keeping stride with typical periods of "raced" study. There is little mention of a distinctly Chicago aesthetic phenomenon between 1932, the year Richard Wright joined Chicago's John Reed Club, and 1945, the year Wright published his autobiography *Black Boy (American Hunger)*, Gwendolyn Brooks published *Street in Bronzeville*, and St. Clair Drake and Horace Cayton published *Black Metropolis*. For example, *Norton Anthology of African American Literature* divides the African American literary tradition into six chronological periods: "The Literature of Slavery and Freedom," "Literature of the Reconstruction to the New Negro Renaissance," "The Harlem Renaissance," and, most importantly for my study, "Realism, Modernism, and Naturalism," covering the years from 1940 to 1960, "when black authors sought to adapt the conventions of these literary movements to new formal modes that would be adequate to the complex interplay of race and class and gender in modernity." The next period is "The Black Arts Movement," and they conclude the anthology with "Literature Since 1970." Another anthology, *Within the Circle: An Anthology of African American Literary Criticism from the Harlem Renaissance to the Present*, encounters the same oddity. Its introduction, entitled "Voices within the Circle: A Historical Overview

of African American Literary Criticism," journeys from the Harlem Renaissance to the Humanistic/Ethical Criticism and the Protest Tradition (covering the 1940s and 1950s but with no distinct mention of Chicago). It proceeds on to the Black Arts Movement; a Structuralism, Post-Structuralism, and the African American Critic period; ending with Gender, Theory, and African American Feminist Criticism. This omission contributes to the loss of an entire aesthetic movement.

8. Flug, "Chicago Renaissance 1932–1950. Literature."

9. Ibid.

10. Ibid., 22.

11. Flug, "Chicago Renaissance 1932–1950. Music."

12. Floyd, *Power of Black Music*, 111.

13. Ellison, *Shadow and Act*, quoted in Sklaroff, *Black Culture*, 161.

14. Ibid.

15. Rout Jr., "Reflections," 144.

16. Ibid.

17. Flug, "Chicago Renaissance 1932–1950. Music."

18. Flug, "Chicago Renaissance 1932–1950. Journalism."

19. Ibid.

20. Ibid.

21. Ibid.

22. Sklaroff, *Black Culture*, 195.

23. Ibid., 243.

24. Ibid.; "Flug, "Chicago Renaissance 1932–1950. Institutions."

25. Ibid.

26. Boyd, *Jim Crow Nostalgia*, 36, 37.

27. Ibid.

28. Chicago's artists, with the exception of Richard Wright, have not seen the accolades or been credited with the historical significance enjoyed by artists of the Harlem Renaissance or the Black Arts Movement. Between 1932 and 1945 Chicago was bursting with artists who theoretically challenged overly atomistic modes of study and traditional methods of scholarly inquiry. As mentioned previously, Robert Bone's essay "Richard Wright and the Chicago Renaissance," written in 1986, is the first articulation of a distinctly Chicago-based artistic flowering after the Harlem Renaissance. His main thesis is that there was in fact an identifiable generation of black writers holding ascendancy from 1935–1950, and this generation found its locus in the city of Chicago. Moreover, he stresses that the current version of Afro-American literary history is in need of serious revision. The prevailing wisdom postulates a Harlem Renaissance to the 1920s and a second literary flowering associated with the Black Arts Movement of the 1960s. But he wrote in 1986, "our sense of the intervening years is at best vague and indistinct." A recent anthology, *Black Chicago Renaissance*, edited by Darlene Clark Hine and John McCluskey Jr., and Robert Bone and Richard A. Courage's *Muse in Bronzeville*, are among the first books since Bone's 1986 essay to focus exclusively on the Renaissance movement in Chicago as the chronological follow-up to the Harlem Renaissance.

Chapter 1. From Black Belt to Bronzeville

1. Baldwin, *Chicago's New Negroes*, 43.
2. Stewart, *Migrating to the Movies*, 9.
3. Drake and Cayton, *Black Metropolis*, 379.
4. See Grossman, *Land of Hope*; Grossman, *Chance to Make Good*; Spear, *Black Chicago*.
5. Wright, *Black Boy*, 262.
6. Ibid.
7. Ibid.
8. Ibid., 261. For Wright's impressions of the migratory experience, see also his more rhetorical and stylized *12 Million Black Voices*, 93, 98; Grossman, *Land of Hope*, 2.
9. Ibid., 3.
10. Gates Jr., "New Negroes," 17, quoted in Stewart, *Migrating to the Movies*, 2; see Marks, *Farewell*, 2.
11. Stewart, *Migrating to the Movies*, xviii.
12. Ibid., 6.
13. Bachin, *Building the South Side*, 250.
14. Grossman, *Land of Hope*, 4.
15. Reed, *"All the World Is Here!"* xxi.
16. *Chicago Defender*, December 13, 1919, quoted in Grossman, *Land of Hope*, 4.
17. Grossman, 4.
18. Wright, *Black Boy*, 262, quoted in Grossman, *Land of Hope*, 116.
19. Ibid.
20. Ibid.
21. Ibid., 175.
22. Baldwin, *Chicago's New Negroes*, 23.
23. Bachin, *Building the South Side*, 57, 58.
24. Ibid., 58.
25. Reiff, "Contested Spaces." Virulent puts it mildly. On Sunday, July 27, 1919, seventeen-year-old Eugene Williams went for a swim at Lake Michigan's 29th Street beach. The African American teenager was unaware of a confrontation earlier that day when black Chicagoans had walked onto a space conventionally limited to whites. Spotting him in the water, a group of bathers began throwing stones at Williams, who struggled, disappeared, and drowned. As news of his death spread, further violence erupted on the beach and extended out from it. Four days of rioting followed, engulfing large sections of the city. When the violence subsided, 38 persons were dead, 537 were injured, and over 1,000 were left homeless.
26. Hirsch, "Restrictive Covenants." Weaver, "Racial Restrictive Covenants."
27. Baldwin, *Chicago's New Negroes*, 23.
28. Sugrue, *Sweet Land of Liberty*, 76, 208.
29. Ibid., 207.
30. Ibid., 208.

31. Ibid.

32. Grossman, *Land of Hope*, 117. Hughes, *Big Sea*, 33.

33. *Chicago Whip*, August 15, 1919, quoted in Grossman, *Land of Hope*, 117.

34. Grossman, *Land of Hope*, 117.

35. Stewart, *Migrating to the Movies*, 116.

36. Ibid., 7.

37. White, "Stroll"; White and White, *Stylin'*, 225; Baldwin, *Chicago's New Negroes*, 22.

38. Stewart, *Migrating to the Movies*, 107.

39. Ibid., 4.

40. Ibid., 116–118.

41. Ibid., 10.

42. Ibid. Grossman, *Land of Hope*, 16.

43. Stewart, *Migrating to the Movies*, 9.

44. Rebecca Lauren Sklaroff notes that by 1944, black patrons contributed approximately 10 percent of box office receipts for Hollywood films (Sklaroff, *Black Culture*, 238).

45. Stewart, *Migrating to the Movies*, 130.

46. *Chicago Defender*, February 12, 1910, 1, quoted in Stewart, *Migrating to the Movies*, 130.

47. Stewart, *Migrating to the Movies*, 131.

48. White and White, *Stylin'*, 228.

49. Geertz, *Interpretation of Cultures*, Chapters 1, 15, quoted in Kenney, *Chicago Jazz*, xi.

50. For an excellent analysis of the Levee and the vice-sex districts of Chicago, see Mumford, *Interzones*.

51. Reed, *"All the World Is Here!"* 92.

52. Kenney, *Chicago Jazz*, 14.

53. Reed, *"All the World Is Here!"* 78–79.

54. Condon and Sugrue, *We Called It Music*, 114, quoted in Kenny, *Chicago Jazz*, 14.

55. Reed, *"All the World Is Here!"* 92.

56. Ibid.

57. Stewart, *Migrating to the Movies*, 131–141.

58. Kenney, *Chicago Jazz*, 15.

59. Spear, *Black Chicago*, 116.

60. Kenney, *Chicago Jazz*, 16.

61. Burgett, "Vindication as a Thematic Principle," 33, 34.

62. Kenney, *Chicago Jazz*, 151.

63. *Variety*, March 28, 1928, quoted in Kenney, *Chicago Jazz*, 152.

64. Kenney, *Chicago Jazz*, 155.

65. Ibid., 61.

66. Ibid.

67. Ibid., 162.

68. *Chicago Tribune*, August 19, pt. 3, 1, quoted in Semmes, *Regal Theater*, 17.

69. Kenney, *Chicago Jazz*, 162.

70. Ibid.

71. Ibid., 42.

72. *Chicago Defender*, October 29, 1927, pt. 1, 13; November 19, 1927, pt. 1, 8; November 26, 1927, pt. 1, 10; July 26, 1930, 6; April 18, 1931, 6; August 8, 1931, 7; September 19, 1931, 6; October 21, 1933, 5; December 16, 1933, 4.

73. Ibid.

74. *Chicago Defender*, January 28, 1928, 11; April 5, 1928, 10–11; April 19, 1928, 11; May 11, 1929, 9, quoted in Kenney, *Chicago Jazz*, 164.

75. Wright, "Amusements," quoted in Stange, *Bronzeville*, 193–195.

76. Page, "Short Tour," quoted in Stange, *Bronzeville*, 8.

77. Semmes, *Regal Theater*, 2006, 1.

78. Ibid., 11. The Regal Theater's first Black owner, Ken Blewett, directed from 1939–1959, longer than any other manager in the Regal's history. Black business pioneer S. B. Fuller purchased the entire complex in 1963. However, he lost the Regal in 1968. This tragedy was compounded, Semmes writes, in 1973 when the subsequent owners tore down the Regal and built a parking lot in its place.

79. Semmes, *Regal Theater*, 33, 34.

80. Ibid., 39.

81. Wright, *Native Son*, 35, 36.

82. Semmes, *Regal Theater*, 16–17.

83. Reed, *Rise of Chicago's Black Metropolis*, 141, 142.

84. Mullen, "Don't Buy."

85. *Chicago Defender*, December 24, 1927, pt. 1, 6, quoted in Semmes, *Regal Theater*, 24, 25.

86. Wright, "Amusements," quoted in Stange, *Bronzeville*, 194.

87. Ibid.

88. Drake and Cayton, *Black Metropolis*, 380.

89. Ibid., 380, 381.

90. [Author unknown], "Number of businesses."

91. Harris, "Negro Employees," quoted in Stange, *Bronzeville*, 103.

92. In 1928, Jones began a long association with the newly founded South Center Department Store, first as a floorwalker and then as personnel director and, eventually, vice president. Jones was very conscious of his position as one of the race men on Chicago's South Side. In an interview conducted by the Federal Writers' Project, he stated, "I did not make myself. I make no speeches. I believe in fair play. When the final division comes I must be on the side of the Negro. I know that." As an attendee of Pilgrim Baptist Church, he stated, "I hear them preach against the white man. But, I know that the Negro has no business. Were it not for stores like this, there would be no Negro business." South Center Department Store was really more than just a store—one entire floor became the training ground for Madame C. J. Walker,

whose school became a fixture in the community, helping many men and women become independent business owners. He was well aware that stores like his served as fixtures combatting what he himself termed the African American's infancy: "We need more businesses like this. The Negro is an infant, and don't know it. He gets up every Sunday and cusses the white man. On Monday he asks the white man for bread." Wilson, "Interview with Dick Jones."

93. Best, "Bud Billiken Day Parade." Since the 1940s, the Bud Billiken Day Parade has been sponsored by the *Chicago Defender* Charities and has become known as the oldest African American parade in the country. Participants in the parade, which proceeds south on Dr. Martin Luther King Jr. Drive from 39th to 51st Streets and culminates with a picnic in Washington Park, have included Presidents Truman, Kennedy, and Johnson; Nat King Cole; Michael Jordan; and Muhammad Ali. Toward the late 1990s, spectator estimates of the Bud Billiken Day Parade, held on the second Saturday of August, ran into the millions, and the event was routinely considered one of the largest of its kind in the United States.

94. Travis, "Bronzeville."

95. Thompson, "Short History."

96. Drake and Cayton, *Black Metropolis*, 379, 380.

97. Ibid., 382.

98. Brooks, "Sundays of Satin-Legs Smith," 27.

99. Ibid.

100. Ibid.; Brooks, *Report from Part I*, 155.

101. Anderson, *This Was Harlem*, 322.

102. Ibid., 339.

103. Ibid., 322.

104. Johnson, "One Puts on One's Best," 163, quoted in Anderson, *This Was Harlem*, 322.

105. Brooks, "Sundays of Satin-Legs Smith," 26.

106. Ibid.

107. Ibid.

108. Ibid.

109. Zack, "That No Performance."

110. Brooks, "Sundays of Satin-Legs Smith," 30.

111. Knupfer, *Chicago Black Renaissance*, 3.

CHAPTER 2. THE SOUTH SIDE COMMUNITY ART CENTER AND SOUTH SIDE WRITERS GROUP

1. Burroughs, "Saga," 2, quoted in Mullen, *Popular Fronts*, 86.

2. Knupfer, *Chicago Black Renaissance*, 2.

3. For a more thorough look at racial politics and black culture during World War II, consult Sklaroff, *Black Culture*.

4. Stewart, *New York/Chicago*.

5. Park and Markowitz, *New Deal for Art*, xiii.

6. Blair Bolles, "Federal Writers' Project," *Saturday Review of Literature*, July 9, 1938, 4, quoted in Sklaroff, *Black Culture*, 88; Penkower, 30, quoted in Sklaroff, *Black Culture*, 88.

7. Borglum, quoted in Sherwood, *Roosevelt and Hopkins*, 58, quoted in Sklaroff, *Black Culture*, 30.

8. Sklaroff, *Black Culture*, 30.

9. Barnes, "I'd Rather Be," 53. Horace Cayton, St. Clair Drake, Katherine Dunham, E. Franklin Frazier, Charles S. Johnson, and Ira De A. Reid received Rosenwald Fellowships for cultural anthropology and sociology. Marian Anderson, Ralph Bunche, Charles Drew, Ralph Ellison, Jacob Lawrence, Gordon Parks, Pearl Primus, and William Grant Still number among other famous fellowship recipients.

10. To delineate properly the dynamics of the cultural output of the period, this chapter employs a methodology bringing together literary analysis and social history within the rubric of cultural studies. It is important to recognize that a blending of cultural studies together with literary theory opens up the prospect of significant advances in the cultural retheorizing of the past. Traditionally, primary sources have been viewed as points of access to events or states of mind—to what had an "objective" or demonstrable existence beyond the text. Literary theory teaches us to focus on the text itself, because its value lies less in any reflection of reality than in revealing the categories and historical moments through which reality was perceived. Terry Eagleton writes in his seminal work, *Literary Theory*, "All literary works, in other words, are 'rewritten,' if only unconsciously, by the societies which read them; indeed there is no reading of a work which is not also a 're-writing.' . . . [T]his is one reason why what counts as literature is a notably unstable affair." From this perspective, primary sources and archival elements—in this chapter the literature, visual arts, and mass media from the Chicago Black Renaissance—are essentially unstable categories of cultural evidence—testimonies of rhetorical strategies, codes of representation, social metaphors, political struggles, and so on. Thus, literary theory, understood most broadly to include creative works outside the realm of mere prose to include any "text," even archival documents, material artifacts, visual images, and community institutions together with cultural studies, gives me the confidence to move beyond the letter of the "text" to a wider range of voices. This leads one to focus on the aesthetic ideologies and representations widely conceived by literature, visual art, and mass media. Michael Denning's exploration of aesthetic ideologies in his work *Culture Front*, discussed in the next chapter, serves as the foundation from which I will formulate an articulation of the Chicago Black Renaissance's aesthetic ideology—or what Eagleton refers to as *rhetorical strategies*.

11. Rotella, *October Cities*, 3.

12. Hughes, "Negro Artist," quoted in Mitchell, ed., *Within the Circle*, 55–59.

13. DuBois, "Criteria of Negro Art," quoted in Mitchell, ed., *Within the Circle*, 60–68.

14. DuBois, *Crisis* 31, October 1926, 115.

15. Ibid.; DuBois, *Crisis* 22, June 1921, 55.

16. Ibid.; DuBois, "Criteria of Negro Art," *Crisis* 32, October, 1926, 292.

17. Judy, "New Black Aesthetic," 248.

18. DuBois, "Criteria of Negro Art," 292.

19. Rampersad, "W. E. B. Du Bois"; DuBois, *World and Africa*, 24; DuBois, "Criteria of Negro Art," 290–297.

20. DuBois, "Krigwa Players," 134, quoted in Sklaroff, *Black Culture*, 44.

21. Ibid.

22. Locke, "Steps toward the Negro Theatre," *Crisis*, December 1922, 66, quoted in Sklaroff, *Black Culture*, 44.

23. Gates Jr. and McKay, eds., "Gwendolyn Brooks," 1577.

24. Pollack, "Forward."

25. Tyler, "Planting and Maintaining," 31.

26. Ibid.

27. Pollack, "Dinner Speech."

28. Ibid.

29. Ibid.

30. Knupher, *Chicago Black Renaissance*, 67.

31. Ibid., 68.

32. Pollack, "First Year's Work."

33. Ibid.

34. Knupher, *Chicago Black Renaissance*, 68.

35. Tyler, "Planning and Maintaining," 31.

36. Lloyd, *Flowering African American Artists*.

37. Tyler, "Planning and Maintaining," 35.

38. Mullen, *Popular Fronts*, 3.

39. Motley, *Gettin' Religion*.

40. Levinsohn, "In the Heart."

41. Ibid.

42. "Opening Exhibition," December 15, 1940, to January 28, 1941, Exhibition Catalogue, William McBride Papers, Vivian Harsh Research Collection, Carter Woodson Regional Library, Chicago.

43. Mullen, *Popular Fronts*, 83, 84.

44. Ibid., 84.

45. Burroughs, "Saga," 1, quoted in Mullen, *Popular Fronts*, 85.

46. Burroughs, "Saga," 2, quoted in Mullen, *Popular Fronts*, 86.

47. Tyler, "Planning and Maintaining," 35.

48. Mullen, *Popular Fronts*, 87–89.

49. Many African Americans found a friend in Mrs. Roosevelt and showed profound faith in her and her husband's White House policies toward African Americans. In *Black Culture*, Sklaroff notes an editorial from the *Pittsburgh Courier*: "Perhaps more than any couple ever occupying the White House, President and Mrs. Roosevelt have demonstrated their friendliness and interest in the problems of colored Americans. . . . The couple is setting an example of tolerance, sympathetic understanding

and lack of color bias which all white America should follow." Editorial, *Pittsburgh Courier*, May 26, 1934.

50. Eleanor Roosevelt, May 7, 1941, McBride Papers.
51. Alain Locke, "Foreword."
52. Ibid.
53. Ibid.
54. Rotella, *October Cities*, 3.
55. "Major Divisions."
56. Tyler, "Planning and Maintaining," 35.
57. Ibid., 25.
58. Lloyd, *Flowering*, 4.
59. Pollack, "First Year's Work."
60. Ibid.
61. Ibid.
62. Ibid.
63. Ibid.
64. Lloyd, "Legacy."
65. Tyler, "Planning and Maintaining," 36.
66. "Major Divisions."
67. Mullen, *Popular Fronts*, 81.
68. Ibid.
69. Walker, *Richard Wright*, 68.
70. Ibid., 70.
71. Ibid., 72.
72. Knupher, *Chicago Black Renaissance*, 193, n. 1. The Abraham Lincoln Center was an interracial social settlement, similar to the Parkway Community House. There, Dr. Rudolf Dreikurs, an Adlerian psychiatrist, had established a child guidance clinic in 1939 that used both psychiatric and group work methods with parents of "maladjusted" children. Although the clinic closed by 1942, over half of its clients were poor blacks (Knupher, *Chicago Black Renaissance*, 39). As early as 1935 there was concern that the ALC was involved with communism. However, as one staff member countered, the ALC had always been liberal and inclusive, and so it supported organizations for workers and the unemployed, such as the SSWG, just as other settlements did. He knew of no activities "bent upon the destruction of the capitalistic system." There were some interracial problems, although the nature of those problems were not disclosed.
73. Walker, *Richard Wright*, 72.
74. Knupher, *Chicago Black Renaissance*, 53.
75. Walker, *Richard Wright*, 72–78.
76. Walker, "Midwest Federation."
77. Ibid.
78. Ibid.; Walker, *Richard Wright*, 80.
79. Walker, "Midwest Federation."
80. Barnes, "I'd Rather Be," 52.

81. Walker, *Richard Wright*, 335, n. 18.

82. Wright, "Blueprint for Negro Writing," quoted in Mitchell, ed., *Within the Circle*, 97–106.

83. Ibid., 104.

84. Ibid., 106.

85. Ibid.

86. Ibid.

87. Ibid., 59.

88. Ibid.

89. Mullen, "Popular Fronts," 7.

90. Barnes, "I'd Rather Be," 53.

91. Bontemps, "Expect Next Literary Renaissance."

92. Takara, "Frank Marshall Davis," 215–227, 220. In addition to documenting the impact of segregation on football, basketball, and boxing, Davis reported on the movement toward desegregation in other sports as well. He covered the first annual National Professional Basketball Tournament in 1939, featuring the two best African American teams in the nation—the New York Rens of Harlem, and the Harlem Globe-trotters of Chicago (who played at the Savoy Ballroom at the corner of 47th Street and South Parkway)—claiming that their "initial success" during this "national test of strength was the first step toward breaking the color barrier in this pro sport."

93. Knupher, *Chicago Black Renaissance*, 53, 54; "Radio Log." Radio became another medium of expression for black Chicago literature. One could find the voices of many in the SSWG on Richard Durham's "Destination Freedom" black radio program. Airing from 1948 to 1950, the program's opening announcement reflected the postwar disillusionment felt by Durham: "D. F., dramatizations of the great democratic heritage of the pages of history and of America's own DES-TINATION FREEDOM!" Durham's historical episodes dramatized how Harriet Tubman, Frederick Douglass, Sojourner Truth, Ida B. Wells, Mary Church Terrell, and Carter G. Woodson, among others, had traveled the road to freedom. Other episodes portrayed those who had followed in their footsteps: Langston Hughes, Richard Wright, Lena Horne, Gwendolyn Brooks, Mary McCleod Bethune, Paul Robeson, and W. E. B. DuBois.

94. Walker, *Richard Walker*, 80, 81.

95. Mooney, *Archibald J. Motley, Jr.*, 83.

96. Motley Jr., "How I Solve," 3, quoted in Harris, "Color Lines," 169.

CHAPTER 3. POLICY, CREATIVITY, AND BRONZEVILLE'S DREAMS

1. Haller, "Policy Gambling," 719.

2. Bachin, *Building the South Side*, 285.

3. Illinois Writers Project: Negro in Illinois Papers, 1936–1942. Chicago Public Library, Woodson Regional Library, Vivian G. Harsh Research Collection of Afro-American History and Literature.

4. Bachin, Building the South Side, 250.

5. Herman Clayton, "Game Policy," Illinois Writers Project, October 1, 1940, Box 35, Folder 13, Harsh Research Collection; Andrew G. Paschal, "Policy: Negroes' Numbers Game," Illinois Writers Project, n.d., Box 35, Folder 15, Harsh Research Collection; Mathilde Bunton, "Policy," Illinois Writers Project, n.d., Box 35, Folder 11, Harsh Research Collection; Haller, "Policy Gambling," 720; Drake and Cayton, *Black Metropolis*, 472.

6. Herman Clayton, "Local Policy Barons," Illinois Writers Project: Negro in Illinois Papers, October 30, 1940, Box 35, Folder 17, Harsh Research Collection.

7. Drake and Cayton, *Black Metropolis*, 474.

8. Ibid., 477.

9. Bachin, *Building the South Side*, 247, 248.

10. Ibid., 256.

11. Ibid., 250.

12. Ibid.

13. Ibid.

14. Bone and Courage, *Muse in Bronzeville*, 185.

15. Ibid., 264, quoting *Chicago Defender*, August 17, 1918.

16. Ibid., 250.

17. Ibid.

18. Paschal, "Policy: Negroes' Number Game."

19. Thompson, *Kings*, 13, quoting "Center of US Negro Business," *Time Magazine*, 1938, and *Our World Magazine*, 1947.

20. Schatzberg and Kelly, *African-American Organized Crime*, 71–73.

21. Bachin, *Building the South Side*, 271.

22. Drake and Cayton, *Black Metropolis*, 481.

23. Ibid., 480.

24. Ibid.

25. Ibid., 481.

26. Ibid.

27. Ibid.

28. Ibid., 487.

29. Ibid.

30. Ibid.

31. Thompson, *Kings*, 96, 152.

32. According to Thompson, the 1905 law imposed sanctions on "all persons involved in the game from the policy racketeer to the caretaker of the building in which the gambling was conducted." Johnson quickly closed his current gambling den, the Emporium, but on May 1, 1906, with Tom McGinnis and Bill Lewis, Johnson opened Frontenac Club on 22nd Street. During the first year, the owners took in about two hundred dollars a day and divided the profit.

33. Schatzberg and Kelly, *African-American Organized Crime*, 21.

34. Ibid.

35. Ibid., 86.

36. Bachin, *Building the South Side*, 281.

37. Drake and Cayton, *Black Metropolis*, 485.

38. "Mrs. Binga, Wife of Ex-Banker, Is Dead," *Chicago Defender (National Edition)*, April 1, 1933, 1, 4.

39. Bone and Courage, *Muse in Bronzeville*, 76.

40. "Binga-Johnson Wedding the Most Brilliant Ever Held in Chicago," *Chicago Defender (National Edition)*, February 24, 1912, 1.

41. "Try Binga. Banker for Embezzlement," *Chicago Defender (National Edition)*, May 27, 1933, 13; "Binga Downfall Ends Spectacular Career," *Chicago Defender (National Edition)*, June 10, 1933, 10; "Binga Represented a Business Era That Was Crude, Rough, Uncultured," *Chicago Defender (National Edition)*, June 24, 1950, 7; "Business Men, Laboring Classes Staggered by Closing of Binga Bank," *Associated Negro Press*, August 6, 1930, Claude Barnett Papers, Box 261, Folder 3, Chicago History Museum; Luix Virgil Overbea, "Jesse Binga Represents Vanishing Race of Self-Made Men," *Associated Negro Press*, June 21, 1950, Claude A. Barnett Papers, Box 261, Folder 3, Chicago History Museum.

42. Drake and Cayton, *Black Metropolis*, 490.

43. Ibid., 492, 493.

44. Ibid., 494.

45. Baldwin, *Chicago's New Negroes*, 50.

46. Drake and Cayton, *Black Metropolis*, 488.

47. Thompson, *Kings*, 104.

48. Ibid., 226.

49. Ibid., 233.

50. *Chicago Daily Tribune*, February 23, 1964; *Chicago Daily Tribune*, August 31, 1959.

51. *Chicago Daily Tribune*, February 23, 1964.

52. *Chicago Daily Tribune*, July 17, 1960.

53. *Chicago Daily Tribune*, December 1, 1961.

54. Ibid.

55. Caldwell, *Policy Game in Chicago*, 29.

56. *Chicago Daily Tribune*, February 23, 1964.

57. Drake and Cayton, *Black Metropolis*, 494.

58. Caldwell, *Policy Game in Chicago*, 29, 30.

59. Drake and Cayton, *Black Metropolis*, 486.

60. Ernest W. Burgess Papers, "Characters, Gambling," April 7, 1937, Box 23, Folder 13, University of Chicago Special Collections.

61. Ibid.

62. Caldwell, *Policy Game in Chicago*, 47.

63. Ibid., 48.

64. Ibid., 50.

65. Ibid., 50, 51.

66. Drake and Cayton, *Black Metropolis*, 487.

67. Bachin, *Building the South Side*, 281.

68. Brooks, "Kitchenette," 3; Brooks, "Song in the Front Yard," 12.

69. Baldwin, *Chicago's New Negroes*, 52.

70. Ibid., 35.

71. Ibid., 45.

72. Ibid., 48.

73. Ibid., 45.

74. Ibid., 50, 51.

75. Ibid., 51.

76. Ibid., 51, 52.

77. Fabian, *Card Sharps and Bucket Shops*, 144.

78. Ibid.

79. Ibid., 145, 146.

80. Reed, *Rise of Chicago's Black Metropolis*, 23.

81. Ibid., 42. Equally crucial were media of visual and literary art and radio, which continued to find both aesthetic inspiration and institutional support from the Stroll consumer marketplace. As an example, Archibald Motley Jr. used the formalist training he acquired from the Art Institute of Chicago to shift from the dominant respectable images of southern folk landscapes toward the urban streetscapes of a new settler life. He powerfully depicted Stroll nightlife in his paintings *Black Belt* and *Barbecue* (both in 1934); nightclub and vaudeville scenes in *Blues* (1929), *Saturday Night* (1935), and *Between Acts* (1935); and *Sanctified Church Life in Tongues (Holy Rollers)* (1929).

82. Fabian, *Card Sharps and Bucket Shops*, 148.

83. Ibid.

84. "Aunt Sally's Policy Players Dream Book." http://www.luckymojo.com/aunt-sallys.html (accessed November 24, 2011).

85. Paschal, "Policy: Negroes Number Game."

86. Clayton, "Local Policy Barons."

87. Fabian, *Card Sharps and Bucket Shops*, 149.

88. Harris, "Playing the Numbers," 75, 76.

89. Ibid., 76.

90. Ibid., 78.

91. Wolcott, *Remaking Respectability*, 95.

92. Drake and Cayton, *Black Metropolis*, 475.

93. Ibid.

94. Ibid., 476.

95. Ibid., 476–478; Mathilde Bunton, "Interview with Edward H. Lowe, Conjurer," Illinois Writers Project: Negro in Illinois Papers, July 10, 1941, Box 35, Folder 22, Harsh Research Collection.

96. Fabian, *Card Sharps and Bucket Shops*, 143.

97. New York State, Senate [Lexow Commission], *Report and Proceedings of the Senate Committee appointed to investigate the Police Department of the City of New York* (Albany, N.Y., 1895), 3246, quoted in Fabian, *Card Sharps and Bucket Shops*, 143.

98. Fabian, *Card Sharps and Bucket Shops*, 144.

99. Ibid., 150.

100. Denning, *Cultural Front*, 462.

101. White et al., *Playing the Numbers*, 21.

102. Illinois Writers Project: Negro in Illinois Papers, 1936–1942, *Harsh Research Collection*, "*Number of Businesses Operated by Negro and White Proprietors on 47th Street between State and Cottage Grove, 1938*," Illinois Writers Project, Harsh Research Collection; Rotella, "Federal Writers' Project," 288, 289.

103. Bunton, "Policy."

104. Clayton, "Negro In Illinois."

105. Paschal, "Policy."

106. Clayton, "Local Policy Barons"; Chauncey Spencer, "Interview with George Jones, Ben Franklin Store," Illinois Writers Project: Negro in Illinois Papers, August 26, 1938, Box 35, Folder 24, Harsh Research Collection.

107. Spencer, "Interview with George Jones."

108. Bunton, "Interview with Edward H. Lowe," Illinois Writers Project: Negro in Illinois Papers, July 10, 1941, Box 35, Folder 22, Harsh Research Collection.

109. Ibid.

110. "Cavalcade of the American Negro." http://www.loc.gov/exhibits/african/afamo13.html (accessed December 23, 2011).

111. Green, *Selling the Race*, 20.

112. Quoted in Hathaway, "Native Geography," 46.

113. Margolin, "African American Designers."

114. Ibid.

115. Hughes, "From the International House."

116. White et al., *Playing the Numbers*, 21.

117. Ibid.

118. Baldwin, *Chicago's New Negroes*, 42, 43.

119. Ibid., 21, 22.

120. Ibid., 22.

121. Ibid., 42, 43.

122. Ellington, *Music Is My Mistress*, quoted in Thompson, *Kings*, 135, and Baldwin, *Chicago's New Negroes*, 21.

123. Thompson, *Kings*, 146.

124. Ibid., 146, 147.

CHAPTER 4. TWO BRONZEVILLE AUTOBIOGRAPHIES

1. Stavros, "Interview with Gwendolyn Brooks," 6.

2. Ibid., 15.

3. Bone and Courage, *Muse in Bronzeville*, 139.

4. Brooks, "Bean Eaters: A Bronzeville Mother," and "Bean Eaters: Last Quatrain," 317, 324.

5. Bone and Courage, *Muse in Bronzeville*, 207.

6. Green, *Selling the Race*, 2,

7. Here I make reference to the Negro Spiritual, "I Got a Home in That Rock." "Poor old Lazarus, poor as I, Don't you see? Don't you see? (repeat) Poor old Lazarus, poor as I, When he died had a home on high. He had a home in-a-that Rock, Don't you see? Rich man, Dives, lives so well Don't you see? Don't you see? (repeat) Rich man, Dives, lived so well. When he died he found home in hell, Had no home in that Rock, Don't you see?" Quoted in Tidwell, "Two Writers Sharing," 399–408.

8. Lewis, *When Harlem Was In Vogue*, 48.

9. Locke, *Negro Art*, 47.

10. Locke, "American Negro Exposition."

11. Wright to Barnett, Chicago.

12. Ibid.; Wright, "I Tried to Be a Communist."

13. Ibid.; Wright to Barnett.

14. Ward, Introduction, xii.

15. Ibid., xv.

16. Ibid., xi, xii.

17. Ibid., xii.

18. Wright, *Black Boy (American Hunger)*, 279.

19. Ibid., 281.

20. Sklaroff, *Black Culture*, 250.

21. Ibid., 88. Frank Yerby also worked with the FWP in Chicago; Sklaroff, *Black Culture*, 95.

22. Monty Noam Penkower, *Federal Writers' Project: A Study in Government Patronage of the Arts* (Urbana: University of Illinois Press, 1977), 62, quoted in Sklaroff, *Black Culture*, 88.

23. Members of the SSWG included Richard Wright, Arna Bontemps, and Margaret Walker.

24. Bone and Courage, *Muse in Bronzeville*, 130, n. 79. Alain Locke to Peter Pollack, September 5, 1941, Locke Papers, Box 164-78, Folder 6, Manuscript Division, Moorland-Springarn Research Center, Howard University.

25. Cayton, *Long Old Road*, 250. Quoted in *Bone and Courage*, 130.

26. Wright, *Black Boy (American Hunger)*, 100, 101.

27. Ibid., 74.

28. Ibid., 100.

29. Ibid.

30. Ibid., 204.

31. Ibid., 194.

32. Walker, *Richard Wright*, 190.

33. Ibid., 189.

34. Wright, *Black Boy (American Hunger)*, 198.

35. Ibid., 201.

36. Ibid.

37. Ibid., 301.

38. Ibid., 282.

39. Ibid.

40. Ibid., 300.

41. Ibid., 298.

42. Ibid., 267.

43. Ibid., 383.

44. Ibid., 37.

45. Ibid., 384.

46. For a wonderful discussion of Wright's blend of literary realism and the "documentary mode," please consult Bone and Courage, *Muse in Bronzeville*, Chapters 6 and 7. They make the claim that stemming from lifelong friendships with members of the Chicago School of Sociology and his experience with the Federal Writers' Project, Wright developed his own literary style, allowing him to move fluidly between imaginative literature and the literature of fact. This documentary mode would eventually morph into a second mode: Afronaturalist vision embraced words as weapons and books as vehicles for social justice.

47. Walker, *Richard Wright*, 189.

48. Wright repeatedly used the phrase "poetic realism" to describe his style, mode, and temper, Walker, *Richard Wright*, 365, n. 85.

49. Ibid., 189, 190.

50. Kent, Preface, 14.

51. lee, Preface, 14.

52. Cited as a major influence on her early writing, World War II dominates Brooks in the 1940s. She approached the subject of war during a time of great optimism—optimism she was cautious to accept and her poetry pressed hard upon the current optimism. "Streets" poems, such as "Gay Chaps in a Bar" or "Negro Hero," asked difficult questions of the United States, demanding an answer to as to what the post–World War II world would look like for African Americans. Artists, writers, and community activists explored this question in many different ways. Every institution in Bronzeville, whether it was the YMCA, SSCAC, or the SSWG, held meetings to reflect on what post–World War II life would be for African Americans. These meetings often focused on what was dubbed the "Double V Campaign," a fight for an American victory abroad but an African American victory at home. These issues continually found expression in the Renaissance's painting, music, and literature (*Chicago Defender*, December 1942).

53. lee, Preface, 15, 16.

54. Reed, *"All the World Is Here!"* 89.

55. Brooks, *Report from Part I*, 47.

56. Ibid.

57. Ibid.

58. Ibid.

59. Ibid., 44.

60. Drake and Cayton, *Black Metropolis*, 658, quoted in Kent, *Life of Gwendolyn Brooks*, 4.

61. Reed, *"All the World Is Here!"* xv, 89.

62. Kent, *Life of Gwendolyn Brooks*, 4.

63. Ibid., 5.

64. Brooks, *Report from Part I*, 40.

65. Ibid., 40, 41.

66. Ibid., 55.

67. Ibid., 41.

68. Kent, *Life of Gwendolyn Brooks*, 5.

69. Ibid., 43. Biographer George Kent describes the NAACP Youth Council at the time as "the most militant organization for black youth except for organizations of the Left. . . . The Council had been established in 1936 by Jeanette Triplett Jones, civic leader and dean of girls at DuSable High School. By 1937 the advisorship passed to Mrs. Frances Matlock." Brooks found herself in company with Margaret Taylor Burroughs, painter and founder-director of the DuSable Museum of African American Art, and John H. Johnson, former head of Johnson's Publications—publisher of *Ebony* and *Jet* Magazines. For a detailed study of Chicago's NAACP, see Reed, *Chicago NAACP*.

70. Brooks, *Report from Part I*, 58.

71. Bone and Courage, *Muse in Bronzeville*, 164, 165.

72. Kent, *Life of Gwendolyn Brooks*, 52. According to Kent, by 1940, the area where blacks lived in the city would nearly halt its expansion. During World War II, however, sixty thousand would migrate into the city—as had forty thousand during the Depression. Near the end of the war, the area would increase by one square mile.

73. Brooks, *Report from Part I*, 59.

74. Ibid.

75. Ibid., 69.

76. Ibid.

77. Brooks, "Interviews: Summer, 1967," 136.

78. Ibid., 72.

79. Bone and Courage, *Muse in Bronzeville*, 165; Kent, *Life of Gwendolyn Brooks*, 53. Brooks joined Cunningham's class in June, 1941. She wrote, "1941. June. This woman who loved poetry and valued the minds that made it, had just announced a dismaying thing. She, socially acceptable, wealthy, protected, a member of the 'Gold Coast,' where her black friends were sent to the rear by royal elevator boys, was going to instruct a class of Negro would-be poets, in the very *buckle* of the Black Belt" (Brooks, *Report from Part I*, 65–67). The faithful among the students were William Couch, John Carlis, Margaret Taylor Goss (Burroughs), Margaret Danner Cunningham, Brooks, and her husband Henry Blakely.

80. lee, Preface, 26. He explained this process this way: "if one defines one's self as a Russian poet, immediately we know that things that are Russian are important to him and to acknowledge this is not to *leave out the rest of the world* or to limit the poet's range and possibilities in any way."

81. Quoted in Bone and Courage, 164, 165, n. 23; Brooks, "How I Think Poetry Should Be Written with an Original Poem," September 11, 1938, typescript, Gwendolyn Brooks Papers, Carton 3, Bancroft Library, University of California, Berkeley.

82. According to Kent, the letter from Harper and Brothers Publishing company accepting Brooks's first collection was accompanied by Wright's enthusiastic evaluation. Brooks's poems are "hard and real," he wrote. "She easily catches the pathos of petty destinies, the whimper of the wounded, the tiny accidents that plague the lives of the desperately poor, and the problem of color prejudice among Negroes." Brooks wrote to thank Wright for his support (Kent, *Life of Gwendolyn Brooks*, 48, 49).

83. Wright to Aswell, 62.

84. Ibid.

85. Ibid.

86. Ibid., 63.

87. Ibid., 76.

88. lee, Preface, 15.

89. Ibid., 16–17. lee wrote, "*Annie Allen* (1949), important? Yes. Read by blacks? No. *Annie Allen* more so than *Street in Bronzeville* seems to have been written for whites." I find lee's comments disturbing and my advisor, Dr. Jonathan Smith, made the comment that lee dangerously assumed "black people cannot appreciate high art"; I agree with Dr. Smith here and stress that Brooks's work strove to create high art out of the entirety of black life—both its simplicities and dreams.

90. lee, 16.

91. Ibid.; lee stressed that Brooks's "winning the Pulitzer Prize in 1950 is significant for a number of reasons other than her being the first person of African descent to have done so. One unstated fact is obvious: *she was the best poet, black or white, writing in the country at the time.* Also winning the Pulitzer she became internationally known and achieved a following from her own people whereas normally she would not have had access to them. She attracted those 'negro' blacks who didn't believe that one is legitimate unless one is sanctioned by whites first. The Pulitzer did this. It aided her in the pursuit of other avenues of expression and gave her a foothold into earning desperately needed money by writing reviews and articles for major white publications." lee's Preface focused on Brooks's coming to consciousness of her "Africanness" in the spirit of the Black Arts Movement. I surmise that by "own people" he meant Africans—not African Americans. A considerable amount of scholarship has been done stressing that Brooks's real poetic age came about during the Black Arts Movement of the 1960s and that her early poetry fails in comparison to her more African-centric work of the 1960s. This book employs as one of its premises that Brooks's early work is just as powerful and aware.

92. Kent, *Life of Gwendolyn Brooks*, 102.

93. lee, Preface, 26, 27.

94. Kent, *Life of Gwendolyn Brooks*, 84.

95. Ibid., 85.

96. Brooks, "*Annie Allen*," 83.

97. Ibid., 84.

98. Brooks, "Maud Martha," 127, 128.

99. Brooks, "John Stavos Interview," 158, 159.

100. Ibid.

101. Ibid.; Brooks, *Annie Allen*, 86.

102. Ibid.; Brooks, "Poets Who Are Negroes," 296.

103. Wright, "Blueprint for Negro Writing," 102.

104. Kent, *Life of Gwendolyn Brooks*, 74.

105. Ibid., 62; Wright to Aswell, quoted by Kent, *Life of Gwendolyn Brooks*.

CHAPTER 5. KITCHENETTES

1. Green, *Selling the Race*, 1.

2. Drake and Cayton, *Black Metropolis*, 379.

3. Wright, *12 Million Black Voices*, 101.

4. Drake and Cayton, *Black Metropolis*, 383.

5. Wright, *12 Million Black Voices*, 104.

6. Ibid., 105.

7. Brooks, *Report from Part I*, 32.

8. Baker, *Workings of the Spirit*, 50.

9. Ibid., 104.

10. Wright, *Native Son*, 19, quoted in Baker, *Workings of the Spirit*, 103.

11. Ibid., 103, 104.

12. Drake and Cayton, *Black Metropolis*, 379.

13. Green, *Selling the Race*, 8, 9.

14. Ibid., 9.

15. Wright, *12 Million Black Voices*, 31.

16. Ibid., 40.

17. Goodwin, "Depression Era," 283.

18. Green, *Selling the Race*, 9.

19. Wright, Introduction, xix.

20. Ibid., xiii.

21. Ibid., xviii.

22. Ibid.

23. Ibid.

24. Goodwin, "Depression Era," 281.

25. Ibid.

26. Ibid., 282.

27. Wright, *12 Million Black Voices*, 30.

28. Ibid., 93.

29. Wright, "Shame of Chicago," 24, quoted in Stange, *Bronzeville*, xxi.

30. Ibid., 107.

31. Wright, *12 Million Black Voices*, 105.

32. Ibid., 103.

33. Ibid.

34. Ibid., 105.
35. Ibid.
36. Ibid., 107.
37. Ibid.
38. Ibid., 111.
39. Stange, *Bronzeville*, xxiv, xxv.
40. Wright, *12 Million Black Voices*, 152.
41. Wright, Introduction, xxv.
42. Williams, "World of Satin-Legs," 53.
43. Ibid., 55.
44. Gates Jr. and McKay. eds., "Gwendolyn Brooks," 1577.
45. Williams, "World of Satin-Legs," 55.
46. Gwendolyn Brooks, "Kitchenette," 3.
47. Williams, "World of Satin-Legs," 57.
48. Ibid., 62.
49. Smith, "Paradise Regained," 130.
50. Guy-Sheftall, "Women of Bronzeville," 154.
51. Lattin and Lattin, "Dual Vision," 183.
52. Brooks, *Report from Part I*, 186, quoted in Guy-Sheftall, "Women of Bronzeville," 154.
53. Brooks, "Mother," 4.
54. Guy-Sheftall, "Women of Bronzeville," 157.
55. Brooks, "Mother," 5.
56. Ibid., 4.
57. Wright, *12 Million Black Voices*, 106.
58. Ibid., 108.
59. Ibid.
60. Brooks, "Song in the Front Yard," 12.
61. Ibid.
62. Ibid.
63. Ibid.
64. Ibid.
65. Said, "Reflections in Exile," 357, quoted in Konzett, *Ethnic Modernisms*, 2.
66. Ibid.
67. DuBois, *Souls of Black Folk*, 162.
68. Ibid., 10.
69. Wright, "I Choose Exile," quoted in Fabre, *Unfinished Quest*, 296.
70. Prescott, "Review of *The Outsider*," 29.
71. Wright, *Outsider*, 109.
72. Ibid., 16.
73. Ibid., 585.
74. Christian, *Black Feminist Criticism*, 13, 14.
75. Ibid.

76. Brooks, "Maud Martha," 188–190.
77. Ibid., 195.
78. Ibid., 196.
79. Ibid., 196, 197.
80. Ibid.
81. Christian, *Black Feminist Criticism*, 129.
82. Ibid.
83. Brooks, "Maud Martha," 289.
84. Stange, *Bronzeville*, xv.
85. Williams, "World of Satin-Legs," 69.
86. Wright, *12 Million Black Voices*, 130.

CONCLUSION

1. Reardon, " Can Bronzeville Reclaim?" 10–16.
2. Boyd, *Jim Crow Nostalgia*, 36–37.
3. Green, *Selling the Race*, 200, 214.
4. Drake and Cayton, *Black Metropolis*, 794.
5. Ibid.
6. Hunt, "What Went Wrong," 96.
7. Boyd, *Jim Crow Nostalgia*, 37.
8. Reardon, " Can Bronzeville Reclaim?" 10–16.
9. Timuel Black, quoted in Reardon, "Can Bronzeville Reclaim?" 10–16.
10. Bone and Courage, "*Muse in Bronzeville*," 229, 230.
11. Ibid., 225.
12. Ibid.
13. Ibid., 226.
14. Ibid., 4.
15. Hyra, *New Urban Renewal*, xiii–xvi.
16. Dickerson, "DuSable Museum of Art," 249, 250.
17. http://www.southsidecommunityartcenter.com (accessed October 10, 2010).
18. Drake and Cayton, 12, quoted in Hyra, *New Urban Renewal*.
19. Hyra, *New Urban Renewal*, 6.
20. Boyd, *Jim Crow Nostalgia*, 36, 37.
21. Ibid.
22. Semmes, *Regal Theater*, 216.
23. Green, *Selling the Race*, 214.
24. Ibid., 215.
25. Baldwin, *Chicago's New Negroes*, 236.
26. Sklaroff, *Black Culture*, 247.
27. Locke, *Negro Art*, 47.
28. Ibid., 8.

BIBLIOGRAPHY

Anderson, Jervis. *This Was Harlem: A Cultural Portrait, 1900–1950*. New York: Farrar Straus Giroux, 1981.

Bachin, Robin. *Building the South Side: Urban Space and Civic Culture in Chicago 1890–1919*. Chicago: University of Chicago Press, 2004.

Baker, Houston. *Workings of the Spirit: The Poetics of Afro-American Women's Writing*. Chicago: University of Chicago Press, 1991.

Baldwin, Davarian L. *Chicago's New Negroes: Modernity, The Great Migration, and Black Urban Life*. Chapel Hill: The University of North Carolina Press, 2007.

Barnes, Deborah. "'I'd Rather Be a Lamppost in Chicago': Richard Wright and the Chicago Renaissance of African American Literature." *Langston Hughes Review* Vol. 14, 1, 2 (1996): 52–61.

Barnett, Claude H. "Expect Next Literary Renaissance to Come from Chicago Group." *Associated Negro Press*. March 10, 1938. Claude H. Barnett Papers, Chicago History Museum, Chicago.

Becker, G. J. *Documents of Modern Literary Realism*. Princeton: Princeton University Press, 1963.

Best, Wallace. "Bud Billiken Day Parade." *The Encyclopedia of Chicago*. http://www.encyclopedia.chicagohistory.org/pages/175.html (accessed July 20, 2007).

Bone, Robert A. "Richard Wright and the Chicago Renaissance," in "Richard Wright: A Special Issue." *Callaloo* Vol. 28 (Summer 1986): 446–468.

Bone, Robert A., and Richard Courage. *The Muse in Bronzeville: African American Creative Expression in Chicago, 1932–1950*. Newark: Rutgers University Press, 2012.

Bontemps, Arna. "Review of the Outsider." *Saturday Review*, March 28, 1953, 15.

Boyd, Michelle R. *Jim Crow Nostalgia: Reconstructing Race in Bronzeville*. Minneapolis: University of Minnesota Press, 2008.

Brooks, Gwendolyn. *A Street in Bronzeville*. New York: Harper and Row, 1945.

———. "Poets Who Are Negroes," in "The Negro in Literature," Special Issue. *Phylon* 4th Quarter (1950): 296.

―――. "The Kitchenette." *Selected Poems: Gwendolyn Brooks.* 6th ed. New York: Harper and Row Publishers, 1963.

―――. "The Sundays of Satin-Legs Smith." *Selected Poems: Gwendolyn Brooks.* 6th ed. New York: Harper and Row Publishers, 1963.

―――. "Song in the Front Yard." *Selected Poems: Gwendolyn Brooks.* 6th ed. New York: Harper and Row Publishers, 1963.

―――. "The Mother." *Selected Poems: Gwendolyn Brooks.* 6th ed. New York: Harper and Row Publishers, 1963.

―――. "*Annie Allen*: The Anniad." *The World of Gwendolyn Brooks.* New York: Harper and Row Publishers, 1971.

―――. "Maud Martha." *The World of Gwendolyn Brooks.* New York: Harper and Row Publishers, 1971.

―――. "The Bean Eaters: A Bronzeville Mother Loiters in Mississippi. Meanwhile, a Mississippi Mother Burns Bacon." *The World of Gwendolyn Brooks.* New York: Harper and Row Publishers, 1971.

―――. "The Bean Eaters: The Last Quatrain of the Ballad of Emmett Till." *The World of Gwendolyn Brooks.* New York: Harper and Row Publishers, 1971.

―――. *Report from Part I.* Detroit: Broadside Press, 1972.

―――. "John Stavos Interview." *Report from Part I.* Detroit: Broadside Press, 1972.

―――. "Interviews: Summer, 1967, in my home; with Illinois historian Paul. M. Angle, Illinois Bell Interview." *Report from Part I.* Detroit: Broadside Press, 1972.

Burgett, Paul. "Vindication as a Thematic Principle in the Writings of Alain Locke on the Music of Black Americans." *Black Music in the Harlem Renaissance: A Collection of Essays, Volume I.* Samuel A. Floyd Jr., ed. New York: Greenwood Press, 1990, 29–40.

Burroughs, Margaret Taylor. "Saga of Chicago's South Side Community Art Center 1938–1943." *The South Side Community Art Center 50th Anniversary. 1941–1991.* Vivian G. Harsh Research Collection, Carter G. Woodson Regional Library, Chicago Public Library, Chicago.

Caldwell, Lewis A. H. *Policy Game in Chicago.* Dissertation submitted to the Department of Social Work. Northwestern University. Evanston, Illinois. 1940.

Cayton, Horace R. *Long Old Road: Back to Black Metropolis.* New Jersey: Trident Press, 1965.

Christian, Barbara. *Black Feminist Criticism.* New York: Teachers College Press, 1997.

Condon, Eddie and Thomas Sugrue, eds. *We Called It Music: A Generation of Jazz.* New York: Holt, 1992.

Cruse, Harold. *The Crisis of the Negro Intellectual.* New York: Bantam, 1967.

Denning, Michael. *The Cultural Front: The Laboring of American Culture in the Twentieth Century.* New York: Verso, 1996.

Dickerson, Amina J. "DuSable Museum of Art." *Encyclopedia of Chicago.* James R. Grossman, Ann Durkin Keating, and Janice L. Reiff, eds. Chicago: The University of Chicago Press, 2004.

Drake, St. Clair, and Horace Cayton. *Black Metropolis: A Study of Negro Life in a Northern City.* 3rd ed. Chicago: University of Chicago Press, 1970.

DuBois, W. E. B. *Crisis* (June 22, 1921): 55.

———. "Criteria of Negro Art." *Crisis* (1926): 290–297.

———. *Crisis* (October 31, 1926).

———. "Krigwa Players Little Negro Theatre." *Crisis* (July 1926): 134.

———. *The World and Africa.* New York: International Publishers, 1965.

———. *The Souls of Black Folk.* New York: Norton Critical Edition, 2001.

Eagleton, Terry. *Literary Theory.* 2nd ed. Minneapolis: University of Minnesota Press, 2003.

Ellington, Edward Kennedy. *Music Is My Mistress.* New York: Da Capo Press, 1931.

Ellison, Ralph. *Shadow and Act.* New York: Vintage Books, 1972.

Fabian, Ann. *Card Sharps and Bucket Shops: Gambling in Nineteenth-Century America.* New York: Rutledge, 1990.

Fabre, Michel. *The Unfinished Quest of Richard Wright.* 2nd ed. Urbana: University of Illinois Press, 1993.

Floyd, Samuel. *The Power of Black Music.* New York: Oxford University Press, 1995.

———, ed. *Black Music in the Harlem Renaissance: A Collection of Essays.* Westport, Conn.: Greenwood Press, 1990.

Flug, Michael. "Chicago Renaissance: 1932–1950. Introduction." Vivian Harsch Digital Collections. 01/2000. http://www.chipublib.org/digital/chiren/introduction.html (accessed November 11, 2005).

———. "Chicago Renaissance: 1932–1954. Literature." Vivian Harsch Digital Collections. 01/2000. http://www.chipublib.org/digital/chiren/literature.html (accessed November 11, 2005).

———. "Chicago Renaissance: 1932–1954. Music." Vivian Harsch Digital Collections. 01/2000. http://www.chipublib.org/digital/chiren/music.html (accessed November 11, 2005).

———. "Chicago Renaissance: 1932–1954. Journalism." Vivian Harsch Digital Collections. 01/2000. http://www.chipublib.org/digital/chiren/journalism.html (accessed November 11, 2005).

———. "Chicago Renaissance: 1932–1954. Institutions." Vivian Harsch Digital Collections. 01/2000. http://www.chipublib.org/digital/chiren/institutions.html (accessed November 11, 2005).

Gates, Henry Louis, Jr. "New Negroes, Migration, and Cultural Exchange." *Jacob Lawrence: The Migration Series.* Elizabeth Hutton Turner, ed. Washington: Rappahannock, 1993.

Gates, Henry Louis, Jr., and Nellie Y. McKay, eds. *The Norton Anthology: African American Literature.* New York: W. W. Norton and Company, 1997.

———. "Gwendolyn Brooks." *The Norton Anthology of African American Literature.* Henry Louis Gates Jr. and Nellie Y. McKay, eds. New York: W. W. Norton and Company, 1997.

Geertz, Clifford. *The Interpretation of Cultures.* New York: Basic Books, 1973.

Goodwin, James. "The Depression Era in Black and White: Four American Photo-Texts." *Criticism* Vol. 10, 2 (Spring 1998): 273–308.

Green, Adam. *Selling the Race: Culture, Community, and Black Chicago: 1940–1955.* Chicago: University of Chicago Press, 2007.

Grossman, James R. *Land of Hope: Chicago. Black Southerners. and the Great Migration.* Chicago: University of Chicago Press, 1989.

———. *A Chance to Make Good: African Americans 1900–1929.* New York: Oxford University Press, 1997.

Guy-Sheftall, Beverly. "The Women of Bronzeville." *A Life Distilled: Gwendolyn Brooks, Her Poetry and Fiction.* Maria K. Mootry and Gary Smith, eds. Urbana: University of Illinois Press, 1987.

Haller, Mark. "Policy Gambling, Entertainment, and the Emergence of Black Politics: Chicago from 1900 to 1940." *Journal of Social History* Vol. 24 (Summer 1991): 719–740.

Harris, Ardis. "Negro Employees in Stores and Offices" [South Center Department Store, 421 East 47th Street]. Federal Writers' Project: Negro Studies Project. Library of Congress.

Harris, LaShawn. "Playing the Numbers: Madame Stephanie St. Clair and African American Policy Culture in Harlem." *Black Women Gender and Families* Vol. 2, 2 (Fall 2008): 53–78.

Harris, Michael D. "Color Lines: Mapping Color Consciousness in the Art of Archibald J. Motley Jr." *Colored Pictures: Race and Visual Representation.* Chapel Hill: The University of North Carolina Press, 2003.

Hathaway, Rosemary. "Native Geography: Richard Wright's Work for the Federal Writers' Project in Chicago." *African American Review* Vol. 41, 1 (Spring 2008): 91–108.

Hirsch, Arnold R. "Restrictive Covenants." *Encyclopedia of Chicago.* http://www.encyclopedia.chicagohistory.org/pages/1761.html (accessed July 20, 2007).

Howe, Irving. "Of Black Boys and Native Sons." *Dissent* (Autumn 1963).

Hughes, Langston. "The Negro Artist and the Racial Mountain." *Nation* 122 (1926): 692–694.

———. "From the International House Bronzeville Seems Far Away." *Chicago Defender* (June 11, 1949).

———. "Un-American Investigators" (1967). *The Black Poets.* Dudley Randall, ed. New York: Bantam, 1972, 79–80.

———. *Big Sea.* Columbia: The University of Missouri Press, 2002.

Hunt, D. Bradford. "What Went Wrong with Public Housing in Chicago: A History of the Robert Taylor Homes." *Journal of the Illinois State Historical Society* Vol. 94, 1 (Spring 2001): 96–123.

Hyra, Derek S. *The New Urban Renewal: The Economic Transformation of Harlem and Bronzeville.* Chicago: The University of Chicago Press, 2008.

Johnson, James Weldon. "One Puts On One's Best." *Black Manhattan* (1930): 162–163.

Judy, Ronald A. T. "The New Black Aesthetic and W. E. B. DuBois, or Hephaestus, Limping." *Massachusetts Review* Vol. 35, 2 (Summer 1994): 248–270.

Kenney, William Howland. *Chicago Jazz: A Cultural History 1904–1930.* New York: Oxford University Press, 1994.

Kent, George E. Preface. *Report from Part One.* Detroit: Broadside Press, 1972.

———. *A Life of Gwendolyn Brooks.* Lexington: The University Press of Kentucky, 1990.

Knupher, Anne Meis. *The Chicago Black Renaissance and Women's Activism.* Urbana : University of Illinois Press, 2006.

Konzett, Delia Caparoso. *Ethnic Modernisms: Anzia Yeziersk, Zora Neale Hurston, Jean Rhys, and the Aesthetics of Dislocation.* New York: Palgrave/Macmillan Press, 2002.

Lattin, Patricia H., and Vernon E. Lattin. "Dual Vision in Gwendolyn Brooks' *Maud Martha." Critique* Vol. 25 (Summer 1984): 180–188.

lee, don l. Preface. "Gwendolyn Brooks: Beyond the Wordmaker—The Making of an African Poet." *Report from Part I.* Detroit: Broadside Press, 1972.

Levinsohn, Florence Hamloish. "In the Heart of the Heart of the City." *The Flowering African-American Artists and Friends in 1940s Chicago: A Look at the South Side Community Art Center.* Illinois Art Gallery. April 7–May 28. 1993. Curated by Judith Burson Lloyd in collaboration with Anna Tyler. William McBride Papers. Vivian G. Harsh Research Collection, Carter G. Woodson Regional Library, Chicago Public Library, Chicago.

Lewis, David Levering. *When Harlem Was in Vogue.* New York: Random House, 1982.

Lloyd, Judith Burson. *The Flowering African American Artists and Friends in 1940s Chicago: A Look at the South Side Community Art Center.* Illinois Art Gallery. April 7–May 28. 1993. Curated by Judith Burson Lloyd in collaboration with Anna Tyler. William McBride Papers. Vivian G. Harsh Research Collection, Carter G. Woodson Regional Library, Chicago Public Library, Chicago.

———. "The Legacy." *The Flowering.* Illinois Art Gallery. April 7–May 28, 1993. Vivian G. Harsh Research Collection, Carter G. Woodson Regional Library, Chicago Public Library, Chicago.

Locke, Alain. *Negro Art: Past and Present.* Washington, D.C.: Associates in Negro Folk Education, 1936.

———. "American Negro Exposition." July 1940. McBride Papers. Vivian G. Harsh Research Collection, Carter G. Woodson Regional Library, Chicago Public Library, Chicago.

———. Foreword. *We Too Look at America.* May 1941. McBride Papers. Vivian G. Harsh Research Collection, Carter G. Woodson Regional Library, Chicago Public Library, Chicago.

Mahoney, Olivia. *Images of America: Douglas/Grand Boulevard, A Chicago Neighborhood.* -Chicago: Arcadia Publishing, 2001.

"Major Divisions of . . . Art Center Program." McBride Papers. Vivian G. Harsh Research Collection, Carter G. Woodson Regional Library, Chicago Public Library, Chicago.

Manning, Marable. *Race, Reform, and Rebellion: The Second Reconstruction in Black America: 1945–1990.* 2nd ed. Jackson: University of Mississippi Press, 1991.

Margolin, Victor. "African American Designers: The Chicago Experience Then and Now." Lecture presented at *Looking Closer: AIGA Conference on History and Criticism*, February 2001.

Marks, Carole. *Farewell—We're Good and Gone: The Great Black Migration.* Bloomington: Indiana University Press, 1989.

Marx, Leo. *The Machine in the Garden.* 2000 ed. Oxford: Oxford University Press, 1964.

Mitchell, Angelyn, ed. *Within the Circle: Anthropology of African American Literary Criticism from the Harlem Renaissance to the Present.* Durham: Duke University Press, 1994.

Mooney, Amy. *Archibald J. Motley, Jr.* San Francisco: Pomegranate Communications, 2004.

Morgan, Stacy I. *Rethinking Social Realism: African American Art and Literature. 1930–1953.* Athens: The University of Georgia Press, 2004.

Motley, Archibald J., Jr. "How I Solve My Painting Problems." n.d. Archibald J. Motley Papers. Archives and Manuscripts Collection. Chicago History Museum.

———. *Gettin' Religion.* Oil on Canvas. 1948.

Motley, Willard. "Negro Art in Chicago." *Opportunity* Vol. 18, 1 (January 1940): 19–31.

Mullen, Bill V. "Popular Fronts: *Negro Story* Magazine and the African American Literary Response to World War II." *African American Review* Vol. 30, I (1996): 5–15.

———. *Popular Fronts: Chicago and African-American Cultural Politics, 1935–1946.* Urbana: University of Illinois Press, 1999.

———. "Don't Buy Where You Can't Work Movement." *The Encyclopedia of the Great Depression, Volume 1.* Robert S. McElvaine, ed. New York: MacMillan Reference, 2004.

Mumford, Kevin J. *Interzones: Black/White Sex Districts in Chicago and New York in the Early Twentieth Century.* New York: Columbia University Press, 1997.

"Number of Businesses Operated by Negro and White Proprietors on 47th Street between State and Cottage Grove. 1938." Negro in Illinois Papers. Vivian Harsh Collection, Carter G. Woodson Regional Library, Chicago Public Library, Chicago.

"Opening Exhibition of Paintings by Negro Artists of the Illinois Art Project. Work Projects Administration." December 15, 1940, to January 28, 1941. Exhibition Catalogue. William McBride Papers. Vivian G. Harsh Research Collection, Carter G. Woodson Regional Library, Chicago Public Library, Chicago.

Page, William M. "A Short Tour of Points of Interest on the South Side." n.d. Federal Writers' Project: Negro Studies Project. Library of Congress, in Maren Stange, *Bronzeville: Black Chicago in Pictures 1941–1943.* New York: The New Press, 2003.

Park, Marlene, and Gerald E. Markowitz. *New Deal for Art: The Government Art Projects of the 1930s with Examples from New York City and State.* Hamilton, N.Y.: The Gallery Association of New York State, 1977.

Pollack, Peter. "The First Year's Work." William McBride Papers. n.d. Vivian G. Harsh Research Collection, Carter G. Woodson Regional Library, Chicago Public Library, Chicago.

———. "Forward." South Side Community Art Center. n.d. Illinois Art Project. William McBride Papers. Vivian G. Harsh Research Collection, Carter G. Woodson Regional Library, Chicago Public Library, Chicago.

———. "Dinner Speech." Willliam McBride Papers. May 7, 1941. Vivian G. Harsh Research Collection, Carter G. Woodson Regional Library, Chicago Public Library, Chicago.

Prescott, Orville. "Review of *The Outsider*." *New York Times*, March 18, 1953, 29.

"Radio Log: Destination Freedom. 1948–1950." Richard Durham Papers. Vivian Harsh Research Collection, Carter G. Woodson Regional Library, Chicago Public Library, Chicago.

Rampersad, Arnold. "W. E. B. DuBois as a Man of Literature." *Critical Essays on W. E. B. DuBois*. William L. Andrews, ed. Boston: G. K. Hall and Company, 1985.

Reardon, Patrick. "Can Bronzeville Reclaim Its Soul?" *Chicago Tribune Magazine* (May 21, 2000): 10–16.

Reed, Christopher Robert. *The Chicago NAACP and the Rise of Black Professional Leadership, 1910–1966*. Bloomington: Indiana University Press, 1997.

———. *"All the World Is Here!" The Black Presence at White City*. Bloomington: Indiana University Press, 2000.

———. *The Rise of Chicago's Black Metropolis, 1920–1929*. Urbana: The University of Illinois Press, 2011, 141, 142.

Reiff, Janice L. "Contested Spaces." *Encyclopedia of Chicago*. http://www.encyclopedia.chicagohistory.org/pages/332.html (accessed July 20, 2007).

Ronald, A. T. Judy. "The New Black Aesthetic and W. E. B. DuBois. or Hephaestus. Limping." *Massachusetts Review* Vol. 35, 2 (1994): 248.

Roosevelt, Eleanor. May 7, 1941. McBride Papers. Vivian G. Harsh Research Collection, Carter G. Woodson Regional Library, Chicago Public Library, Chicago.

Rotella, Carlo. *October Cities: The Redevelopment of Urban Literature*. Berkeley: University of California Press, 1998.

———. "Federal Writers' Project," *The Encyclopedia of Chicago*. James R. Grossman, Ann Durkin Keating, and Janice L. Ruff, eds. Chicago: University of Chicago Press, 2004, 288, 289.

Rout, Leslie B., Jr. "Reflections on the Evolution of Post-War Jazz." *The Black Aesthetic*. Addison Gayle Jr., ed. Garden City: Anchor Books, 1972.

Said, Edward. "Reflections in Exile." *Out There: Marginalization and Contemporary Cultures*. Russell Ferguson et al., eds. New York: The New Museum of Contemporary Art, 1990.

Schatzberg, Rufus, and Robert J. Kelly. *African-American Organized Crime: A Social History*. Newark: Rutgers University Press, 1997, 71–73.

Semmes, Clovis E. *The Regal Theater and Black Culture*. New York: Palgrave Mac-Millan, 2006.

Sherwood, Robert E. *Roosevelt and Hopkins: An Intimate History*. New York: Harper and Brothers, 1949 1.

Sklaroff, Lauren Rebecca. *Black Culture and the New Deal: The Quest for Civil Rights in the Roosevelt Era*. Chapel Hill: The University of North Carolina Press, 2009.

Smith, Gary. "Paradise Regained: The Children of Gwendolyn Brooks' *Bronzeville*." *A Life Distilled: Gwendolyn Brooks, Her Poetry and Fiction*. Maria K. Mootry and Gary Smith, eds. Urbana: University of Illinois Press, 1987.

"South Side Community Art Center." http://www.southsidecommunityartcenter.com (accessed October 10, 2010).

Spear, Allan H. *Black Chicago: The Making of a Negro Ghetto, 1890–1920*. Chicago: The University of Chicago Press, 1967.

Stange, Maren. *Bronzeville: Black Chicago in Pictures 1941–1943*. New York: The New Press, 2003.

Stavros, George. "An Interview with Gwendolyn Brooks." *Contemporary Literature* Vol. XI (1969): 6.

Stewart, Jacqueline Najuma. *Migrating to the Movies: Cinema and Black Urban Modernity*. Berkeley: University of California Press, 2005.

Stewart, Ruth Ann, guest curator. *New York/Chicago: WPA and the Black Artist*. n.d. Chicago History Museum.

Sugrue, Thomas J. *Sweet Land of Liberty: The Forgotten Struggle for Civil Rights in the North*. New York: Random House, 2008.

Takara, Kathryn Waddell. "Frank Marshall Davis: A Forgotten Voice in the Chicago Black Renaissance." *Western Journal of Black Studies* Vol. 26, 4 (Winter 2002): 215–227.

Thompson, Nathan. "A Short History of the Mayor of Bronzeville." http://palmtavern.bizland.com/palmtavern/Mayor_of_Bronzeville_story.html (accessed July 20, 2007).

———. *Kings: The True Story of Chicago's Policy Kings and Numbers Racketeers, An Informal History*. Chicago: The Bronzeville Press, 2006.

Tidwell, John Edgar. "Two Writers Sharing: Sterling A. Brown, Robert Frost, and 'In Dives's Dive.'" *African American Review* Vol. 13, 3 (Autumn 1997): 399–408.

Tosh, John. *The Pursuit of History.*, rev. 3rd ed. New York: Pearson Education Limited, 2002.

Travis, Dempsey J. "Bronzeville." *The Encyclopedia of Chicago*. http://www.encyclopedia.chicagohistory.org/pages/171.html (accessed July 20, 2007).

Tyler, Anna M. "Planting and Maintaining a 'Perennial Garden': Chicago's South Side Community Art Center." *International Review of African American Art* Vol. 11, 4 (1994): 31–37.

Walker, Margaret. "The Midwest Federation of Arts and Professions." September 9, 1936. Federal Writers' Project. Abraham Lincoln Presidential Library. Springfield, Illinois.

———. *Richard Wright: Daemonic Genius*. New York: Warner Books. Inc, 1988.

———. Ward, Jerry W. Introduction. *Black Boy (American Hunger)*. New York: Perennial Classics, 1998.

Washington, Robert E. *The Ideologies of African American Literature: From the Harlem Renaissance to the Black Nationalist Revolt*. New York: Rowman and Littlefield Publishers, 2001.

Weaver, Robert. "Racial Restrictive Covenants on Chicago's South Side, 1947." The Newberry Library, 2004. Chicago, Illinois.

White, Shane. "The Stroll." *Encyclopedia of Chicago*. www.encyclopedia.chicago history.org/pages/1212.html. (Accessed 3 June 2007).

White, Shane, and Graham White. *Stylin': African American Expressive Culture from Its Beginnings to the Zoot Suit*. Ithaca: Cornell University Press, 1998.

White, Shane et al. *Playing the Numbers: Gambling in Harlem between the Wars*. Cambridge: Harvard University Press, 2010.

Williams, Kenny J. "The World of Satin-Legs, Mrs. Sallie, and the Blackstone Rangers: The Restricted Chicago of Gwendolyn Brooks." *A Life Distilled: Gwendolyn Brooks, Her Poetry and Fiction*. Maria K. Mootry and Gary Smith, eds. Urbana: University of Illinois Press, 1987.

Wilson, G. R. "Interview with Dick Jones. Manager of South Center." n.d. Negro in Illinois Papers. Vivian Harsh Collection, Carter G. Woodson Regional Library, Chicago Public Library, Chicago.

Wolcott, Victoria W. *Remaking Respectability: African American Women in Interwar Detroit*. Chapel Hill: The University of North Carolina Press, 2001.

Wright, Richard. "Blueprint for Negro Writing." *New Challenge* Vol. 11 (1937).

———. Richard Wright, Brooklyn, New York, to Claude Barnett, Chicago, Illinois. February 5, 1941. Claude Barnett Collection, Chicago History Museum, Chicago.

———. Richard Wright to Edward C. Aswell. September 18, 1944. Harper and Row Author files. Princeton University Library.

———. "I Tried to Be a Communist." *Atlantic Monthly* (August-September 1944): 61–70; 48–56.

———. "I Choose Exile." Kent: Kent State University Library, 1950.

———. "The Shame of Chicago." *Ebony* Vol. 7 (December 1951): 24–32.

———. *Native Son*. New York: Harper and Row, 1966.

———. Introduction. *Black Metropolis: A Study of Negro Life in a Northern City*. St. Clair Drake and Horace R. Cayton, 3rd ed. Chicago: University of Chicago Press, 1970.

———. *12 Million Black Voices*. 3rd ed. New York: Thunder's Mouth Press, 1992.

———. *The Outsider*. New York: Harper Collins Books, 1993.

———. *Black Boy (American Hunger)*. New York: Perennial Classics, 1998.

———. "Amusements in Districts 38 and 40." n.d. Federal Writers' Project: Negro Studies Project. Library of Congress, in Maren Stange. *Bronzeville: Black Chicago in Pictures 1941–1943*. New York: The New Press, 2003.

Zack, Michael Z. "That No Performance May Be Plain or Vain: Self as Art in Gwendolyn Brooks' Bronzeville." *Timbooktu: Stories. Poetry and Essays with an*

African American Flavor. Memphis Vaughn Jr., ed. http://www.timbooktu.com/ zjack/bronzevl.htm (accessed September 8, 2007).

Newspapers

Chicago Bee
Chicago Defender
Chicago Tribune
Chicago Whip

Collections

Claude H. Barnett Papers, Chicago History Museum.

Ernest W. Burgess Papers, University of Chicago Special Collections.

Federal Writers Project, Abraham Lincoln Library, Springfield, Illinois.

Illinois Writers Project: Negro in Illinois Papers, Box 35, Folder 17, Vivian G. Harsh Research Collection of Afro-American History and Literature, Woodson Regional Library, Chicago Public Library.

Alaine Locke Papers, Manuscript Division, Moorland-Springarn Research Center, Howard University.

William McBride Papers, Vivian G. Harsh Research Collection of Afro-American History and Literature, Woodson Regional Library, Chicago Public Library.

New York State, Senate [Lexow Commission], *Report and Proceedings of the Senate Committee appointed to investigate the Police Department of the City of New York*, Albany, N.Y., 1895.

INDEX

nature of work, 76; South Side Community Art Center (SSCAC), 40–41, 88, 89; South Side Writers Group (SSWG), 46; specificity of place, 113–114; struggles of early married years, 88; "The Sundays of Satin-Legs Smith" (Brooks), 21–23, 73; on Wright, 49; Wright comparison, 77; Wright on, 93
Bud Billiken Club and Parade, 19–20, 74
Building the South Side (Bachin), 3
Bunton, Mathilde, 69, 70
Burgess, Ernest W., 61
Burroughs, Margaret Goss: Arts Crafts Guild membership, 32; Associated Negro Press journalist, 48; Brooks relationship, 88; Mexico relocation, 42, 121; Pollack relationship, 31; professional background, 31–32; South Side Community Art Center (SSCAC) commitment, 25, 29–30, 32–33, 35, 37

Caldwell, Lewis A., 44, 60, 61–62, 72–73
Carney, J. Lawrence, 67
Carter, William, 32, 35
The Cavalcade of Negro Theater, 71
Cavalcade of the American Negro (Illinois Writers' Project publication), 70–71
Cayton, Horace. See *Black Metropolis* (Cayton and Drake)
"Chicago, Illinois. Scene in Negro section" (Lee), 106
Chicago Black Renaissance: absence of scholarship regarding, 123; aesthetic formula overview, 49; black aesthetic consciousness, 27; complexity, 123; creative accomplishment overviews, 118, 123; cultural output analysis methodology, 133n10; disintegration, 119–122; financial support sources, 25–28; Harlem Renaissance relationship, 27–30, 47–48, 49; legacy, 122–125; literary theory documentation, 46–47; origins, 27–30; radio expression, 136n93; South Side Community Art Center (SSCAC) commitment, 35; time frame, 118–119
Chicago Cultural Collective, 46
Chicago Daily Tribune, 60
Chicago Defender: Hughes' policy treatment, 72; location and importance, 6–8;

on policy and its uses, 57; on the Regal Theater, 17; respectability, 55; on the Savoy Ballroom, 13–14; on the Stroll, 8–9
Chicago Housing Authority, 120
Chicago Jazz (Kenney), 8, 11
Chicago Real Estate Board, 4–6
Chicago Repertory Group, 46
Chicago's New Negroes: Modernity, the Great Migration, and Black Urban Life (Baldwin), 5
Chicago Sunday Bee, 19
Chicago Tribune, 12
Chicago Vice Commission, 54–55
Chicago Whip, 6, 16–17
Chicago Writers Group, 45, 46
Chicago Writers Project, 43–44
"Children playing under the elevated on the southside of Chicago" (Lee), 106
Chimes of Normandy, 71
Christian, Barbara, 113
Clayton, Herman, 69, 70
Cold War, 121
Cole, Grace Carter, 31
Cole, Nat "King," 40
Coleman, Buddy, 59
Coleman, Irene, 59
Collier, John, 35
Columbian Exposition of 1893, 3, 9
Communist party, 44, 121–122
Condon, Eddie, 9, 11
Conroy, Jack, 69, 71
Contemporary Literature, 75
Cortor, Edward T., 35
Cortor, Eldzier, 32, 35
Cosmopolitan Orchestras Booking and Promotion Offices, 12
Courage, Richard A., 88, 121–122
Cre-Lit Club, 88
Crisis, 28–29, 30
Crisis and Opportunity (DuBois and Locke), 30
"The Criteria of Negro Art" (DuBois), 28
cultural output analysis methodology, 133n10
cultural studies, 133n9, 133n10

Daddy Was a Number Runner (Meriwether), 73
Danner, Margaret, 46

ELIZABETH SCHROEDER SCHLABACH is an assistant professor of history at Earlham College.

THE NEW BLACK STUDIES SERIES

The University of Illinois Press
is a founding member of the
Association of American University Presses.

_____

Composed in 10/13 Sabon
by Lisa Connery
at the University of Illinois Press
Manufactured by Cushing-Malloy, Inc.

University of Illinois Press
1325 South Oak Street
Champaign, IL 61820-6903
www.press.uillinois.edu